HOOLEY*GAN*
MUSIC, MAYHEM, GOOD VIBRATIONS

TERRI HOOLEY was born and brought up in Belfast. In 1978 he opened a record shop, and later founded the music label, Good Vibrations. The shop quickly became the hub of the music revolution sweeping Northern Ireland and soon the label had an impressive portfolio of bands. In spite of bankruptcy, arson, and other setbacks, the label, the shop and Terri survived.

RICHARD SULLIVAN is Deputy Editor with the *Sunday World* in Belfast. He spent eight years on the staff of the *News Letter* where he became News Editor, and has worked on a freelance and full-time basis for a number of other newspapers, including the *Sunday News*, *Irish Times*, *Sunday Tribune* and *News of the World*. As a teenager, he hung out in Good Vibrations record store and has been an avid follower of Hooley's chequered fortunes ever since.

HOOLEY*GAN*

MUSIC, MAYHEM, GOOD VIBRATIONS

TERRI HOOLEY & RICHARD SULLIVAN

BLACKSTAFF PRESS

First published in 2010 by
Blackstaff Press
4c Heron Wharf, Sydenham Business Park
Belfast BT3 9LE
with the assistance of the Arts Council of Northern Ireland

Designed by Lisa Dynan, Belfast

Printed in Belfast by W. & G. Baird, County Antrim

A CIP catalogue record for this book is available from the British Library

ISBN STANDARD EDITION 978-0-85640-851-9
ISBN COLLECTOR'S EDITION 978-0-85640-859-5

www.blackstaffpress.com

TERRI

To my children
Anna and Michael

RICHARD

To Val, Niamh,
Jacob and Roly

CONTENTS

THE ART OF STORYTELLING WITH TERRI HOOLEY
GLENN PATTERSON

To tell a story you must have a story.

If you are blessed with many stories tell one at a time.

If you must tell the many, hold one fixed point in mind. Range where you will, but try always to come back to it.

Try harder next time ... the time after that.

The ambition one day to come back to the point will do to be going on with.

The truth, the whole truth and nothing but the truth only applies in a court of law.

The unlikely, the improbable, the frankly incredible, are acceptable if the punch line is good enough.

Punch line in this instance will always include a bona fide punch.

Revision is positively to be encouraged, even five hours after the story has been told; even five hours after midnight. Even by phone.

Revisionism, conversely, is never to be countenanced; revisionists are always to be denounced. History is not safe in their hands.

Brandy is the begetter of intimacy.

Brandy is the enemy of chronology.

Swings. Roundabouts.

Twin sisters go a long, long way.

But that is a whole other story.

PLEASE BE UPSTANDING ...

I cried the night John Peel played 'Teenage Kicks' by The Undertones on his late-night show on Radio 1, and that was before he uttered the words I will never forget: 'Isn't that the most wonderful record you've ever heard in the world? In fact I'm going to play it again.'

I cried because, until that point, I thought the music industry had beaten me. I had just returned from London doing the rounds flogging 'Teenage Kicks' to the record companies and none of them had wanted to know. I couldn't understand it, this was a great song from a great band. Recorded in a back-street studio in Belfast for only two hundred pounds over a few cans of beer, several bags of crisps and some stale sandwiches, it was two minutes and thirty-two seconds of immaculate guitar and great vocals, but those arseholes in the Big Smoke just didn't get it. I cried because I thought I'd let the band down; this was our chance to put Northern Ireland back on the music map and it had gone down the tubes.

But John Peel got it. He got it straight away, got what the Good Vibrations record label was all about. He could hear the energy in the record and he knew it was going to become one of the greatest songs of all time. 'Teenage Kicks' was the first record in the history of BBC radio to be played twice in a row and it would remain Peel's all-time favourite.

In the late seventies Northern Ireland was a no-go area, bombs were going off left, right and centre. It was a very grim time for everybody, but for our young people in particular. By playing The Undertones and other Good Vibrations artists, John Peel proved to people that there was more to Northern Ireland than bombs and bullets.

Thirty years after 'Kicks' was released I was doing a gig in a Belfast pub and at the end of the night I said, 'Ladies and gentlemen, please be upstanding for the National Anthem.' The bar manager nearly shit himself, 'You can't do that in Belfast, what national anthem are you going to play?'

I played 'Teenage Kicks' and the place erupted! That's a legacy.

ONE IN
THE EYE

I suppose I have always been heavily influenced by music; many of the really important events of my life even seem to have come with their own soundtrack. Perhaps the most significant of these came on a summer's day in 1954 when an accident with a toy bow and arrow resulted in the loss of my left eye.

I was six years old and we were living in a small bungalow in Garnerville, a residential area on the outskirts of east Belfast. We were right on the edge of the city and had a nice big garden. At the back there was also a huge field that provided us with a natural playground, which we exploited to the full. I spent my days building forts and playing soldiers in the wide-open space. We didn't have much money but they were happy times and I look back on them with great fondness.

My dad, George, was an active trade unionist and member of the Labour Party, and it was before the elections of that year – which saw my dad run for office – that the accident happened. One of our neighbours had been trying to shoot a biscuit tin off a wall with a bow and arrow but, when he finally managed it, the arrow hit the tin, rebounded … and shot straight into my left eye.

My mum Mavis was hysterical as we waited for the ambulance to arrive but I don't really remember being in much pain. It was a nice sunny day and I can recall thinking how daft it was for the ambulance men to bandage both my eyes, I'd only hurt one of them! I felt a bit stupid as they helped me into the vehicle because I could see perfectly well; the sunlight was shining through my bandages, and all I could think of was the Hank Williams song, 'I Saw the Light'. It came from nowhere, from deep within the recesses of my memory, but it was very appropriate in the circumstances.

I remember that moment very clearly, and I am convinced that my love of Hank Williams came from listening to

Our bungalow in Garnerville

Dad adopting an enigmatic pose for an election poster

programmes like *Forces Favourites* on a Sunday morning at home with Mum and Dad. But almost fifty years later I would discover that this was not the case at all.

For me, Hank Williams will always be the undisputed king of country music, and so I was thrilled when, in 2003, the BBC rang me up and asked me to take part in a radio programme to mark the fiftieth anniversary of his death. They had been looking for someone to take part in the programme for a while, but couldn't find anybody suitable until my name came up. People often mistakenly assume that my musical taste is restricted to punk when, in truth, I am as happy listening to gospel, reggae, blues, folk and country. So when the researcher on the programme rang me she said, 'I can't believe the Godfather of Punk is a Hank Williams fan!'

I went on the show and told the story of my earliest musical memory, but I couldn't really explain to the listeners why the song had come into my head at such a traumatic moment. Some days after the programme, however, I got a phone call from a lady who had heard the item on the radio – she had asked the BBC for my number – and she told me she could solve the mystery of my Hank Williams obsession.

It turned out that her aunt had run a guesthouse in the Botanic Avenue area of south Belfast and her family had been members of the same Methodist Church my family had belonged to. She told me that, because of their business, they weren't always able to attend services and so my grandfather would often call down to see them and collect their donation to the church. According to this lady, my grandfather took me with him one day – I could only have been about three years old – and on this particular day the family were playing a Hank Williams 78 on a big old gramophone player. I had been mesmerised and wouldn't leave until they had played it again. There was something about his voice that had captivated me and three years later his song came to comfort me as I was loaded into the back of an ambulance.

As a six year old the journey to Belfast's Royal Victoria Hospital was full of dread. I didn't fancy the idea of staying there and I remember just focusing my energies on getting out as quickly as I could. It soon became very clear that I had lost my eye but, thankfully, they only kept me in for one night. My mum took me to a park on the

Me with big brother
John, 1949

Falls Road, just across from the hospital, and I remember playing on the swing, just so happy that I was going home. The missing eye never caused me a second thought.

I've heard some really weird stories about how I lost the eye and it has sort of become my trademark, in fact it went a long way to making me the person I am today. When I was a young boy, for example, my brother stole my glass eye and hid it. I couldn't find it for two whole days, despite searching the whole house. I was distraught and was stuck indoors until the heartless bastard finally owned up to where it was. There have, of course, been other times when I have become separated from it; I've even shocked a few people by answering the door without it first thing in the morning. A few years ago I was without it for a full thirty-six hours because it had been accidentally thrown in the bin.

Despite numerous stories to the contrary, I have never put my glass eye in anybody's pint – I'm too afraid of losing it! Besides, do you have any idea how long it actually takes to get a new glass eye made? It's just not worth it!

Of course, I have been known to take it out on-stage at times, and it has always helped me work out if a girl liked me. I would test the water by asking them, 'Do you mind if I take out my glass eye?' and then if they offered to hold it I knew I'd scored, but if they said, 'I'd rather you didn't,' I knew nothing was going to happen!

My parents first met in Belfast during the Second World War. My grandfather let rooms in Cameron Street in the south of the city and he had sent my mum down to place an ad in the *Belfast Telegraph*. My dad always joked that the ad wasn't for a room, but that it was actually for someone to take Mavis off my grandfather's hands, because it was on her way to the *Telegraph* offices on Royal Avenue that they met.

George Hooley was a handsome man, very popular and very active in the Labour and trade union movements. Originally from England, he spent the early years of the war in the Merchant Navy. There was one story he used to tell us, about a time when his ship had docked in Houston, Texas. He had caught a bus going into the main town but the driver refused to leave the terminus because he was sitting on the 'black' side of the bus. It was the first time that he had had any experience of that sort of bigotry, and I think it shaped a lot of his political thinking in

The cowboy from Leek,
Dad in his uniform

Mum and Dad taking a seaside stroll following a trade union conference

years to come. Anyway, as I said to him years later, 'No wonder you were asked to move, what self-respecting black person would be seen dead sitting beside you!'

A few years into the war he jumped ship, and signed up to the Royal Irish Fusiliers, who were then posted to Belfast for a brief period. The rest, as they say, is history! However, meeting my mum was not Dad's only stroke of luck during his war days – his skill as a bridge player would keep him safe when nothing else could.

His unit was in India, preparing to move to Burma where they were to take on the Japanese, when he caught malaria.

He made a quick recovery but when it came time for his unit to move out, the doctors wouldn't let him go – it turned out he was a great fourth man in their bridge team!

Dad never really spoke in any detail about his wartime experiences, and I can only imagine how dangerous it must have been. His brother was killed during the war and he must have lost many friends, but he chose to keep all those memories bottled up inside. Even in his later years, when he and Mum found his brother's war grave during a holiday in Italy, he didn't speak about it to me. I know it must have been a very emotional time for him and Mum said it had been very difficult. I admired him all the same; he was undoubtedly a brave man.

Mum and Dad were married in 1945. They moved to a small house in Leek in Staffordshire, where my dad got a job in the local textile mill and he soon ended up as the trade union rep. Shortly after, he joined the local Labour Party and, in 1947, was even selected as a candidate for local council elections, which he won by narrowly defeating the sitting Tory councillor. He told me once that the day after his election victory he went to work at the mill only to be greeted by the owner who told him that had he been late he would have been sacked. I'm guessing he was a Tory voter!

In 1946, my brother John was born and the family were very happy for a while. But my mum was homesick and just couldn't handle revolution in her living room: there were always people coming to the house and Dad's door was always open. Besides, Dad was very good looking and was always drawing attention from the ladies, which I know made Mum feel very uncomfortable. Even years later, when they went back to Leek to visit old friends, Dad was treated like a returning hero. Mum missed having her family round her, and by 1948 she was pregnant with me, so she moved home to Belfast.

I came into the world on 23 December 1948. I had missed the hungry thirties, two World Wars and arrived just in time for rock 'n' roll and the swinging sixties! My father was still in England at the time waiting for a suitable replacement candidate for his council seat, so it was left to my uncle Wilf to act the part of the surrogate father. He got the doctor when my mum was giving birth, and for his journey through the snow-filled streets of Belfast he was granted the dubious honour of having the new arrival named after him – Terence Wilfred Hooley. Inevitably people shortened this to Terry and, in 1967, following an article in the New York newspaper, *The Village Voice,* in which they misspelt my name as Terri, I began to use the 'i' spelling myself – becoming, once and for all, the man with one 'i'!

As soon as he was able, Dad stood down and came back to Belfast. He got a job as a Post Office engineer, but his trade union calling was never far away and he soon began working for the Post Office Engineers Union, with which he served for many, many years. Our house was always full of trade union officials!

I often wonder how Mum and Dad's marriage lasted so long, Mum was a committed Christian with a deeply held faith which she maintained till her dying day while Dad was never a churchgoer. However, he had a strong sense of justice and cared passionately about human rights, often doing his best to stick up for the little guy. He was always organising things for the Labour Party and frequently ran whist drives, beetle drives and social evenings, and occasionally he would get up and sing. He could be a great entertainer. I remember one night about twelve years ago he took to the stage during an event at the Royal Ulster Rifles Club in North Street and did a fantastic version of the Tiny Tim number, 'Tiptoe Through the Tulips', but then he spoilt it by asking the band to play 'The Birdie Song'! Dad was actually the first man to sing the

Me and John, 1954

Labour standard, 'The Red Flag', in Belfast City Hall, which caused a bit of a stir, and my memories of him centre on his political activities.

I'll always remember us going to anti-apartheid rallies and on anti-nuclear marches for CND together. And he didn't like Spain. I often say to people that in our family the Troubles never meant much but we never got over losing the Spanish Civil War!

He travelled the world as a trade union activist and was a committed socialist, standing for election as a Labour Party candidate in east Belfast on more than one occasion.

However, he soon found that it wasn't the same political scene as it was in England. In Belfast, Labour candidates would often get beaten up at election time because Labour was perceived to be Catholic. People used to gather outside our house and shout, 'Go back to Cork you fenian bastards', which always amused me with my dad being English! He was a very proud man though, and every time he lost an election he would put on his suit and walk down the road with his head held high – you would have thought that he'd won it.

Like me, Dad always loved his music – and being surrounded by girls! This is him leading the Leek Youth Circle Jazz Band.

Having said that, in 1958 the local Labour parliamentary candidate, David Bleakley, actually did win his seat. I remember the unionists parachuted Roy Bradford in to contest the election and they had a van going round the area with loud speakers exhorting people to vote for him. So me and my mates used to go round the streets singing, 'Vote, vote, vote for David Bleakley. Let us put him in again, Bleakley's win will be our gain' to the theme tune from *Z Cars*!

We were living in Garnerville at the time and we were happy. Dad used to grow his own vegetables and the neighbours would come round if they had forgotten to buy a lettuce or whatever and my dad would always give them what they wanted at no charge, even though these were the same people who used to shout at us at every election!

I can't, in all honesty, say that he was a great father. I respected him enormously, but he was fairly strict and wasn't really an affectionate person. He was away a lot, and the house would always be a lot more relaxed when he wasn't there – I would sit in his big chair and put on a cross face and mimic him, 'I'm Daddy and I'm in bad form!' which was something he would say when he didn't want us bothering him.

Worst of all was his tendency towards violence. He had always had an aggressive streak and was often verbally, and sometimes physically, threatening towards us – you knew not to cross him or you might feel the rough side of his hand. It wasn't all the time, but it was enough to put us all on edge; we all knew it was there, just beneath the surface.

Dad never went anywhere
without his pipe!

I remember one incident when I was a teenager when I had to lift the poker and warn him to leave Mum alone after he had lost his temper with her one afternoon. I was terrified he would hit her, and from that moment I was very protective of her and a little scared of Dad.

Tragically in later years Dad contracted Alzheimer's – ultimately it was to claim his life, but he lived with it for a long time and it was devastating to see his character change. His speech deteriorated and he began to ramble incoherently, quite often he would even order Mum out of the house, and it soon got to the stage where he didn't even know who she was. Despite all the difficulties, Mum loved him dearly all her life and in his rare moments of clarity she would try and help him remember the days when they were young and in love. On one visit to their house I was playing a Bryan Ferry album, when the song 'You Are My Sunshine' came on. Mum's face lit up and she turned to Dad, 'Do you remember you used to sing this to me when we went for walks along the Lagan towpath?' she asked him. It was when he snapped, 'No', and I saw how it crushed Mum that I knew he couldn't stay in the house any more.

Dad was placed in a home in 2005 and we visited him constantly, but the visits grew further apart and eventually it all became too much for Mum and she stopped going with me. He was in his nineties when he died on 5 March 2009 and we gave the oul' fella a real workers' send off with plenty of song and drink to see him on his way.

I prefer to remember him as the kind, generous person he could be. I was certainly influenced by his political activism, and in many ways he was the one responsible for my interest in music as he bought me my first transistor radio when I was ten. That radio opened a whole new world for me – I loved lying in bed with my earpiece in, listening to the late-night music stations as I snuggled under my bedclothes. I think in the end he was proud of me and what I did with my life.

I was a lot closer to my mum than I was to my dad. She was very religious and we were regular attendees at Sydenham Methodist Church in east Belfast. Mum was also politically motivated and often went with Dad to Labour Party conferences and protest marches, but I always say my dad brought me up a socialist and my mother brought me up a Christian.

Sunday was a big day in our house, Mum wouldn't even bake a cake on the Sabbath and my brother and I weren't allowed out to play. Church dominated everything. There was a service in the morning, then Sunday school and church again in the evening. We always went to church meetings, and every week we would go to the Grosvenor Hall in town to watch a religious film. There they always had a 'silver collection', which meant you had to put silver money in the collection tray, coppers wouldn't do!

Believe it or not, I was very keen on religion as a child and at one point I even wanted to become a missionary so I could go to Red China to 'save' the masses – it was a time when the Christian world viewed the rest of humankind as needing to be saved from themselves. Having said that I ended up supporting the Great Proletarian Cultural Revolution in 1966 and the Marxist-Leninist ideologies of Mao Tse-Tung. China probably had a lucky escape!

I stayed close to my mum all my life – she looked after me and she was always concerned about my friends in case they got into trouble. She even said we could smoke dope in her house so that the police wouldn't catch us. I know she despaired about me many, many times. On 6 June 2009, just three months after my father had passed away, Mum lost her battle against cancer. She had lived to the ripe old age of eighty-six. After she died I found a scrapbook that she had kept, full of press cuttings all about me, it brought a tear to my eye – it was proof that she had been proud of me after all.

Mum on a stroll through one of our favourite places, Belfast's Botanic Gardens

Her funeral in east Belfast was a dignified and deeply religious affair. A lot of my punk friends and drinking buddies turned up, and I have to say it raised a smile to see those boys singing hymns. I always loved the music in church. My favourite hymn was, and still is, William Blake's 'Jerusalem' and I love gospel music. In fact, as a teenager I went to the Church of God in Belfast because their music was much livelier, featuring tambourines and the like.

When I look back on my early years I can see clearly that everything I did was drawing me ever closer to a career in music. My earliest memories are of music: while other kids my age were spending their pocket money on sweets, I was always saving up for the next record.

It was becoming an obsession. I loved it when Mum and Dad went out to political meetings as it meant I would be able to sneak downstairs and listen to Radio Luxembourg. As far as I was concerned, radio was simply the greatest invention ever and I spent a lot of time in friends' houses listening to rock 'n' roll, folk music and whatever other music I could get access to.

I realised very early on in my teens that I couldn't play an instrument of any sort, even a comb and paper seemed beyond my capabilities. I did own a guitar but though I tried and tried, I just couldn't seem to get there: I couldn't find my muse. Soon my attention turned to DJ'ing.

In my mid-teens I joined the Presbyterian Boys Brigade and it wasn't long before I started DJ'ing at their youth club, which led to gigs at people's parties. At that time Bangor Rugby Club held a 'Saturday Night Scrum' and I would do their music and even book bands for them – I was a familiar sight walking down to the Strand Presbyterian Church Hall with my Dansette record player and a bagful of records.

I honestly believe I was born at the right time and in the right place. Growing up in the sixties was remarkable. Free music, free drugs, free love – what more could you ask for? People talk about the promiscuity and drug taking that the younger generation were indulging in during that period, but not everybody was taking drugs and making love – I was just one of the lucky ones!

Sex wasn't a big deal for me and really I think it was because it was so readily on tap in those days. Before I had even reached my sixteenth birthday I'd already spent an afternoon in bed with three girls from a well-known Belfast school, though that was by no means my first sexual experience.

That would have been during the school holidays in the summer of 1962. Being the Protestant end of town, the community was gearing up for the annual Twelfth of July celebrations. It was a good few years before the Troubles started and I don't ever remember it being a time of particular tension – the Prods lit their bonfires on the Eleventh Night, got pissed, marched on the Twelfth, bashed the Pope a few times (metaphorically of course) then went home. Perhaps I was too young to recognise the overt bigotry that hung over the so-called 'marching season', but then I have a very different reason for remembering the Glorious Twelfth of 1962.

There was much merriment and celebration round the bonfire that Eleventh Night, and of course we were all hanging around enjoying the craic. The wife of a well-known robber seemed to have taken a shine to me – her husband was in jail at the time having been found guilty of holding up the local post office. She was only nineteen, but to me she may as well have been twenty-nine. It didn't take much effort on her part, but she managed to talk me into bed. Like most people, my first experience wasn't up to much, I fumbled around not really knowing what to do, but she seemed quite happy, and the next morning I dandered home wondering how on earth I'd managed it. My dad demanded to know where I'd been so I told him I'd slept in a garage. I thought that I'd be able to keep my guilty secret for life, but a few weeks later Dad answered the door to find the newly released bankrobber and another man on the doorstep – they had come round to sort me out. I was ready to take my beating, but didn't want it to happen in front of Mum and Dad, so I told him and his mate to fuck off and stop annoying my parents.

But Dad had overheard everything and, ever the trade unionist, brought them in to sort it out. The robber announced, 'Your son had intercourse with my wife', or words to that effect, and I protested my innocence claiming I had never even heard the word 'intercourse'! I went to hit him but he actually backed away – and this is a guy who had come round to knock ten shades of shit out of me! So my dad asked, 'What age is your wife?' and, when the robber told him, he said he was going to take her to court for molesting a minor. That was the end of the matter. I couldn't believe it; it was the first and only time my father ever stuck up for me. But I'll never forget her, or that shag at the bonfire – she rolled her own tobacco, was drop dead gorgeous and was every schoolboy's dream!

It was not long after this that I fell in love for the first time, with a beautiful, intelligent young woman called Doreen Hewitt. But, like all true-love stories, it was to end in tragedy.

Our story actually began, however, with another girl. I was walking along the Belmont Road in east Belfast with my mate Tommy, when I saw someone standing at the bus stop. She was the most beautiful girl I had ever seen, like Sophia Loren, Brigitte Bardot, Gina Lollobrigida all rolled into one, and so Tommy dared me to ask her out.

I was really nervous, but rather than lose face I went over and told her that my mate had dared me to talk to her. She told me she had a boyfriend that she was actually on her way to see, but that she would be at the Belmont Tennis Club dance the following night if I wanted to come along.

I spent the whole of the following day getting ready – I had three baths and shaved, even though I didn't have any facial hair. I put on so much aftershave you could smell me three streets away! I used my dad's Brylcreem and put on my brother's Teddy Boy jacket and drapes, then set out for the tennis club. I had never been to a dance before but I felt cool as fuck. My cockiness did take a bit of a knock when I arrived however – not only was I the only Teddy Boy there, but the girl from the bus stop had stood me up! My mood soon lifted though when I spotted Doreen across the room. She was there with two other girls, Valerie Hewitt and Pauline Harrison, who were to become dear, dear friends of mine. They had a right laugh when they first saw me, but soon we were all chatting away – we got on so well.

Doreen and I became inseparable. I'd never met anyone like her. At twenty-one, she was seven years older than me, but we just clicked. She introduced me to writers such as J.D. Salinger and Nietzsche and it was Doreen who bought me my first pint of Guinness with a brandy chaser, which as many of you may know is still my choice of poison.

It wasn't long before Doreen and I became lovers, but barely eighteen months into our relationship my world came crashing down. One day, while I was busy putting up anti-Vietnam War posters – a cause I had become very heavily involved in – she came round to see me. She wanted me to go with her to a party in Bangor as Billy Harrison, who played with Van Morrison, was going to be there. I was too involved in the Vietnam thing to go with her, so she went on her own. On the way back, as she was travelling along the Bangor bypass, a drunk-driver hit the car she was in and she was killed outright. I still have pictures of her and I think about her a lot.

I'm sure it will come as no surprise to hear that I hated school and that I left at fifteen, which was as soon as I was able. I attended Ashfield Boys School and I have very bad memories of that place – there were some real evil bastards there. Corporal punishment was the norm, and children were regularly battered for no real reason. It was appalling and still upsets me when I think about it.

As a way of getting out of class I would tell teachers that I had an appointment at the hospital about my eye. Whether it was because they didn't like to talk about it I don't know, but I was never questioned and it always worked. Of course I had no intention of going to hospital, instead I would head down to the Plaza Ballroom in the city centre for lunchtime sessions. The Plaza was a huge ballroom on Chichester Street, right in the centre of Belfast, and they would open for three hours between 12 p.m. and 3 p.m. on a Wednesday and a Friday. It had a massive revolving stage and there were often bands on, so it would always be packed. I even remember the Royal Showband teaching us to 'do the Hucklebuck' there.

By this stage, we had moved house to Clarawood, an east-Belfast housing estate which I didn't really like so I started spending a lot of time in Botanic Avenue where my grandparents lived. It was in the south of the city and a lot of artists and musicians lived there. To me it was like a Paris boulevard – I loved it. The well-known artist Mercy Hunter and her sculptor husband George McCann lived there and I got to know them very well. I was very fond of Mercy. It was the mid-sixties and at that time she was head of the Art Department at Victoria College, a posh girls school in south Belfast. She used to send for me to pose as a life model for her art class, which was a bit embarrassing but she would make up for it by taking me down to John Rath's off-licence to buy gin, and then we would get drunk. Now that was a proper education.

By the time I was sixteen there was another interest in my life as well as music and girls. My school life was over and I was determined to indulge my new-found passion for photography – I suppose at that time the thought of a career in the music industry didn't seem like a realistic proposition, so photography it was. The trouble was I had no qualifications. I remember going for a job in the Queen's University Photographic Department. They required that I passed a medical examination but I think I embarrassed the doctor when he put a card over my right eye and asked me to read the chart on the wall, 'Are you fuckin' stupid?' I said, 'I've got a glass eye!' Needless to say, he failed me.

I did, however, manage to get a job in the photographic department at the W. Erskine Mayne department store in Belfast city centre. My department was situated right next to the record section, which was fantastic. The reps used to give me promotional copies, which meant I had them weeks before they were released and my music collection was growing apace.

The Plaza Ballroom was damaged by fire in 1975 – it was being prepared for demolition when this photo was taken.

I was working and, for the first time, I had money in my pocket. I would get paid on a Friday and on my way home I would buy a couple of singles. I bought some real classics at that time, stuff by The Big 3, The Searchers, The Animals, The Rockin' Berries, The Hollies, The Dave Clark Five, The Nashville Teens and Wayne Fontana and the Mindbenders. After tea I would head up to my room, stick on the new singles, and read *New Musical Express*. Then at seven I would head for the bathroom with Radio Luxembourg blasting out of the transistor. I would take a quick bath in my mum's bath salts, and follow that up with a dousing in Dad's Imperial Leather aftershave. I would always be warned not to stay out late, I was still a teenager and the front door would be locked if I wasn't home by midnight. But I never listened because I felt like a million dollars.

So off I would go to meet my mates in a coffee bar and listen to a bit of Elvis, Roy Orbison, Cilla Black or Dusty Springfield on the jukebox. We'd either score a bottle of cheap wine or a gallon of scrumpy at The Spanish Rooms and head for one of the dozens of clubs in Belfast city centre – Betty Staff's, The Maritime, Clarkes, The Astor, The Elizabethan, The Plaza, the list was endless.

Saturday mornings however were shit, Dad was off work and seemed to have nothing better to do than stop me lying in bed. I couldn't see why he wouldn't let me lie in bed and listen to *Children's Favourites* with Uncle Mac instead of making me sit downstairs with him to listen to the same programme. Perhaps he was afraid I would discover masturbation and go blind in my good eye! All I knew was that I would rather have had a wank than face one of his bread and dripping fries.

Saturday afternoons were spent in Smithfield Market looking for second-hand records or playing snooker with my mates. If I was lucky I'd go to the flicks with a girl in the evening, or hit the clubs again. Sundays were often boring and so I'd take my transistor radio to the grounds at Stormont or up to Cave Hill, to listen to the Top Twenty.

I was getting more and more DJ'ing gigs. The Maritime Hotel near the city centre had a weekly Jazz Club where I would DJ quite regularly, and I remember doing a gig at Bangor's Co-Op hall where they put up a poster hailing me as, 'Ireland's Top DJ'. I knew I had to have it to show my mum but, as I was trying to tear it down, I was interrupted by a cop. I thought I was in big trouble, but when I explained the situation he actually helped me rip it down before sending me on my way. These were happy times and Belfast seemed like a very good place for a teenager to live.

PARTIES AND POLITICS

February 2003 and there are still things worth protesting about.

NO WAR ON IRAQ
JUSTICE FOR PALESTINE

During the sixties you really felt you could go out and make a difference. The world had changed and the music changed with it: this was the age of protest and of the protest song. Hootenannies replaced the skiffle of the fifties, and we crowded into the strangest places to listen to Folkniks and their songs. Joan Baez reassured us that 'We Shall Overcome', Bob Dylan reminded us that 'The Times They are A-Changin'' and it was Dylan again – through Peter, Paul and Mary – who told us that the answer was 'Blowin' In The Wind'.

People used to say that a lot of Britain's ills stemmed from the hippies of the sixties but, as I always contend, it wasn't a case of us being the first generation of people with opinions, it was just that we were the first working-class generation who could afford to buy drink and drugs and also to have the independence to do our own thing. And of course, thanks to my mum and dad, I had always been very politically motivated anyway.

I had marched with CND from an early age, but it was the Cuban Missile Crisis in 1962 that really politicised me. It may have seemed far away but I knew that our futures were inextricably linked with what was going on across the pond. I had always felt that the British government was spending too much money on nuclear weapons and power stations; money which I believed could have gone on better things like the NHS and housing, but the events in Cuba had me really worried, and so I became an avid supporter and fully-fledged member of CND.

Our branch hired rooms over a billiard hall in Upper North Street near the city centre to hold their meetings and for a while, I did everything I could to raise our profile. Every Saturday I would stand at the front of Belfast City Hall selling *Sanity*, the CND newspaper, and at night I would be out collecting funds for the campaign. In fact, I would even give them a slice of my earnings if I got a gig as DJ.

On Saturday afternoons, wearing our polo necks, duffle coats, jeans and sandals, we would march and demonstrate. We would sit down in the middle of the road, get arrested and, when released, meet in the Lido Café in the city centre to organise the following week's escapade. The Lido was across the street from the Great Northern Railway station where the Europa Hotel now stands, and every week we would leave our banners in the left-luggage department for collection the following week.

CND was important to me and I was very active in giving my support, but it soon seemed that every time I gave our local committee a donation they would go straight down to the pub to buy rounds, and I began to suspect that these guys were just drinking the money. I had always got the feeling that our leaders just liked the idea of being in an organisation but weren't really committed to its ideals.

It was 1965. I was seventeen years old and had become increasingly frustrated with the way CND in Belfast was being run. And so, during one particular meeting with the support of hundreds of people from the Jazz Club at The Maritime – which also seemed to double up as a sort of soap box/political think tank for me – I tried to vote off the committee and take control.

Sadly however, our bloodless coup failed. It turned out that not everybody I had brought with me were fully paid-up members of CND, and we were told that they would not be able to vote. Of course, it turned out that a few members of the committee weren't paid-up members either, but it didn't matter, we had failed in our mini uprising and so we decided to leave the group.

I suppose I never was one to shy away from confrontation, I knew it was too important to stand up for what you believe in, and I guess that was why I didn't last too long as a member of the Peace Pledge Union either. I had joined this group earlier that same year and had signed their pledge to renounce war and to never take part in, or sanction another. I sold their pamphlets, I sold their badges and I thought that was all I had to do in order to be a member but, a little while after joining, I was surprised to receive a letter from London telling me they had thrown me out. Apparently a few of my fellow members had informed the organisation that I wasn't a pacifist – I guess they hadn't liked me too much. 'Fair enough,' I thought and wrote back to tell them I would never just sit back if the storm troopers came walking down my street, and that was the end of that.

But it was that experience with CND that encouraged us to set up our own breakaway group, the Northern Ireland Youth Campaign for Peace and Nuclear Disarmament (NIYCPD). We were very active in organising anti-war and disarmament demonstrations and marches and at just seventeen I became chairman – the Josef Stalin of the peace movement in Belfast you might say.

I remember one demonstration where we blocked off Wellington Place just down the road from the City Hall, and which ended up with me, and my fellow campaigner Paul Murphy, being arrested. The cops had tried to smash his guitar as he sang 'We Shall Not Be Moved', then they roughed us up and dragged us to the nearby Queen Street police station. We were the first people to be arrested under the terms of the new Civil Disobedience Act in 1966.

But far from being nervous, I thought this was great! I saw our scheduled court appearance as my chance at martyrdom, so I spent weeks working on the speech I was going to make in the courtroom. I would tell them how I believed in the fight to abolish nuclear weapons, in the preservation of humanity and in the end of the war of aggression on men, women and children in Vietnam, then I planned to attack the British government about their involvement. I went down to the courts and I was dismayed to find that neither Paul nor any of our supporters had turned up. I sat there for about an hour, wondering what was going on, when a policeman approached me and said, 'Don't tell me you're married son.'

'Not fuckin' likely,' I replied, 'I'm only seventeen and I think I've got a few years before I head down that road.'

'Why are you here then?' he asked.

Well that was my cue! I launched into my pre-prepared speech and the cop listened patiently to the whole lot before telling me that I was in the wrong court; I had been sitting for over an hour in the maintenance court! Some revolutionary I was.

By the time I got to the magistrates' court, Paul and I had been fined twenty pounds and a couple of friends of ours, Pauline Harrison and Valerie Hewitt, had already paid it! I suppose they couldn't bear the thought of me being locked up!

So in the end, while I never did get to make my speech in court or do some time in jail where I could write page after page of inspirational prison letters, at least I did get to show the girls who paid my fine how grateful I was!

On 6 August 1966, our group wanted to mark the anniversary of the dropping of the nuclear bomb on Hiroshima, so I wrote a letter to the authorities asking for permission to stage a protest. They agreed to let two of us hold a banner at City Hall, but warned that if anybody else joined us they would be arrested. Sid Little and I were the two members chosen for the demo though, despite the orders, a good few other supporters did arrive. We grew a little concerned, but then some Paisley supporters turned up calling for Northern Ireland Prime Minister Terence O'Neill to stand down. The authorities' focus was now on them and they were quickly arrested and taken away. Very amusing!

Of course, my dad was very pleased with my antics and joined me on marches on many occasions, and my parents were quite happy for me to have people round to the house, to sit in the kitchen and organise protests. I remember David Bleakley – Labour MP for east Belfast – coming up to my room where I was painting anti-nuclear banners for a protest march in Belfast.

It soon came to our attention however, through friends we had in the police, that our phone was tapped. This came as no great surprise, given that my father was a senior trade unionist, but he was dismayed to learn that it had nothing to do with his trade union activities at all, but with his son's protest politics! I don't think he ever got over the disappointment of me upstaging him.

Unlike my dad, however, I was never an official member of any political organisation. I did often go along to the parties held by the Communist Party, where they would sell drink to raise money – although we often arrived with bottles of scrumpy up our coats, which totally wound them up. We were always very careful to ensure the NICYPD was not given a political label. Everybody reckoned we were commies but we did our best to ensure that whoever joined our movement was not involved in a political party.

At that point our main rival for support was actually the World Socialist Party (WSP), which consisted of four members – two of them survivors of the 1950s IRA border campaign. They believed in a society without a class system or the need for salaries or money, and they were always trying to get us to go to their meetings. They had great premises at 53 High Street, close to where the world famous Morning Star pub still stands today in Belfast city centre. The building is gone now but at the time the WSP had two rooms, a big one and a small one, and I knew there was potential for making money!

So I approached them and offered them 12s 6d per week for the big room, which they accepted. I told them I was planning to use the space for political meetings but I actually used it to run an underground folk club, charging girls 1s 6d and boys 2s to get in. We had some great nights there – a lot of sex and drugs – and word soon spread about the excellent parties we were throwing. Before long we had around one hundred people crammed in there and I was making a fortune, though most of the money went to the anti-nuclear and anti-Vietnam War groups we were associated with.

It did get a bit crazy at times. I think it was Easter 1967 when we planned to have Belfast's first happening: it would be thirty-six hours of love, peace and joyous liberation. We got high to the music of Jimi Hendrix, The Move, Pink Floyd, and The Temperance Seven and people started painting the walls, and themselves, with flowers – some even formed a new free-love movement called Indecent Exposure!

One night the WSP came down to find three hundred people in the building – they were beside themselves! I don't know if they were more pissed off about us using one of their rooms to run a club or the fact we had so many people there while they could barely muster a quorum. It didn't really matter in the end though as the building's landlord decided not to let them renew their lease and effectively chucked them out. This, however, worked out well for me as I was quick to go to the landlord and arrange to take both rooms myself on a full-time basis.

By that time I had pretty much moved away from home. Dad was strict about me being home for midnight and sometimes our parties were only starting at that time, so I would just stay in the city centre. I moved myself into the building, setting up a bed and a small stove and started to lead a sort of beatnik lifestyle, with lots of loving and lots of drugs.

The anti-Vietnam War movement was probably the biggest single issue that I was involved in. The NICYPD, thanks to our folk club, used to collect money for medical aid to relieve the pressure on the Vietnamese people – the horrors they had to endure were atrocious. We would march and we would demonstrate, anything to raise awareness. We would make sure to always mark International Vietnam Week, which was held in March every year, and still is in some parts of the world. For the 1967 event, we printed up some big display boards and set off for the city centre to demonstrate. On the way back to my grandfather's house – I was going to leave the boards in his shed – we decided to stop off in Lavery's for a pint. We left the banners in the back entry and somebody actually stole them! I can only hope the thieves used them to protest the war too!

The British government, thanks to their 'special relationship' with the US, did not want to appear to be encouraging opposition to the Vietnam War and so we did encounter some resistance, but in truth the Irish government wasn't much better. In

1967 I was invited to address a protest rally outside the American Embassy in Dublin. I was pleased to have been asked and I knew it would be a big moment for me but, much to my disgust, I never made it. We got the train from Belfast to Dublin but no sooner had we arrived into Connolly Station than I was arrested and taken away without explanation. I was thrown in a cell, left there overnight, and the next morning was fed the worst breakfast I have ever tasted before they kicked me out.

Members of the Communist Party protesting the Vietnam War in Belfast in the late sixties

I also remember holding a vigil outside City Hall one Sunday afternoon. I was proudly waving a Viet Cong flag when suddenly all these Orangemen arrived. There were always those who would turn up at our demonstrations and give us a bit of stick, but when this particular crowd showed up I thought, 'This is it, we're going to be battered!' Luckily one of them realised what we were doing and said, 'It's OK they're not fenians.'

We used to go to the Ambassador Cinema on the Cregagh Road in east Belfast – a cinema better known for showing soft-porn movies – and watch films that weren't being broadcast on TV; films that were banned by the censors. I remember one in particular, *The War Game*, a drama which showed the effects of a Soviet nuclear attack on Britain. It had been banned by the BBC in advance of its scheduled screening. It was all Cold War stuff and it fascinated me, it still does to this day.

I even lost one of my regular DJ'ing gigs, in The Maritime Hotel, because I was always making anti-Vietnam War speeches. What made it worse was the fact that the person who got me barred was our next-door neighbour Eddie Kennedy! From that point on, we used to glare at each other over the garden fence.

I also used to protest outside the US Consulate all the time, to the extent the Consul must have been fed up with the sight of me. I used to turn up and demand to speak to him about the latest bombing outrage in Vietnam. I remember being in the audience of a TV discussion programme in which he was a panel member, and he refused to speak to me. Every time I asked a question he pleaded the Fifth. You have to remember the Americans were losing the war at this point, and I was convinced they would drop a nuclear bomb on Hanoi as a last resort.

I'm still very passionate about that time and those protests, and I've never forgiven the Americans for what they did in Vietnam. Americans in the sixties seemed to have no idea what was going on in the world outside, let alone inside their own country, and I think it's still a bit like that. You can't tell me that the fact so many soldiers came out of Vietnam hooked on smack was an accident – how the fuck did they get it all? In my opinion, the US government sowed the seeds of the mass drug addiction in America that we see today and if you're looking for the drug-dealing godfather, look no further than the CIA. In fact, it was this staunch, anti-American feeling that led, in part, to my queuing all night outside the ABC for tickets to see Bob Dylan in May 1966.

My musical taste has always been extremely varied, but back then I was very much into folk music and the protest songs of Dylan and of Joan Baez. At this stage, Dylan was just breaking into the big time but he was a renowned protest artist who had given his voice to many campaigns over the years. On this particular occasion he had arrived in town on the back of a controversial confrontation with his fans at the 1965 Newport Folk Festival in America, where he had lifted an electric guitar for the first time, prompting many of his fans to accuse him of abandoning his folk roots. Dylan was moving in more of a 'rock' direction, so the first part of his Belfast show was acoustic and the second half was with his band. During the interval, all the folkies actually walked out, but they missed what turned out to be a sensational show.

Dylan in Belfast, May 1966

The main reason I went to the gig was also to protest, though not against his use of the electric guitar. I was making a statement against the war in Vietnam. Dylan had always been very vocal about his opposition to the war, so a dismayed tour manager came out to ask us why we had been heckling Dylan when he too was opposed to America's involvement. I told him it was because Bob had refused to withhold his taxes, which were being used to pay for the war in Vietnam. Believe it or not, this led to me being invited to come and meet him after the gig which, of course, I did. I told him that Joan Baez and other artists had refused to pay their taxes in protest against the war and I asked him why he wouldn't do the same. He just looked at me and said in a slow drawl, 'Why don't you just fuck off?'

When I went outside the other protestors wanted to know if I had met him. 'I did,' I told them, and they cheered. 'What did he say?' they asked. 'He told me to fuck off,' I said, and they cheered even louder!

Not that Bob Dylan was my first brush with musical genius. Only a year before, in 1965, the Rolling Stones had played Belfast. It just shows what we all chucked away when we started shooting each other, Belfast was firmly on the concert circuit and all the big acts were starting to come here, it's only in the last few years that we have been truly back on the map as a proper destination for a touring band.

Anyway, in the mid-sixties the Stones were just beginning to make it big and by the time they hit our town they were riding the crest of a wave. Mick Jagger had already become one of the most iconic figures of the decade and, along with The Who and The Beatles, the Rolling Stones were one of the biggest bands in the world, putting the UK at the top of the heap.

They were booked to play the Ulster Hall, and it was the most eagerly awaited concert Northern Ireland had ever seen, but nobody got to hear very much of the set! The lads were mobbed as they arrived at the venue, which was swamped with hysterical girls screaming and crying. After reaching the relative safety of their dressing room they then took to the stage, but less than twenty minutes into the gig they had to run for their lives as screaming female fans launched a stage-invasion.

I suppose I was a bit of a groupie too, and I was determined to meet the band, so I headed towards the Grand Central Hotel where they were staying. I didn't really know how I was going to get to meet them but I did have a few contacts that I was planning to exploit! Being involved in the jazz and folk clubs had its advantages; I was already doing gigs round the country and putting on bands, so I was well known to the promoters. To be fair, it was also easier to get backstage then than it is these days, so my hopes were high. I was having a coffee in Café Lido close to the hotel when I got my chance. I got talking to this bloke called Jim Hurst who turned out to be part of the tour management, and he invited me over to meet the band.

I have to say they were lovely guys. Jagger even bought me a Coke, which I thought was extremely generous as it would have cost 1s 6d in the local shop but in the Grand Central it was 12s 6d, which just seemed outrageous to me. Brian Jones was with them at that stage and I remember him being such a pleasant man. They were all so generous, giving me autographs and guitar strings, posing for pictures – it really was a memorable day.

During the late sixties, my own music career was starting to take off. I was getting bigger DJ'ing gigs in hotels and word had got round about our underground folk club in High Street, though this had folded by then, after we had received a letter warning us we risked prosecution for operating without an entertainment licence.

If I was involved in organising a gig or putting on a band, people would often expect me to get on-stage and do something myself, so I began to perform fairly regularly – I couldn't resist getting on-stage whenever the opportunity presented itself. I had been contributing to a few underground poetry magazines at the time, so on one occasion I got up on-stage with Creative Mime and did some psychedelic poetry. Once I even got on-stage with the blues band, Fickle Pickle!

On top of that, I was approached by Dougie Knight, the owner of Knight's Music Shop on Botanic Avenue, to see if I was interested in setting up a blues club – as if I would have turned him down – and so I became secretary of the new Belfast Blues Society. On Sunday afternoons we would clear away all the racks in Dougie's store and get in some fantastic acts to play. We had people like Denny Warwick, who was a great blues guitarist; the Jim Daly Blues Band; Shades of Blue with a guy called Brian McCaffrey who could play the guitar with his teeth; Memphis Slim; my personal favourite, Champion Jack Dupree; and we even had Arthur Crudup who wrote the Elvis classic, 'That's All Right, Mama'.

Sadly, our secret sessions at Dougie's shop came to an end in 1967 when the police shut us down, again for operating without an entertainment licence, but by then we were putting on gigs at various other venues around the city. We used to go to a club in Ann Street in the centre of Belfast called Betty Staff's Ballroom. It was an unusual place in that if you started kissing a girl, or even if you got too close to one, Betty Staff herself would come round with a can of hairspray and spray you in the face to separate you! If you were smoking a joint that was OK, but woe betide if you were too amorous with the girls. There was none of that allowed at Betty Staff's.

In 1968 we booked the War Memorial Building, a few streets away from the city centre, and put on a concert with American blues singer, Juke Boy Bonner. Riots had broken out all over the city that particular day, and all the pubs were shut by teatime. We weren't even sure if Bonner could avoid all the trouble and make it down from the airport, and we had a huge crowd waiting to see him, so it was a long, nervous wait before he finally arrived. We were all so relieved when he did, that Pauline Harrison gave him a big kiss on the cheek. The next day Bonner went to London and recorded a track called 'Belfast Blues'. But that was the last concert we did and, for me, that was the night the party ended.

I was still very active in politics and the underground music scene – I used to get magazines like the *International Times*, *Oz* and *Friends* and sell them at local pubs, or at Queen's University alongside my own poetry mags. Though when I say 'mags' I really mean pamphlets, which I would run off at a printers' shop and distribute free of charge! The anti-Vietnam War movement still had a lot of support in Belfast, but this was the time of the Northern Ireland Civil Rights movement and it wasn't long before public demonstrations were banned within a certain radius of City Hall. Northern Ireland was changing and tensions were definitely running high. We had no idea what was round the corner for us all.

It was 1968 and the party wouldn't start again until punk came along.

The night we knew the party was over
– Bonner played at the end of an era

For Super Snapshots

KODAK
PANCHROMATIC FILMS

- Finest Grain
- Highest Speed
- Longest Tone Scale

IKB

BOMBS,
BULLETS
AND
EX-BEATLES

Our world changed forever in the seventies and the Northern Ireland I knew became almost unrecognisable. As the violence increased, many of our best people decided to leave; musicians, artists, writers, they all got out – it was the original brain drain.

One by one, all the weird and wonderful clubs that I had loved when I was a teenager began to disappear. As people retreated into their own areas there was little need for the Fiesta Ballroom, the Plaza or Betty Staff's and they soon closed. Belfast became a ghost town.

The biggest shock to me was how ghettoised the city became. The Troubles brought about an end to cross-community contact and it seemed that the notion of Protestants and Catholics sharing this tiny place was a step too far for many. I couldn't believe how so many freethinking people I knew became utterly single-minded, adopting an us-against-them mentality. Some members of my own family, who were members of the Orange Order, even began to lose contact with all their Catholic friends. It really was the start of the dark ages.

I often wonder if I should have left too but I think I would have felt too much like a traitor, as I have always loved Belfast and her people. Luckily, I was one of the few people who could have lived anywhere in the city and, despite growing up in the predominately loyalist east Belfast, I knew as many people from the nationalist community as from my own.

When I first moved out of my mum and dad's I shared a number of houses and flats with friends of mine on Claremont Street and Wolsey Street in the university area of the

Getting to grips with the student body on QUB rag day, 1971

city, and then on the Malone Road – in the posh end of town – before ending up in a flat on the Donegall Road, a staunch Protestant enclave and a hotbed of support for loyalist paramilitary organisations. We had a poster up on the wall which a certain UVF commander took a real shine to. It was a picture of the Rvd Ian Paisley alongside the words, 'Paisley for Pope'. I handed it over, and as far as I know it is still on the wall of his living room! In fact, I knew all the loyalist paramilitary leaders in that area; some of them had even asked me to edit their organisation's magazine – an offer I politely declined!

On another occasion, a prominent loyalist offered me a different type of job; to start taking his wife out socially in an attempt to distract her from the fact that he was having an affair. This all came with the strict instruction that I was to keep everything platonic and that there was to be no funny business! I, of course, had the best of intentions, but one night, having made plans to go to a house party in the university area, she came round early to my flat while I was still getting ready. One of the lads I was sharing with let her in, and before I knew it she had joined me in the shower! I tried, but I couldn't resist her, and since her husband was continuing to pay me I continued to take her out. Of course, I was constantly terrified we would be found out though!

Years later, I ended up living in Andersonstown in west Belfast which was, and still is, a predominantly nationalist area. Most of the women I knew in this district had husbands who were in jail, and so they were lonely and in need of male company. But by then I had learned my lesson – I had skated close to the line in the past by getting involved with women who were married to paramilitaries and had sworn never to do so again, so I made sure to keep everything non-physical. And it was actually great! The women of the area looked after me and I was a regular visitor in a good few houses. Sundays were a particularly busy day for me as I was expected for dinner in about six homes. It was exhausting eating that much food! But I always felt safer in republican areas – there was a greater sense of community and togetherness and, once you were accepted, you became one of them. When I moved to Andytown it was a bit of a novelty having a Protestant living in the middle of such a staunchly republican area, but I can honestly say there was never a problem. There was no question of being excluded because of your perceived religion.

That wasn't always the case in loyalist areas where you always felt certain that people would look for any excuse to give you a kicking. One time, for instance, I was DJ'ing at the Maple Leaf Club in east Belfast when this man weaved his way to the stage and ordered me to play the National Anthem. I have never played any National Anthem so I told him to fuck off. He just stood there looking at me, rocking back and forth on his heels for what seemed like an age before turning away. I must admit that I felt a little scared, and was convinced I would get a beating before the night was through. But, amazingly, what had been a sea of drunken terrorists not two minutes before, formed an orderly line of gents who stood to attention and sang 'God Save the Queen' themselves! Rather than provoke any fresh controversy I quietly stood to attention too.

It was because of that stubborn streak I had, as well as my mingling with people from both communities, that people hadn't a clue whether I was Protestant or Catholic. I just used say that I opposed oppression in all its forms, and that applied to all sides.

But there was no denying that the civil situation in Belfast had worsened and, to be honest, I didn't really want to get involved. I was spending all my time with my friends, and my reputation as a DJ was such that I was getting regular gigs around the town and further afield. I was also so bound up in international issues and protests that I had little patience or time for Northern Ireland politics, such as it was. To me it was the territory of the narrow-minded and bigoted.

Anyone who knows me at all will know that my politics are very simple. We have to ensure the world is fed and that oppression in all its forms is stamped out – it wouldn't take long to write my manifesto! I know it may be a fairly naïve and simplistic view, but then that's me all over and I don't understand why we have to complicate things unnecessarily.

In fact, one of the only local political issues in which I ever got involved was in 1967, when I marched to protest the banning of Republican Clubs. Their close links to the IRA made the establishment uneasy, but I believed that the party was legitimate and politically motivated. I may not have actually agreed with those politics but I was willing to support their right to practice them. However, even in the late sixties it was becoming increasingly obvious that no matter what cause, project or principle you became involved in, it came with a sectarian tag.

I suppose that's why, around a year later, the RUC Special Branch came to the door with warnings for me to take a step back from protesting. They told my dad that I needed to cool it, that there would be bombs going off in this country and that there would be no room for our protests. They were not trying to intimidate us, they just told us they couldn't guarantee our safety and, looking back, I can see their concern – it was all very well lifting anti-Vietnam war protestors off the streets, but now they were faced with the prospect of real political violence. It was a situation the police had never really had to deal with before.

I did take their warning seriously, but it wasn't enough to stop me being concerned about the issues that mattered to me. I – and others like me – continued to protest on the issues we had always cared about, even as it became clear that this country was in real trouble.

One of the ways we made sure our voices were heard was through our very own pirate radio station, Radio Harmony, which I set up in 1970 with my friend Tommy Little. We were complete novices at the pirate radio game but it was such an important medium in those days – throughout the sixties and early seventies you would rarely have seen a hippy without a transistor radio stuck to his or her ear, and a lot of what they were listening to was broadcast by pirate stations – we knew we had to give it a go ourselves.

We broadcast from a derelict house on Rocky Road – in the Gilnahirk Hills on the outskirts of east Belfast – a road which I always thought was well named due to its incredibly steep incline, the top of which offers fantastic views over Belfast. I remember once looking out over the city and finding it hard to believe that down there were bombs, bullets, soldiers, armoured cars and paramilitaries. The city looked so peaceful from up there.

Not that the sight of soldiers on the street was particularly common in 1970. Soon they would be on every Belfast street corner, but when Tommy and I spotted an army patrol making its way up Rocky Road straight for Radio Harmony we thought we had been rumbled.

We watched them getting closer and closer, and Tommy began to shit himself – he could envisage years spent in a Gulag somewhere stretching in front of him – but the revolutionary in me told him to keep broadcasting until the very last second, we wanted to be on air when they burst in and cut us, and our attempt at free speech, off.

Tommy was a mess, he put on a record called 'Alone Again Or' by an American hippy band called Love, and promptly fainted! It was left to me to face the invading forces. As it turned out, however, the squaddies were completely lost and were clearly happy to see a one-eyed hippy who could read a map and send them on their way. They had no interest in our wee pirate station at all – though even if they had, they needn't have worried. Tommy and I were so crap at it that Harmony only lasted a month.

I suppose though, that it was my time as a pirate radio DJ which indirectly led to one of the biggest disappointments of my life, an event which reinforced for me the old adage – you should never meet your heroes. And John Lennon had been my biggest hero for many years. He was the creative force behind The Beatles, he was politically aware and was a fervent peace campaigner – a symbol of the fight against oppression – and so, in the late sixties, I began to write to him, asking him to play in Belfast.

At that time I was still doing my utmost to arrange gigs and music events and so I got involved with members of the Queen's Esoteric Society. They would put gigs on at the University – usually involving bands and artists that I would describe as 'hippy dippy' – and it was all purely self-indulgent.

We knew we could muster enough interest to ensure the gigs paid for themselves, so we encouraged artists to come over to play for the society at Queen's. We were all quite radical at the time so the music reflected that. Acts like Nick Lowe and His Band, Brinsley Schwarz, The Edgar Broughton Band and American folk artist Tim Hardin were probably the best known of those the Esoteric Society brought over.

But I really thought that if Lennon would play here it would make such a huge difference to the place. Of course, in hindsight there was never really any chance of that happening and, even if it had, I very much doubt that it actually would have changed things, but back then we were all so idealistic we thought we could solve the problems of the world and, like I said, Lennon had been a hero of mine. Or at least he was until one fateful trip to London in 1970.

Tommy and I had gone to England to buy equipment for Radio Harmony, but if we thought the capital was going to be a welcome break from the situation back home we were sadly mistaken.

Don't get me wrong, there were enough drugs available to ensure we had a pleasant time, but I found London to be very heavy and tense. I remember a lot of the hippies we met were very upper-middle class; obsessed with the 'revolution' but had never held a job in their lives. A lot of them were connected to the White Panthers, a far-left anti-racist group from America, and they were all seriously radicalised. To be honest I thought their heads were up their arses.

Anyway, it was at a house party on the Portobello Road in west London which was being thrown by one of these people, that I met Lennon for the first time. The Beatles had broken up that April, and Lennon was still probably the world's biggest star, so I wish that I could recall more about that first encounter, but we were all stoned and I don't remember a hell of a lot about it.

What I do remember is talking to a group of people who were obsessed with Northern Ireland. They all seemed to think of Northern Ireland as Britain's Vietnam, and kept talking about sending arms to 'the oppressed'. They were very much pro-IRA without having the first idea about the place or the politics.

There were four big issues of the day as far as they were concerned: the legalisation of cannabis – which I did, and still do, support; an end to anti-gay discrimination – which I supported; American withdrawal from Vietnam – which I supported; and sending guns to Belfast – which I didn't.

So I was particularly disgusted when a couple of guys took Tommy and me to a locked garage and showed us several crates filled with brand-new guns. It scared the fuck out of me, they wanted to send these guns to Belfast. They clearly thought we were 'the boys' – members of the IRA. We were the boys all right, but not those boys! I just looked at Tommy as if to say, 'Let's get away from these mad fuckers.' The whole thing was very scary.

I was beginning to look forward to getting back to Belfast for a bit of peace and quiet, but the next day we were invited to another big house party. I don't remember exactly where it was, but I do recall a very big house, with lots of art on the walls, that was clearly owned by someone very rich. Lennon was there but it was clear he was off his head – he was heavily into speed at that time.

The discussion turned to Northern Ireland and Lennon started spouting what I can only describe as 'green, nationalist, graveyard shit'. We began to argue, it got nasty and I ended up swinging for him. It was a proper haymaker and he landed on his arse. There was a scuffle as the London loonies and Lennon's hangers-on tried to intervene but it was all over very quickly.

I was glad to get back to war-torn Belfast the next day, but my attitude to Lennon had changed completely. He was still an idol but I knew his views on Northern Ireland were ill-informed. In later years he even offered to do a benefit gig for the IRA and encouraged people to send money to help fund the 'struggle' here – it just seemed completely at odds with his pacifist principles, and all I can surmise is that it was the drugs talking. London was a strange place then, full of misdirected revolution.

Many, many years later, in 1994, I won an Irish Music Industry Award and was to be presented with it during a BBC chat show, *Anderson On The Box*, hosted by Gerry Anderson. I was in make-up with another guest and we got chatting – it was Cynthia Lennon, John's first wife! I told her about

John Lennon and Yoko Ono taking part in a Troops Out of Northern Ireland march my encounter with John, warts and all. 'He was a hero,' I told her, 'but our meeting was a disaster and it just goes to show, you should never meet your heroes.' I held my breath and waited for her angry response.

But it didn't come, instead she said, 'Terri, I'm so glad to hear that, people have no idea what a nightmare it was living with John.' We had a great chat after that and became firm friends.

I think what made the whole Lennon encounter all the worse was the fact that the Troubles had been very scary for everyone, and the seventies, at least to me, was the worst decade of all. It seemed that the whole country was having a nervous breakdown and I knew a lot of people who got caught up in it at that time.

On 29 September 1974, a good friend of mine, Gerard McWilliams, took a skinfull of drink and some drugs and decided to walk home from Lavery's bar in the centre of town. Home was Andersonstown, which wasn't really that far but it took him through the staunchly Protestant Donegall Road area. A UDA mob dragged him down an entry off Lecale Street and stabbed him to death. He was only twenty-three years old. He was just an ordinary bloke walking home from the pub and his murder, like so many during the Troubles, was futile and utterly heartbreaking.

In November 1974, another friend of mine, Ivan Clayton – who was originally from McClure Street – was cruelly and nonsensically murdered. Ivan was a great guy, an honest, hard-working man who loved the occasional pint. He worked for the gas company as the person who would call at people's homes to empty their gas meters. People loved to see him coming because he always gave them a few quid back. He had briefly stayed with me when I lived in Camden Street in 1972 and we stayed in touch. We would meet up in Lavery's for a few pints every now and again.

On 4 November 1974, he agreed to do the door on the Club Bar on University Road, and that night a member of a loyalist group walked up and shot him dead. He was only forty-eight years old, and was just one of countless people who were in the wrong place at the wrong time. I heard later that the man who was supposed to work that night, and who was a member of the UDR, had cried off. It seems that he was the one who was to have been shot but, tragically, Ivan took the bullet for him.

There was no denying that the Troubles had well and truly begun and our social lives now consisted of visits to other people's houses, where we would gather to listen to music and smoke a bit of pot. I remember, at one such party, my good friend Geoff Morris told me a story about a girl he knew, Ruth Dowdie, who had once spent a night hidden in a dustbin. I can't remember exactly how or why this story first came up, but I do remember thinking that she sounded like my kind of girl! Little did I know that I was soon going to find that out for myself.

Geoff and another friend of mine, Louis Boyle, worked with the Community Relations Commission and we were all involved in a number of community-based campaigns at the time, one of which was opposing the construction of a bypass – now known as the Westlink – which was going to be pushed through a number of housing areas. Just shows how forward thinking I was! The city would be a nightmare without the Westlink. Anyway, I was invited to a party at Geoff's house on University Avenue in the autumn of 1973 and it was there that I met Ruth.

I knew straight away that I liked her and so I asked her to come with me to see a band who were playing as part of the Queen's Festival. I was actually in a relationship at the time but I knew that Ruth was something special. To be honest, I think she was more interested in the band that were playing than me, but God loves a trier and, in time,

On my best behaviour with Ruth

we started seeing each other. It wasn't long before we were engaged.

My mum and dad loved her, and I got on great with her parents too. Her dad, Tom, worked in the shipyard and was a lovely man, if a little dour. I recall telling him that you hadn't lived unless you had spent the night in bed with a long-legged woman, listening to Barry White. I don't think he ever thought the same way about me after that!

At this time I had managed to land myself a great job with Kodak, working during the day in their processing department in Corporation Street. I really enjoyed my time there, and things were going well for a while, but my politics soon got in the way. The Kodak Group was very anti-trade union, but I felt it was important that the rights of the workers be safeguarded, so I set up a union under the auspices of the Transport and General Workers' Union – 98 per cent of employees joined.

This was the kind of politics I enjoyed, fighting for the rights of the working class. I had no interest in the civil unrest unfolding outside my door, however I would soon find that the two were no longer mutually exclusive. In May 1974, a month before Ruth and I were due to get married, pro-British loyalist groups under the banner of the Ulster Workers' Council, staged a general workers' strike in protest at the Sunningdale Agreement – an attempt to end the Troubles by establishing a power-sharing government between nationalists and unionists.

Electricity, food supplies and postal services were all affected and in some areas it was impossible even to get milk and bread. People were suffering real hardships, while the loyalist paramilitaries manning the barricades made sure the pubs stayed open so they could enjoy a few pints while making their stand. Their women soon put a stop to that by demanding that they stop knocking back pints – if they couldn't get milk and bread, then the lads could definitely do without beer!

I continued to go to work right through the strike, which was very difficult. There were barricades everywhere, and masked men stopped everyone who passed to ask questions. Things were even worse for me, however, as the loyalists knew who I was, and I knew it was only a matter of time before they tried something. I was getting all sorts of threats from them – the fact I was seen as a socialist was nearly as bad as being a Catholic for those guys – and my peace movement activities, and my support for workers' rights didn't seem to sit easily with them!

Persil-White! and working hard at Kodak

But I wasn't about to let those scumbags scare me so, on the seventh day of the strike (21 May 1974), when the Trade Unions Congress announced a 'Back to Work' rally, I made sure I was in attendance. There were over two hundred of us who marched that day, and it brought me into direct conflict with some more loyalists who lined the route shouting, 'We're going to kill you Hooley, you bastard.'

It was very scary, and the fact that only two hundred people took part was an indication to me of just how many people had been intimidated into not coming. TUC General Secretary Len Murray had travelled to Northern Ireland for the march and I think he too was shocked that so few turned out. I don't think he could understand how terrorist groups could exert such control on a major city in the United Kingdom.

Ruth and my family were worried about me – the abuse I had received on the march seemed to set me up as a 'marked man' – and their worst fears were confirmed when, two days after the march, an RUC Special Branch officer visited Kodak and warned me that I was in danger. It seemed that not only had the loyalists objected to my presence at the 'Back to Work' rally, but they were also unhappy about some of the work I was doing at Kodak. We used to get sent rolls of film from prisoners at the Maze prison, which I would process and return, like I would for any other customer, but I guess they weren't too happy with me for that.

In the end, we hit upon the idea that I should go to England for the duration of the strike for my own safety. My boss at Kodak was so worried for me that he agreed and we dressed it up to appear as part of the job. That was easy enough to believe. The

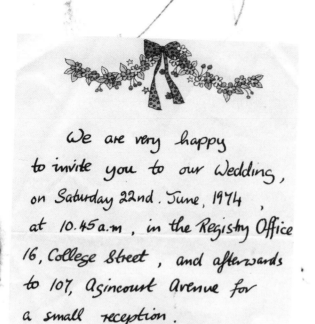

We are very happy
to invite you to our Wedding,
on Saturday 22nd. June, 1974,
at 10.45 a.m, in the Registry Office
16, College Street, and afterwards
to 107, Agincourt Avenue for
a small reception.

Lots of Love,
Terri & Ruth.

workers at the electric power plant were off on strike, so the electricity supply was frequently down and, of course, we couldn't process film with no power, so a backlog soon built up. I was given a huge batch of film and sent to Kodak's plant outside Blackpool to process it. I said goodbye to Ruth and caught the boat to Liverpool.

As it turned out, I was only in England for a few days before the strike ended on 28 May. Northern Ireland Prime Minister Brian Faulkner had resigned after Secretary of State Merlyn Rees refused to meet those behind the strike, marking the end of the Northern Ireland Executive. The UWC had gotten their way.

With things now relatively calm, and with our wedding just a few weeks away, I was keen to come back to Ruth and see the folks back home. I went out on the piss in Blackpool and, slightly hungover, caught the train to Liverpool the next morning. I was just about to board the ferry when the police pulled me aside – it was Special Branch.

I had bought a load of sweets in Blackpool – things like sweetie mice and gobstoppers – and the cops opened all the bags. One of them took out a sweetie mouse, held it by its string tail and asked, 'What's this?' I told him it was a fuse: you just light it and throw it at the army! I don't think they saw the joke. They rang their pals in Northern Ireland who told them that Terri Hooley was known to Special Branch in Belfast, but to let him travel.

I got home and even though I was still a bit worried about my safety I went back to work as normal, and everything seemed to just drop back into place. Ruth and I could now look forward to getting married. Though I must admit to being surprised that, after weeks of drama and uncertainty, Ruth still wanted to get hitched to me! She must have known what she was getting into, but love, as they say, is blind.

I'm sure that most people would assume our wedding day would have been one of the parties of the year with lots of drink, drugs and music, and probably lasting over three days! In truth it was one of the quietest and most civilised weddings I have ever been to.

When I woke on 22 June 1974, it was a beautiful sunny day. I got dressed in my brown corduroy suit, knotted my tie and combed what was an impressively long head of hair. Jimmy Scott was my best man – an Englishman with whom I had become friendly during countless drinking sessions and conversations about revolution – and once I had checked he was up, sober and ready, we headed with Mum and Dad to Belfast City Hall and the Registry Office where a simple ceremony was held. Ruth looked lovely and I felt I was a very lucky man.

Pictures were taken in Botanic Gardens in the south of the city, and somebody recorded the day on 8mm film which, like most married couples, we watched once then put away.

The reception itself wasn't very rock 'n' roll. We invited some friends and family back to Ruth's parents' home in Agincourt Avenue for some sandwiches, sausages rolls and, of course, wedding cake. It was a quiet affair, but we were happy.

I remember standing outside to have a smoke when my old artist friend, Mercy Hunter, walked past on her way back from the off-licence. I don't know if she was a bit tipsy, or just feeling overly generous, but she gave me some money to spend on honeymoon.

Not that our honeymoon was to be in the most glamorous of locations. We, like most newlyweds, were pretty skint so we agreed to stay with my old friend Harry Orr, as he was living in a cottage in Kilkenny in south-east Ireland. Harry was actually growing marijuana in the porch of his cottage, and judging by the six-foot plants on show, it was thriving. In fact, a neighbouring farmer called at the door to ask Harry what the plants were, as he was looking for something fast-growing to thicken the hedges on his land. I suppose the cows would have been very happy at any rate!

Ruth and I stayed for a week with Harry. We went for a lot of walks and went to the local pub – it was a nice relaxing time. We then headed for an overnight stay in Dublin – during which time we visited the Guinness brewery – and then home to our new house in Jerusalem Street, in the Holy Lands area of south Belfast.

Me and Ruth on our big day

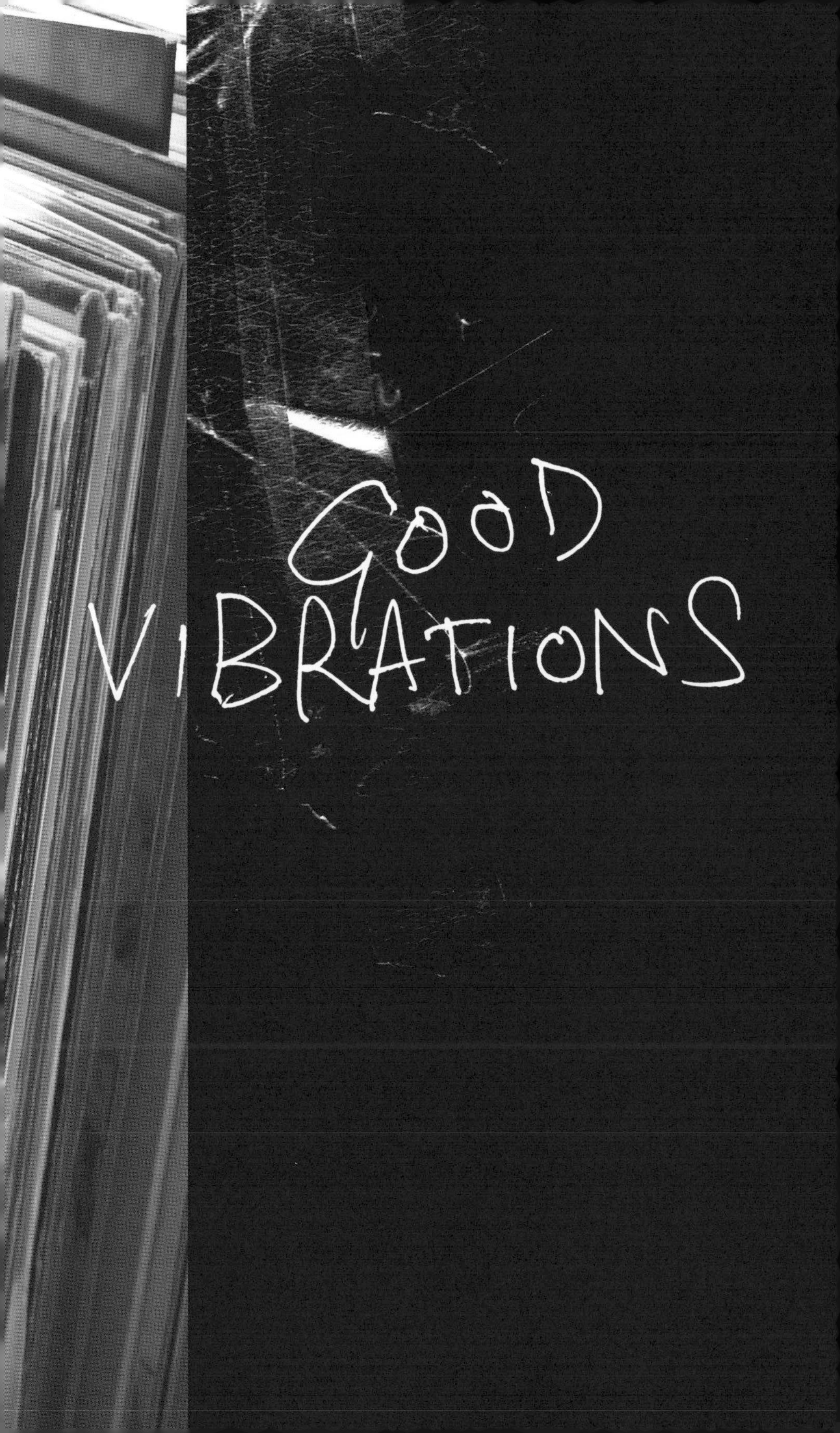
GOOD
VIBRATIONS

One day, one of the boys at Kodak was reading a copy of *Exchange and Mart* and, knowing my passion for music, he showed me an advert – one thousand singles for £40. Too good a bargain to pass up. Of course I didn't have the money, but thankfully Ruth did. The collection contained some real gems. It wasn't long before I learned there's a huge market out there for that sort of stuff – if you have an Elvis record that got to number one, you can be sure there will be a million other copies out there. It's the records that weren't a success that are harder to find and therefore more valuable. I touched lucky and found a lot of non-hits in that thousand and knew I could make a bit of money. That was the start of it – it was 1976 and I quit Kodak.

It was round about that time that I heard that The Ronettes were playing London. I was madly in love with the lead singer, Ronnie Spector – the then wife of Phil Spector, of whom I was also a huge fan, even though it was said that he used to lock her up and not let her out – and I knew I had to go and watch them perform. I went through my new records and decided to take one hundred or so with me, to see if I could sell them to some of the London stores. I thought that if I got at least £1 each for them that it would pay for my trip.

I walked into a collectors' store in London and showed the owner the records. He picked out eleven singles and said, 'I'll give you £110 for those,' pointing at the ones he had set aside, before adding that he simply couldn't afford the rest. I couldn't believe it, those records had only cost me 4p each!

My love for music was finally starting to pay off. The shop owner offered to let me swap the rest of the records I had for stuff in his shop, so I walked away with a live album by Chuck Berry with the Steve Miller Band, and a rare Ronnie Spector import. It was a good lesson in just how much people were willing to pay for some of this stuff.

Operating from the back bedroom in our house, I started trading and swapping records. I would always look in the music press for bargains and then write to record shops in London offering to sell records to them. As the word spread, more and more people would come round to our house to listen to music and to order records.

The house soon started to feel like Piccadilly Circus – people were calling all day every day, and to be honest there was never a twenty-four hour period when we had the place to ourselves. There were very few places to go in those days so, more often than not, when people came round to buy records they would stay on, have a drink and before long we had a full-blown party! Ruth had the patience of a saint but I knew this wasn't fair to her. Quite often she would come home to find Ricky Flanagan – a biochemist at Queen's University who used the lab up there to make the best poteen in Belfast – opening another bottle of the stuff in her kitchen and she would understandably get a bit annoyed. I can't say I blamed her.

But business was booming and I found that I had a real talent for knowing what my customers would want. I ordered stuff like Van Morrison American imports, and I remember going to Dublin on one occasion, where I bought a load of New York Dolls albums for £1 each, selling them on for £2.99. One time I bought seven hundred copies of an album from Hot Wax Records in Edinburgh – *Boogie Bands and One Night Stands* by Kathy Dalton backed by Little Feat and Van Dyke Parks – and I sold every copy, all from my back bedroom. It wasn't long before I started to do the markets.

All the while I was getting a fair idea that there might be enough interest to sustain a

Good Vibrations at 102 Great Victoria Street. The vinyl records on the wall would be worth a fortune now!

business and I began to consider the possibility of opening my own store. It had always been in the back of my head to open a shop and the more involved I became in the music scene, the bigger the idea got until it became an almost unbearable yearning. I suppose I was just waiting on a sign.

It was therefore in keeping with the slightly hectic, drug-influenced life I was leading at the time that the opportunity to fulfill my dream came in the oddest of ways – with an anonymous letter inviting me to meet 'the Man in Black' at the Queen's Arcade bar in the centre of Belfast.

I was dubious and decided not to go – I mean this was Belfast and you just didn't know what you would be walking into if you answered an anonymous invitation, so I ignored it – but shortly afterwards a bloke called Dave Hyndman turned up at my door, announced that he was the mysterious Man in Black and told me that he had wanted to talk to me about getting involved in a sort of cooperative he was planning to set up, a sort of 'Belfast Arts Lab'.

This cooperative would include a record store, a health food shop called Sassafraz, and his own arts group, which would print poetry magazines and such – he had been working at Northern Whig Printers in Belfast at the time and needed to find a vehicle to do the stuff he wanted to.

To this day I don't really know why he approached me in such an unusual way, but his thinking was very similar to mine, and the idea of a cooperative appealed to me as much as it did to him. I loved the idea of having me, the health food store and the print works all working together. It was exactly the sort of message of unity and camaraderie we wanted to convey. I was in.

Initially, we tried to source funding through 'proper channels' – with grant aid and a properly constituted management committee – but in the end we couldn't deal with all the bureaucracy that goes with getting grants, so we abandoned the cooperative project and agreed to just open all three businesses in the same building.

Dave found premises at 102 Great Victoria Street, a street which, in the 1970s, was probably the most bombed piece of real estate in the world. All the windows were boarded up and the landlord was so desperate to have somebody use it, we got the first six months rent free.

For a while the only lights on in that street were ours and the taxi company next door. But I loved the premises. I remembered the building from the sixties, when it

The brass wall plaque that marked Good Vibrations

The King points the way to Good Vibrations. Lots of bands (like The Defects, pictured here) would come to get their photo taken with him.

was sandwiched between an antique shop with a big old cannon sitting outside on the pavement, and a shop which sold Lambeg drums.

Of course we had no money, but with the help of a small army of friends we pilfered enough wood from builders' skips and sites to build racks for the records and a counter. One of the very first things I did was fix up the toilet. Dave couldn't believe it, 'The toilets are fine,' he said, 'why the fuck are you painting them?' I told him, 'Dave, we're having a party and I'm not having girls I know coming in here to use the toilets as they are.' So I painted the toilet seat red and we were ready to go – well you can't have an opening party without a decent loo!

Now all we needed was a name. I struggled to come up with one for a while, until I read that one of my favourite bands, The Troggs, were releasing a version of the Beach Boys classic, 'Good Vibrations'. I thought, 'That's it, that's what it's all about.' We were having such good vibrations; all the people who had helped me get the shop together were after a good time.

We soon decided that we needed something to attract the attention of passers-by so we came up with the now-famous Elvis sign which pointed the way up to the first floor, where the shop was based. Making a pilgrimage to that sign later became a rite of passage for bands visiting Belfast and our Elvis ended up in rock magazines all over the world. He became an iconic symbol of what we were trying to achieve with Good Vibrations. But he had a difficult time. Poor old Elvis was kidnapped three times, and on one occasion we had to pay students at Queen's University a ransom to get him back!

Our doors opened in late 1976, and business soon took off. I never thought for a second that the shop would become as popular as it did but the whole idea seemed to strike a chord with people in Belfast and further afield. It felt as though we were providing something people had been waiting for for a very long time. It was a happy marriage, with

Dave printing fanzines and all our posters. We felt self-sufficient.

It was my passion and with the help of many others it became a way of life – I spent all my time working at the shop. In the mornings people would come in and order records, and I would cycle down – on Dave's butcher's bike – to Symphola, the record suppliers in the city centre. I would get the orders and cycle back up to the shop.

I had such knowledge of music back then, I could get people anything – even the most obscure stuff. And although it's what we became famous for, we didn't just stock punk records. Good Vibrations had the biggest reggae selection in Ireland, and in 1979 I even formed the Belfast Reggae Society. Each week I would DJ a reggae disco at Queen's University; and we started running annual Bob Marley appreciation nights on the anniversary of his death, something we started again in 2010 after a long, long break.

The store also had a great blues section and, even though it might have been hidden away in the corner, we even had a classical section. We did very well in those early days, making up to £2,000 a week, which in those days was a very healthy amount.

The shop had become a hub for people of all ages and creeds. We even had a window seat so that people could sit, have some coffee and listen to music – but little did we know that it would give kids the chance to mitch off school and try to steal anything they could get their hands on! I reckon every teacher within a ten-mile radius of the shop had a wanted poster up on his classroom wall with my picture on it.

The shop was full of some real characters – people like DJ Death Darren, a huge soul fan who once told me he had been really worried about coming to the shop because he thought it would be full of punks. Of course, when he eventually did come in he found a Booker T and the MGs album that he had been after, and so became a regular.

In fact, it was the social element which was the best part of the whole thing. My enduring memory of that time is of lots of parties and lots of good times. Many a time after a night out we would head back to the shop for a few beers and listen to music, and then stumble home at about four in the morning. I often brought people back to our house. Life was a constant party.

BUYING RECORDS
DAVID HOLMES

I was always buying records. Ever since I was twelve years old practically every penny I had would go on music, and my idea of heaven was spending the afternoons after school in Terri's shop, just hanging out and annoying him. I used to hassle him with questions about music, and I rarely had any more than £2 in my pocket – but then ability to pay was never an issue for Terri!

Good Vibrations was a remarkable place. Long before the dawn of the internet, Terri was able to source rare recordings, or albums that had only been released in America. And these weren't re-issues – Terri always had the real thing, he always had something you wanted. Any record collector will tell you that they only want an original pressing in its original or imported sleeve, and Terri always delivered.

One particular day, as a young mod, I went looking for stuff at Good Vibes and struck gold – Terri produced a dusty box of seven-inch singles from under the counter that were all original pressings from Sue, Atlantic, Liberty and London records. There we were, in a dusty record shop in Belfast, looking at original recordings by people like Ray Barretto, The Blendells and The Strangeloves. He even had one by Lee Dorsey, signed by Lee himself. That was twenty-five years ago and in those days I reckon they were worth about £30 or £40 each, but Terri was selling the lot for £30.

These were incredibly rare pressings and I hadn't a pot to piss in, but Terri knew how badly I wanted them. By this stage Terri knew music had become the most important thing in my life. He knew exactly what he was doing when he produced those records, and he knew full well that I wouldn't be able to resist them.

I was fifteen at the time and I would have sold my soul for them. Instead I told him that, if he let me have the records, I would pay him back over a period of time – I'd just keep giving him money from my paper round until he was paid. And so Terri handed me the box of records, and I went away a very happy and excited young man. As I said, some of those records were worth £30 on their own, so I knew that to get the lot for the same money was a steal.

I'm sorry to say that it took me twelve whole years to pay for those records. Twelve years of having to avoid Terri! But when I started making myself some money, I did hand over the dough. By all accounts, Terri didn't have that money for long. Apparently he was chatting to members of a local band called The V-Necks soon after and they mentioned that they needed a new microphone, but that they didn't have the £28 it took to pay for it. Legend has it that as soon as Terri got the money from me, he proceeded to give it to those lads to pay for their mic!

One day I was getting my hair cut in Belfast when this English guy walked in – we'll call him Mr Smyth. We got talking, and he started to tell me about being a mod in London during the sixties, and how he was a regular at top London R & B clubs like The Scene and The Flamingo. This guy was the real deal; he had been a bit of a face round London but then had to take a bit of a holiday at 'her majesty's pleasure'.

He told me how, before he went inside, he had entrusted his record collection to Terri, to look after while he was away – a collection which consisted of Ray Barretto, The Blendells, The Strangeloves and Lee Dorsey. I couldn't believe it! I just shouted, 'I've got those fuckin' records!' and all Mr Smyth could do was shake his head and say, 'That fuckin' Hooley.'

Of course, Terri does maintain to this day that he never met Mr Smyth, and that he bought those records from another party, but it doesn't really matter. If you're lucky you'll meet people in life who will pass on their knowledge and enthusiasm and, for Terri, it's always been about the music. He's still spreading the love.

BIG TIME PUNKS

The Clash on the streets of Belfast after their gig was cancelled, October 1977

By 1977, things in the shop were going really well and we really seemed to have hit our stride. Finally I was doing something I loved! I made sure I was always well up to date with the ever-changing trends in music, and of course the biggest thing by the late seventies was punk.

Dave had recently started printing punk fanzine *Alternative Ulster* from his printers upstairs, so I knew a good bit about the genre, though I hadn't seen any of it performed live. However, I knew its history, and loved its ideals. The only difference that I could see between the punk movement of the seventies and the hippies of the sixties was that instead of being arrested for handing out flowers, punks were arrested for being loud-mouthed and not being afraid to say you were full of crap. To be a punk was to be a pariah, and nothing highlighted this sentiment better than the now-infamous Clash gig, which was scheduled to take place in Belfast on 20 October 1977.

It was the first visit to Ireland by one of the major London punk bands, so hundreds of people had travelled from far and wide for the gig. They waited outside the Ulster Hall, knocking back a few bottles of Olde English and growing more and more excited at the prospect of seeing their punk-rock idols in the flesh. At the very last minute, however, the insurance on the gig was cancelled (by order of Belfast City Council) and, since these were pre-mobile phone days, it was too late to let anyone know.

No one really knew what to do and naturally there were a lot of upset and pissed-off people about. Then rumours began to circulate that the gig might go ahead at Queen's, but while both The Clash and the promoter were trying to get that sorted, the RUC arrived and, no doubt seeing a crowd of rowdy youngsters, went into automatic Belfast 'riot control' mode.

They got pretty heavy-handed as they tried to disperse the crowd but, later, the local press seemed to be more interested in poking fun at the 'wacky' punks than in reporting the police brutality, churning out tediously infantile drivel like, 'one girl had a kettle for a handbag'.

What still rankles to this day was the ridiculous attitude of the local establishment to punk: Belfast City Council had the insurance cancelled simply because they didn't want to let a 'nasty' punk band play in their city. I think what makes me most angry however, is that when the newly refurbished Ulster Hall re-opened its doors in March 2009 it marked the Clash non-gig as a major event in its history!

The irony is that the cancelled gig actually became a catalyst for the punk movement in Belfast, drawing more and more people to the music. Where once local bands had played to just a handful of people, there were now hundreds of fans. My own conversion to the scene however would come just a little later thanks to a shop regular, 'Wee' Gordy Owens.

Gordy – or 'Fangs' as we used to call him, due to some missing teeth – was generally very likeable, even if he could sometimes be a real pain in the arse. He almost never went to school and he tortured us all day long, but it was he who told me about a gig at a local club called The Pound that would change the direction of Good Vibrations forever.

The Pound had been an important music venue right through the sixties, a place where you could have seen some of the big showband stars for a ticket price of £1 – hence the name. It was there that you would have seen the likes of Them – though without Van Morrison – and acts like local soul legend Sam Mahood, or the Jim Daly Blues Band playing in residence.

The Pound was part of Roddy's Bar on Townsend Street, just round

Kids making their way home after partying at The Pound

the corner from the Law Courts, and a shabbier place I have yet to see. Comfort was not high on the list of priorities at The Pound – it had the look and feel of a stable, but in the centre of the city. It had the worst toilets for miles around – which is quite a claim to fame considering some of the dumps I drank in back then – and was even closed down on more than one occasion because of the bogs.

Most pubs and clubs were closed at night during the Troubles as nobody felt safe going into the city centre – East Berlin was probably livelier than Belfast in the late seventies! – but The Pound was one of the few exceptions. With the likes of Light and Sk'Boo playing on a Saturday afternoon it was pulling in big crowds. Although, like most city centre buildings, it hadn't escaped The Troubles unscarred. It was used as a makeshift morgue on 'Bloody Friday' when, on 21 July 1972, the IRA detonated a series of bombs across Belfast killing nine people and injuring dozens more; and it was badly damaged by a bomb at the nearby Oxford Street bus station in 1983, forcing it to close. But for three heady years between 1978 and 1981 it was home to some great punk gigs and for me it will always be the starting place for Good Vibrations' biggest adventure.

So anyway, it was 12 January 1978 and on Fangs' recommendation we went down to The Pound. I can't remember who else was with me, apart from my mate Paul Campbell, and by the time we arrived the place was already packed – there was a real feeling of expectation in the air.

The first band on was The Outcasts and I absolutely hated them! But then a band called RUDI took to the stage and they blew my mind. From the moment the first chords were played I was completely in love with them – hook, line and sinker. They sounded like one of those American garage rock bands from the sixties, like The Standells, Electric Prunes or The Seeds, but what sealed it for me was that, halfway through their set, the RUC came in and tried to break up the gig …

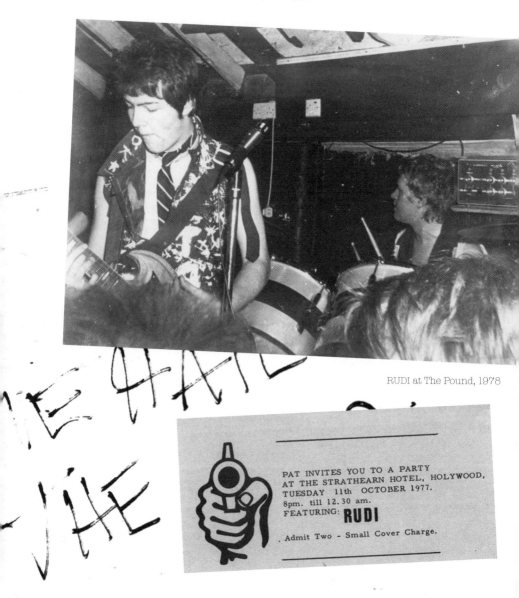

RUDI at The Pound, 1978

PAT INVITES YOU TO A PARTY AT THE STRATHEARN HOTEL, HOLYWOOD, TUESDAY 11th OCTOBER 1977. 8pm. till 12.30 am. FEATURING: **RUDI**

. Admit Two - Small Cover Charge.

In reaction to the cancelled Clash gig three months earlier, RUDI's lead singer, Brian Young, had written 'Cops', the lyrics of which went, 'Go to see the show, just wanna hear some rock 'n' roll. City Council says no, Ulster Hall says no.' Even better was the chorus of 'We hate the cops', and the well known 'SS RUC' chant which served as both intro and outro. It became *the* Northern Ireland punk anthem and always went down a storm live.

When they saw the police enter The Pound, everyone immediately started singing the chant from the song: 'SS RUC' and I thought to myself, 'This is fuckin' great!' I loved the energy and I loved the fact that these kids didn't seem to give a shit about the cops and were prepared to take them on. Punk was anarchy, and I had been waiting for it all my life.

RUDI themselves were no newcomers to punk, however. The band had formed in 1975, though in those early days their influences were glam rock greats such as Marc Bolan, and David Bowie. They were only about fifteen or sixteen years of age at the time and their act was a bit rough and ready – they coloured their hair, wore customised boilersuits, and had a cheap but effective lightshow. But the explosion of punk onto the scene in 1976 meant a complete change in direction for them. At that time RUDI were really the only local punk band doing any gigs in Northern Ireland. The band themselves reckon they played about twenty different gigs throughout 1977, which doesn't sound like much by today's standards, but was quite a significant amount at the time, especially when you consider that venues were so limited. There were absolutely no places to play

RUDI, 1979
L-R: Ronnie Matthews,
Brian Young, Graham Marshall

E.M.S.
PRESENTS

QUEENS

THE
BUZZCOCKS

WITH **RUDI**

THURSDAY, 26th JANUARY, 1978

THE
ADVERTS

THURSDAY, 2nd FEBRUARY, 1978

**BOTH CONCERTS IN
McMORDIE HALL, STUDENTS UNION
DOORS OPEN 7.30 p.m.**

NOW BOOKING **CAROLINE** MUSIC ANN STREET

in the centre of Belfast, so venues like the The Trident in Bangor, the Windsor Hotel in Holywood, or the Glenmachan Hotel and Girton Lodge in east Belfast were about the only ones available.

But RUDI were so good that they were even offered the chance to support The Buzzcocks at their gig at the McMordie Hall at Queen's on 26 January 1978. On the night RUDI arrived early to set up and waited for The Buzzcocks, but they never showed. Eamonn McCann, who ran Queen's entertainments, asked RUDI if they'd play a free gig for everyone and it turned out to be the biggest gig (up to then anyway!) to be headlined by a local band. Everybody thought that The Buzzcocks had chickened out, and even when it was announced that their van had broken down somewhere in Wales on their way to the ferry, no one believed it – at least not until about four years later when RUDI got chatting to a DJ who had actually been in the van heading to Belfast with The Buzzcocks when it broke down, and he was able to confirm that it was all true!

RUDI had been through a few line-up changes since their formation, but by the time I saw them at The Pound the group comprised Brian Young, Ronnie Matthews, Graham 'Grimmy' Marshall and Gordy Blair and they were being managed by Kyle Leitch who worked in Belfast's biggest record shop Caroline Music. RUDI was the first of the local bands to start writing their own material, and I was just so impressed by them.

It was for this reason, and carried away by excitement and enthusiasm, that I found myself battling through the throng of punks pogoing in front of the stage that night and asking RUDI if they fancied putting out a flexi-disc single.

The band knew who I was thankfully. They were regular customers in the shop and while I do think they thought I was just some old hippy from the sixties, lead singer, Brian Young shared my love of sixties girl groups and old rockabilly. After seeing them in action that night, I knew that I wanted to bring this band to the public's attention and to help them in any way I could. I did some investigating and discovered that to make a flexi-disc would cost around 11p per unit, while it was only a few pence extra to press a vinyl 45. I suggested that we do that instead, they agreed, and the Good Vibrations record label was born.

It was perfect – everything I had done in my life seemed to be leading to this moment. I had thought about starting a record label in the sixties and calling it Orbit – because we were all out of our heads! – but with one thing and another, I never did. I always felt that I had missed a great opportunity then, as so many great local acts like The Aztecs or the late great Sam Mahood and The Big Soul Band had failed to get a recording deal. I knew that I couldn't let that happen again – I had to let the world know that there was something vibrant happening here.

We managed to raise the money to make the record from a series of gigs, and there were many late nights in the shop and at my house in Jerusalem Street sorting out the details. Naturally there was always a lot of drink taken. In the end we decided we would produce two tracks, 'Big Time' and 'Number One', so Kyle organised for RUDI to record at Hydepark Studios in Templepatrick on 7 February 1978.

The band borrowed a van, we all piled in, and headed for Templepatrick. George Doherty was the house producer and he really knew what he was doing, even though he spent most of the time talking up Pretty Boy Floyd & the Gems, a local band he was managing. The lads had never set foot in a recording studio before but they simply set up and played the entire backing track as they would play it live. The vocals were recorded separately, and it was all done and dusted in three hours.

Three thousand copies of the record were then pressed by EMI in Dublin. Two friends of mine – Gerry Devlin and John Carson – and I drove down in John's Mini to hear it. It rained most of the way there, and unfortunately the windscreen wipers weren't working properly, so Gerry and I each had to pull wee bits of string attached to the wipers all the way there! I don't know how we made it to the factory in one piece.

When we arrived, they played the record to see if we were happy with it. Happy? We were absolutely knocked out! It was one of the best days of my life.

Me with Good Vibrations'
first-ever record

GOOD VIBRATIONS

FIRST RECORD

RUSH RELEASE

BIG TIME

BY

RUDI

GOOD VIBRATIONS

102 GT. VICTORIA ST
BELFAST BT2 7BE

And it wasn't just us that the record made an instant impression on. I remember a girl who worked in the factory approached me after we had played it. 'Would there be any chance I could get a copy of that?' she said. It was a beautiful moment.

We released 'Big Time' in April 1978 and to this day it remains my favourite song on the Good Vibrations label. I had such faith in the band that I sent a copy off to every record label in England but nobody replied, not even to acknowledge that they had received it. We managed to sell every copy of it anyway though!

I believed so much that something really exciting was happening in Belfast that I didn't give a shit what the record companies thought. More and more kids were coming into my shop, more and more people were forming bands and the general atmosphere was just incredible. It was as if all the shit going on outside didn't matter anymore. These may have been the darkest days of the Troubles, but I honestly believe punk bands saved countless lives then, keeping impressionable young people away from the paramilitaries and giving us all something exciting to focus on.

Although I wanted nothing more than for them to be successful, RUDI broke my heart when, a matter of months after the single was released, they announced they were heading to London. I thought that they were making a mistake by leaving, but they felt this was their chance.

On 9 August 1978, the boys packed a white van with all their gear and caught the ferry to Scotland. They were so skint they had to siphon petrol from parked cars to keep

RUDI, 1978. When their van
died, I had to go over and get
their gear from Birmingham!

the van going, but they finally hit London and set themselves up in a squat in Clapham. They turned to Bernie Rhodes, manager of The Clash, and to the late Malcolm McLaren for guidance, but RUDI found it difficult, and despite gigging with the likes of The Nips, Bitch and Stiff Little Fingers, things just didn't work out. And so, in December 1978, when Ronnie and Grimmy spent a week in jail following a spurious driving offence, they decided to pack up and come home. They were back in Belfast just in time to contribute to a documentary on punk, *Shellshock Rock*, which was being produced that year by local filmmaker, John T. Davis. In January 1979, the band provided interviews for the piece and were filmed playing 'Big Time' at the Glenmachan.

It was around this time that they came to the notice of Polydor Records who offered to sign them, but only on the condition that they dropped their drummer, Grimmy. To their credit the lads refused, knowing that it wouldn't have been right for them.

In August 1979, Cherry Red, the London-based independent record label, asked if they could feature 'Big Time' as the lead track on *Labels Unlimited*, a forthcoming compilation LP. It turned out to be a mixed blessing: in allowing Cherry Red to use the song, we had unwittingly signed away the publishing rights for it, but the album generated such interest that Mike Read, the Radio One DJ took to regularly playing the song on his hugely popular evening show. On top of that, the clip of their Glenmachan gig from *Shellshock* was shown on *Nationwide*, a hugely popular TV news and current affairs magazine programme. It was fantastic exposure.

Never one to miss an opportunity, Good Vibes reissued 'Big Time' in October 1979 with a brand-new sleeve, which I'm sorry to say, the band hated. On the back of the new sleeve we had added this note, 'RUDI/Good Vibrations decided to re-press and re-activate this single in the hope that they now get the recognition they justly deserve. RUDI are one of Ireland's best bands and so far have managed to elude a contract with any of the major labels. Any interested parties can get in touch.'

RUDI continued to release material on Good Vibrations and, through the great contacts they had made in England, they gigged all over the UK. In 1981 they were signed to Jamming! Records in London – the brainchild of long-time RUDI fan, Tony Fletcher, and Paul Weller of The Jam.

They put out a couple of records, but despite a huge fan base it just didn't happen for them the way it should have, and when The Jam split in 1982, the Jamming! label also ceased operation, leaving RUDI high and dry. It was then that they decided to call it a day, though Brian Young, who is still a great friend, continues to gig with a band called The Sabrejets. I tried to talk RUDI into playing together again, but I think they were just worn out. The disappointment was too much for them. They were one of the most popular bands Northern Ireland has ever had and, to be honest, they were the ones we all thought would make it. They had everything.

THE POUND
BRIAN YOUNG

First time I set foot in The Pound I absolutely hated it! And no wonder!
It woulda been sometime early in 1976, and aged just sweet sixteen
I'd ventured down to one of the regular Saturday afternoon gigs with
several of my mates. Starry-eyed after getting to meet Marc Bolan the
previous year, I'd recently got together a band of sorts – which would
eventually become RUDI, Belfast's very first (and, for a very long time,
only!) punk combo – and we reckoned it was about time we checked out
the competition!

In all honesty, our curiosity was probably piqued more by the rumours
that, within this very venue, every illicit substance your heart could
desire – along with acres of willing female flesh – was readily available.
A heady and irresistible mix to impressionable, dumb, horny teenagers
like us!

Sadly, the reality was very different and, after managing to bluff our
way in past the manager, Dermott Moffat, who didn't seem to like the
look of us, we found ourselves in a grimy, dank, whitewashed stable-
like building, packed wall to wall with hordes of long-haired bedenimed
and bearded hippies who didn't exactly welcome us with open arms! To
add insult to injury, it soon became apparent that not only was there
precious little sign of any illicit substances but also that none of the
'hippy chicks' present seemed even remotely interested in talking to,
never mind exchanging actual bodily fluids with, any of our party. Mebbe
if I'd splashed out on a flea-bitten afghan coat and grown a beard I'd have
had more luck? But I guess my spiffy ensemble of sawn-off skinners,
Wrangler coat, and Crombie (with the red pocket lining pulled up!),
all topped off with a particularly scrappy DIY Bowie spiky haircut, was
somewhat out of place in those august environs.

Still, there was always the music? So, after clambering up to the small
upstairs balcony (where you could spit into the band's drink if they
weren't looking!), we waited expectantly for the band to take to the
stage – and at that point things went from bad to worse. Instead of the
no-holds-barred rock 'n' roll action I'd been expecting, we were treated
to a series of lamentably predictable, soulless, American AOR cover
versions – 'album oriented rock' to you and me – which consisted of

long meandering tunes with no real structure, and which were mind-numbingly boring, especially when they were executed, somewhat perfunctorily, by some aging longhairs who apparently included several ex-members of the latter-day, post hit-making, line-up of Them. Back then AOR was the ultimate form of derision and to my way of thinking still is! Don't get me wrong, they sure could play but frankly, to someone raised on Johnny Thunders and Iggy Pop, they looked and sounded dull, boring and very, very old ... and after a while the interminable, self-indulgent guitar/drum/bass solos really started to get on my tits! If I never ever hear 'Reelin' in the Years' again it'll be much too soon. Natch, the hippies loved it and the place went nuts. Natch, I hated every minute of it, and left to get the early bus home, determined never to go back.

But as fate would have it, not that long after, as punk started to rear its spiky lil' head in earnest, The Pound confounded my expectations by staging gigs by acts like Little Bob Story and The Count Bishops. Though both pulled decent enough crowds, the bands still looked positively geriatric, having more in common with the fag end of pub rock than punk rock. Also, let's face it, once you'd seen Dr Feelgood during their Wilko era, every other pub rock band was just pissing in the wind. The Feelgoods had already torn apart the Whitla Hall at Queen's – an oft overlooked catalyst for nascent NI punk – in an event which was every bit as significant as the much lauded Clash visit in October 1977. But for The Pound it was a huge leap in the right direction.

Sadly, once punk lost its underground and alternative status – mainly due to the Sex Pistols and their 'Jubilee' media blitz of 1977 – the scabrous tabloids went into overdrive, hyping up a frenzy of anti-punk sentiment at every opportunity. The Pistols, and indeed every punk band, became the enemy and, for those of us from Northern Ireland, the additional implied religious/political spin added a very real danger – as being seen as pro- or anti-monarchy could have a very real impact on your general well-being, depending on your location at the time!

Now firmly identified in the public eye as one of those 'nasty punk bands', RUDI were kicked out of our regular practice hall on the Albertbridge Road and banned from our regular east Belfast haunts, the Glenmachan Hotel and Girton Lodge – and so we kept on pestering The Pound for the chance to play.

Finally, they relented, agreeing to put on a RUDI/Outcasts double-header on 12 January 1978. They weren't exactly taking a huge risk as this was a weeknight, when most bars would be virtually empty! Nevertheless, as fate would have it, this very night would turn out to be the infamous occasion when wee Gordy finally dragged a certain Mr Hooley down to see RUDI in action, which Terri regularly cites as being the springboard for the whole Good Vibes label.

CELEBRATE THE NEW YEAR AT

THE
POUND
MUSIC CLUB
TOWNHALL STREET
(Opposite Oxford Street Bus Station Car Park)
When in Town, call at The Pound

Wednesday —
LIGHT

Thursday —
BRONCO
Plus SUPPORTING BAND

Friday
RUDI plus OUTCASTS

Saturday Afternoon —
LIGHT

Saturday Night —
BRONCO

All these years later, I can't remember much about that night – apart from the fact that we'd had to hire amps from local company Bairds, which we lugged to and from the gig on the bus and which none of us could figure out how to use properly. We probably sounded more like Bert Weedon on a particularly bad day rather than the intended beefy raunch of the Pistols' Steve Jones!

Unfortunately too, we were still wearing our customised boilersuits, a look we'd come up with in our earliest days to try to give us an identity which would set us apart from all the other local bands who were uniformly visually dull and boring. It did work though, in fairness, we probably looked like a squad of painters on their way home from work! Thankfully the boilersuits' days were soon to be numbered!

Much more impressively, unlike any other contemporary Belfast band back then that I can think of, we had started writing and playing a lot of our own material too – alongside the old rock 'n' roll/glam and sixties garage slop we'd started off with. In fact, if memory serves me right, this was the first time we ever publicly played a brand-new song we'd just written called 'Big Time' – we thought it was pretty good too! But we never did play The Who's 'My Generation' as Terri insists – I never liked that song much and besides it was far too complicated!

Anyway, for whatever reason, even though it was a weeknight, the place was packed and the young punky waver crowd went totally apeshit! In all the excitement a few lights got smashed and both RUDI and The Outcasts were promptly banned, forbidden to set foot on-stage in The Pound ever again! Little did they know …

In fact, RUDI were due to return to The Pound the very next month to be filmed alongside Stiff Little Fingers for the UTV documentary on the local punk scene, *It Makes You Want To Spit,* but were replaced by Victim at the very last minute after some devious double-dealing behind the scenes. Thankfully, it turned out to be a blessing in disguise, as the show turned out to be a hopelessly inept, and unintentionally hilarious, piece of televisual crap, organised by people who clearly had no idea what was going on and who merely viewed the bands as some sort of curiosity.

Meanwhile, an alternative city centre venue was found shortly afterwards in the unlikely shape of The Harp Bar, which quickly became the epicentre of Belfast's punk music explosion. Unwilling to get left behind, and anxious not to miss out on a whole new generation of paying punters, The Pound relented and began to bring in more 'new wave' acts such as The Doomed, Lurkers and Radio Stars in 1978 – though, for now at least, pride of place was still going to the various incestuous line-ups of Light, Sk'Boo and Bronco!

RUDI returned to The Pound at Christmas '78 for a lunchtime gig, with a special guest spot from our chums from London, The Raped. They played their last ever gigs under that unfortunate moniker before opting for the equally lame title of Cuddly Toys.

Again, this event was not without incident, as Pound manager Dermott threw a hissy fit when he discovered that we had also arranged a gig with the same line-up the next evening at The Harp and he was insistent that

A flyer advertising The Pound's Christmas line-up, *c.* 1978

RUDI would never be able to fill two venues so close together! Thankfully we proved him wrong, playing to jam-packed houses on both occasions! An *NME* review even noted that it was the biggest crowd at a gig in The Harp Bar ever! How times had changed!

RUDI didn't get back into The Pound until April 1979, but from then on we played there on a pretty regular basis, particularly when Chris Roddy took over the managerial reins. With its low ceiling rafters – which the more acrobatic singers would swing from – and a relatively big, but low, stage taking up almost one wall, there was plenty of room to jump about, and it was great fun to play. It was easy to get a good sound and the audience was literally right in your face! It was also relatively trouble free and whilst the 'facilities' mighta been rudimentary at best, and you hadda wade in and out of the toilets on occasion, we'd seen much worse. One consolation of that hazardous journey to the toilets was that you could often get a free pint or two, as it wasn't unheard of for the occasional beer keg to be 'liberated' and upended over one of the stinking toilet bowls with free drink dispensed to all and sundry ... those were the days, huh?

Truth is, many of the best gigs I ever played and ever saw were under that roof. You'll just have to take my word for it though, as a proposed live album of RUDI at The Pound had to be scrapped when Davy Wiz – aka Davy Smyth, the owner of Wizard Studios in Belfast – screwed up the recording. Typical!

Later on, as punk began to run out of steam and The Harp switched to hosting country and western nights (strange but true!) more and more local punk bands switched allegiance to The Pound and a notoriously lax door policy allowed a lot of younger punters to see what all the fuss was about first-hand.

Though by now well outside the restrictive identipunk mainstream, RUDI could still pack The Pound and we were offered, and played, several long-running residencies which I recall with a very real fondness. In fact, we'd become such a regular fixture in the place that Chris even allowed us to rehearse in The Pound during the day. Mind you, The Pound in broad daylight was not a pretty sight, and many a time we were interrupted mid-song by the sight of live rats racing across the stage, probably trying to get away from our tuneless thrashings!

Nevertheless, this invaluable on-stage rehearsal time really paid off handsomely when we signed to Tony Fletcher/Paul Weller's Jamming! Label in 1981. It allowed us to hone our chops in preparation for our prestige support slot to The Jam on their massive Trans Global Unity Express UK tour in March and April of 1982 where we actually got encores night after night!

Sound check at The Pound, 1979.
L-R: Gordy, Ronnie, Brian and Graham

Later that same month we set out on our first ever large-scale UK tour as headliners – which proved another great success! Who knows what mighta happened if The Jam hadn't split and the label hadn't had to fold! We called it a day shortly after – and, somewhat ironically, the last-ever RUDI gig took place in The Pound on 30 December 1982 – though we didn't know that's what it was at the time!

Though it's now long gone, on the right night, with the right band, The Pound was a great place to see live music, and despite my initial reservations I spent many a happy night there. It's tragic that there's nowhere in Belfast like it now. It's also well worth remembering that The Pound was very much a neutral, safe venue at a time when those were very thin on the ground, and it most definitely deserves

Paul Weller with Brian and Liz Young

recognition for daring to put on live music in the centre of Belfast all through the very worst days of the Troubles – even if most of it wasn't exactly to my particular taste!

GOOD VIBRATIONS

102 GT. BELFAST

WORKING WITH OUTCASTS

The label was up and running, and its existence changed my whole way of thinking. I could see that we now had a vehicle, a platform for all those bands in Belfast and beyond who were desperate for a chance to show what they could do. The reaction to the release of the RUDI record had underlined to me – as if I needed proof – that, to the record companies at least, Northern Ireland was a music backwater. Kids with real talent and a message to deliver were having to try and kick down a locked door. I was determined that Good Vibrations was to be the key they needed.

It wasn't long before my attention was captured by another vibrant Belfast band, Victim. Like so many who came after them the band was made up of a bunch of lads who hung out in the shop. I actually thought they were more of a mod band than a punk outfit as they were always pretty sharply dressed in suits and ties.

Victim at The Harp, c.1978. L-R: Jeff Beattie, Hugh O'Boyle, Wes Graham and Joe Zero

When I saw them live I thought they were different and, in a way, I almost felt sorry for them because they didn't seem to fit in with the whole punk ethos, but I liked them and so I signed them up anyway. They are credited with being the first band to play a punk gig at The Harp and I remember them playing the Windsor Hotel one night when someone ran on-stage and nicked lead singer Colin 'Ziggy' Campbell's mic while he was still singing!

We released their first single, 'Strange Thing By Night' on 1 June 1978. The whole record cost £90 to record and was the band's only release with Good Vibrations. In July 1979, Victim were offered a record deal by Manchester-based label, TJM Records, and the band moved over to England, where they supported The Damned on their 1979 UK tour.

In 1981, and only for a brief period, Mike

GOOD VIBRATIONS

BIG

2

NEW

WAVES

NOW RELEASED ON THE PUBLIC

BIG TIME
BY RUDI
STRANGE THING BY NIGHT
BY VICTIM

TWO GOOD BELFAST GROUPS
TWO GOOD NEW WAVE SINGLES
TWO GOOD VIBRATIONS RELEASES
TOO GOOD TO MISS

GOOD REVIEWS IN THE PRESS
GOOD AIRPLAY
GOOD VIBES ALL ROUND

Pic sleeves

BIG TIME. BY RUDI (GOT1)
STRANGE THING BY NIGHT
BY VICTIM. (GOT2)
YES GOT 1 & 2
YOU HAVE GOT TO GET THEM

With Getty from The Outcasts
at Downtown Radio

Joyce – later of The Smiths – became their drummer, but by then I had lost touch with them. I know the band broke up around 1990 and that some of the members stayed in England, but I think they left the music scene altogether.

The third band I signed at Good Vibrations was The Outcasts, and if anybody had told me when I had first seen them play that a year later I would be their record label boss and manager, I would have laughed my head off because at that stage I really hated them!

I still maintain that in their early days they were truly awful – they were too aggressive and I'm convinced they were called The Outcasts even before they were a band because nobody would invite them to their parties. But in spite of this, in March 1978, they managed to arrange a one-release deal with IT Records in Portadown, and issued a single called 'You're a Disease'. I'm not exactly sure how well that did, but a few months later Greg Cowan from the band came to see me in the shop and we got to talking. Maybe it was because I was growing fond of the lads themselves, but I began to see a real humour in them and their songs and it was for this reason that I ended up offering them a chance to put out a record with Good Vibrations. So, in the summer of the same year, their song, 'Justa Nother Teenage Rebel' became the third single we released, with 'Love is for Sops' as a B-side.

I think part of the problem at the outset of their career was how awful the band sounded when performing live. The equipment they had at the time was really old, so

The Outcasts

that of course made the band sound terrible. There was one particular gig at The Harp, that thankfully I was not at, where the sound quality was just dreadful apparently. It was so bad that they were getting stick from the crowd, and you had to be pretty terrible to get a bad time from an audience in The Harp! This was a great pity for a band that had built a following based on its live performances and so I decided to buy them a new PA. It's on-stage performance that makes any band, and I knew that they had to sound better or they wouldn't sell any records.

And these guys just loved to get out and play – even if I used to introduce them on-stage as 'the band we love to hate'! The band consisted of Blair Hamilton, Colin 'Getty' Getwood and brothers Martin, Colin and Greg Cowan – they were all totally mad.

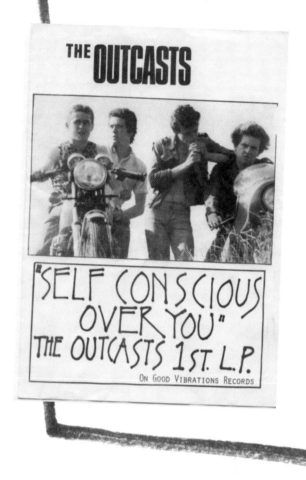

Colin Cowan, for example, had developed a 'burst on-stage routine', which involved him sneaking backstage at gigs in the Ulster Hall or wherever, running on-stage, grabbing the mic and shouting, 'Outcasts!' before diving into the crowd. He managed this guerrilla advertising at Graham Parker and the Rumour, Boomtown Rats and Elvis Costello gigs, making the band very unpopular with the bouncers. I'm convinced that's why, after The Clash gig in October 1978 – a gig in which they were the support act – the bouncers gave them a severe beating.

But they were great guys at heart, and they actually recorded the first album Good Vibrations ever put out, *Self Conscious Over You*. We didn't exactly sell thousands of copies, but we were very proud of it nonetheless. I remember coming down to the shop on Boxing Day 1979 just to make sure everything was all right, and we ended up selling thirty-five copies of the album to all these kids who had been given Christmas money!

Unfortunately, not long after the album release, I began to receive a lot of complaints from venues about the behaviour of one of The Outcasts' fans, a nasty piece of work who was handy with his fists and who was continually causing havoc and picking fights with doormen. I didn't want Good Vibrations to be associated with a character like that so I told The Outcasts that as long as he was around I couldn't manage them anymore. Thankfully, the guys realised that this had been a difficult decision for me to make, so they accepted my position and I resigned as their manager, though I remain close to the boys to this day.

One of our many Good Vibrations flyers

In 1980 the band began recording with French indie label, New Rose, and decided to form their own label, GBH, which later became Outcasts Only, but I always regarded them as our band, and we were all mates – Getty even worked for Good Vibrations for a bit.

Tragically, on 13 May 1982, Colin Cowan was killed in a car accident and I don't think the lads ever really recovered – this loss marked the beginning of the end for the band. They released a few more singles and played a few more gigs, but in 1985 the band decided to break up.

In a way, they became the label's most famous band. They were offered deals by Rak Records and Polydor, and were a really significant act across Europe, becoming especially huge in France, but they always knew their place was in Northern Ireland. They played music for the love of it, and I know they had a ball in the process. As Greg Cowan said, 'It was a magical time to be young when with three chords and a killer haircut you could be a rock star.'

Seasons greetings from GOOD VIBRATIONS

102 GREAT VICTORIA STREET, BELFAST. PHONE 29152

Of course, the biggest problem we had then was trying to find a venue. Up until 1978 most gigs took place in bars and youth clubs, but because of the security situation it was virtually impossible for fans from outside Belfast to travel. Thrown into the mix was the fact that many bar owners wouldn't touch a punk gig with a barge pole, and so we often had to get creative.

We would book hotels or function rooms in bars under false pretences, telling them it was for a birthday party or something, and then, on the night have a band turn up. Sometimes the hotels would try to kick us out, and we were also barred from a few pubs as a result, but on the whole, most places were just happy to have people spending money there. Back then a booking for any kind of function was a bonus and, as long as people behaved themselves, they were happy.

But it was getting more and more difficult to organise anything as people grew wise to our tactics, and it became blindingly obvious that if punk was to survive, it needed a venue of its own.

Enter The Harp Bar. It was located on Hill Street – a stone's throw from St Anne's Cathedral on the north edge of Belfast city centre – and seen from the outside with its metal security grills and blacked-out windows, you could be forgiven for thinking it was a condemned building. It had not escaped the Troubles unscathed and even as early as the mid-seventies had been targeted in a number of terrorist attacks.

By day it was a strip club, and a less glamorous strip joint you will never find. I never actually saw a stripper there but, after hearing reports from those who did, I'm very relieved! The ground floor had two rooms – one with a bar, a pool table and a jukebox, while the back room had a small stage – but upstairs was where the action took place. It was also where the afternoon strippers did their business, or so I'm told.

The room upstairs could hold about 350 people, and had a small stage and a dance floor – which was known as 'murder alley' – over which hung one of those classy ballroom mirrorballs. The bathrooms had to be seen to be believed and, with everybody packed in, the floor was treacherous with spilt drink, sweat and damp. It was a classy joint! The only bother ever came when bands tried to set up their gear in the afternoon with a stripper doing her routine a few yards away. The punters were none too impressed! But by night The Harp came alive and the atmosphere was electric, it was an exciting place, always packed, and it wasn't long before the reputation of The Harp began to grow. At a time when the religious divide in Northern Ireland was most pronounced, we had kids from both sides of the community coming together in the name of music and there was rarely any trouble.

Around that time, some friends and I had set up the Punk Workshop, with the goal of coordinating and booking gigs for the bands on our label, and we saw The Harp as the perfect venue for our 1978 May Day Punk Festival. It was a pretty chaotic affair with only one band, Pretty Boy Floyd & The Gems, turning up to play – some bands were notoriously unreliable and often wouldn't turn up, while others just didn't have access to transport for their gear – but thankfully a few lads in the audience had just formed a band called The Basics and they agreed to do a quick set. Despite the initial hiccups however, we decided to book The Harp on a more regular basis, for the Workshop to put on a band every week. Soon this evolved into a proper club, with paying members and a committee – of which yours truly was a member! – to oversee things. Thursday nights became punk disco nights, and Friday and Saturday were given over to live gigs.

Not that we can take the credit for bringing punk to The Harp. April of that year had already seen The Harp's first-ever punk gig thanks to Victim and a band called The

Androids. In time, just about every punk band in Northern Ireland would come to play there, bands like The Undertones, RUDI, Ruefrex, Protex, The Tearjerkers, The Moondogs and The Idiots, to name but a few.

Soon visiting bands would also take the time to visit The Harp, such was its notoriety. The Clash made a pilgrimage to have their picture taken outside it, and in May 1979 John Peel even made a point of paying it a visit, though I don't think he had ever seen anything like it. In later years, I would bring over bands like The Fall and The Nips – Shane MacGowan's first band – to play at the venue.

It might have been an absolute dump but The Harp kept punk alive, and indeed punk kept it alive. However, The Pound was the bigger venue of the two and it was generally accepted that once bands outgrew The Harp they moved there instead. So, over time, the bands started to move away, more venues began to open up, and The Harp became a country and western club, before eventually closing its doors for good.

The building itself is long gone and the area has now become the very trendy Cathedral Quarter, packed with bars, restaurants and newer music venues. It's sad but the vast majority of people who throng the cobbled streets in that area now have no idea that it was once the location of one of the only clubs putting on live music in Belfast in the seventies and eighties.

I think they should put a special plaque up on the wall to mark the spot where the building once stood – 'Famous Strip Joint and Punk Venue, The Harp Stood Here' – but I don't think the suits on Belfast City Council would wear it!

Direct from LUTON! *THE JETS*

HARP BAR, HILL STREET

Friday 11th January 1980

Support *Rudi*

Saturday 12th January 1980

Support *Outcasts*

ADMISSION £1.00

8p.m.

THE DUBLIN WEEKEND
GREG COWAN

We had released our first single 'You're a Disease' on IT records in 1978 to universal apathy, and had to jealously watch as both Stiff Little Fingers and RUDI got loads of attention for their first singles. We knew the Stiffs had official management, but RUDI were on local label Good Vibes, so we decided to approach them with a view to releasing our next single. After many high-powered meetings – which actually just meant us asking Terri if he was interested, him coming to see us play and then saying he hated what he heard – we released our second single 'Justa Nother Teenage Rebel', and Terri became our manager.

We were offered our first gig in Dublin at McGonagle's bar that same year and Terri decided to use this as an opportunity for a PR assault on the Republic. With a more conventional record company this would have meant a series of meetings, co-ordination of press and radio coverage, culminating with the gig itself, but not Good Vibes. Instead, we loaded the van with whatever equipment we owned, a selection of Good Vibes releases and posters, as many friends as we could squeeze in, and our leader Terri.

Early on a Saturday morning we headed off to Dublin, confident we would be household names by teatime. But things quickly unravelled: the gig itself was pulled as the authorities decided they were having enough trouble with local punks without importing wild men from the north.

This left only the PR push, which consisted of us turning up at the nearest record shop we could find – Golden Discs on Grafton Street – and, while Terri occupied the manager by discussing the possibility of stocking the Good Vibes back catalogue, we spread out, putting up Outcasts posters and menacing as many locals as possible until security escorted us from the building.

Later that night, tails firmly between legs, we retired to our luxurious accommodation to work out phase two – bunking up with Dublin all-girl punk band, The Girl Scouts, who only let us stay because they thought we were RUDI and two of them fancied Ronnie from the band. The girls, taking pity on us, told us there was a two-day festival currently running at Phoenix Park, so the next day, we decided to chance our arm there.

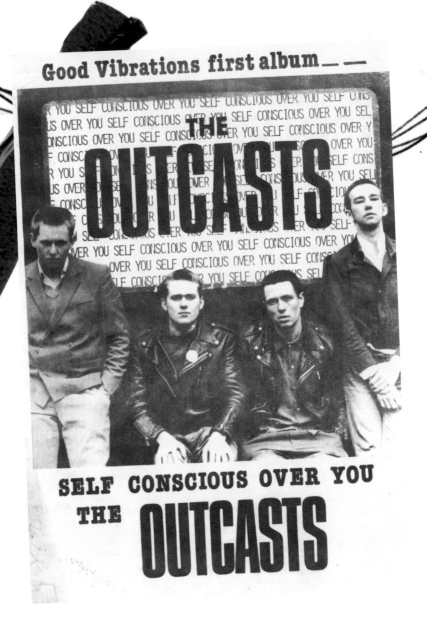

SELF CONSCIOUS OVER YOU

THE OUTCASTS

Sunday morning arrived with torrential rain and we drove through the downpour, expecting to fight our way through thousands of festival-goers. Instead we found a waterlogged stage and a handful of organisers who were bemoaning the fact that the festival would have to be cancelled as all the equipment had been soaked – this being Sunday in Catholic Ireland, there was no danger of getting any replacements! Step forward Terri, the man of the moment. I swear the sun decided to suddenly split the sky as he went into a huddle with the organisers, casually mentioning that not only did we have a complete backline but also a PA! Terri had actually bought our band this PA because he thought it would help our sound and we were very proud to be the only punk band in Belfast to own one, even if Baird Hire had sold it cheaply to prevent any more gear being returned with blood stains and, in one case, teeth embedded in it. It was a Baird two hundred watt, barely enough to fill a phone box and, even in the late seventies, a small festival would expect to have a two to three thousand watt PA, but it would have to do - the show must go on!

The organisers agreed and, just like that, the Phoenix Park festival became the Good Vibrations festival. As such, Terri decided we would not only open the festival but also play anytime we felt like it throughout the day. It's hard to remember just how many people turned up – though years later I was still happily telling people twenty thousand – but the sun stayed out and the sloping hills around the stage quickly filled with expectant music lovers. God help them!

As we had never played Dublin before we decided that we needed a big opening. The plan was to have Terri introduce us, while Blair – our first singer but by now strictly a roadie – would throw cider bottles, which he himself had emptied, over the stage, smashing them on a space in front of the crowd and hopefully causing maximum impact. Sadly this did not all run according to plan, and instead we ended up causing several incidents of grievous bodily harm ...

As we stood on-stage, waiting to begin our first set, Terri appeared unexpectedly in an old-man rubber mask and launched into the first (of many) readings of his autobiographical poem, 'Be My Friend'. Blair, confused as to who this interloper was and believing him to be some chancer from the crowd, decided to launch his first three missiles directly into the audience as a deterrent to others who might follow Terri's example. Of course nobody really had any intention of storming the stage but, even if they did, Blair's bottle missiles soon put the notion out of their heads.

And so, there we were at our first gig in Dublin, with our manager in a rubber mask happily reciting verse sixty-three of his epic and members of St John's Ambulance leading away the wounded – and all before we had even played our first song! Many years later we would still have people claiming to have been at our first Dublin gig where their first cousin twice removed had had their eye put out!

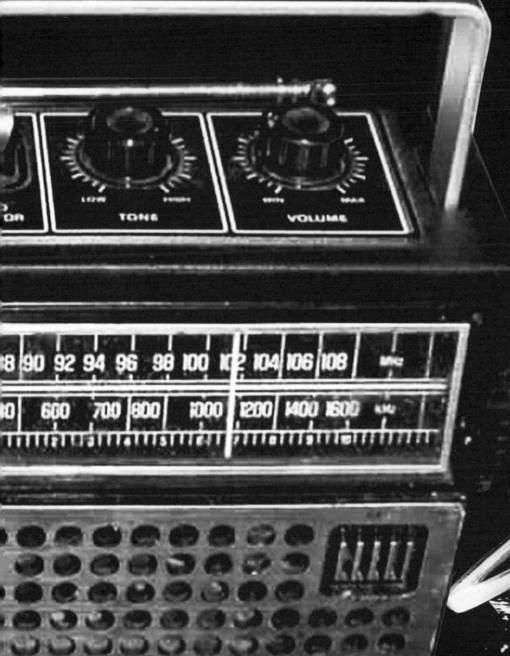

TEENAGE KICKS

Of course, it was the fourth single we released on Good Vibrations that everyone remembers, 'Teenage Kicks' by The Undertones. I wish I had a pound for every person who claimed they were with me when we signed the band to our label – it never ceases to amaze me what people will lay claim to. I guess the world is full of people ready to jump on the bandwagon, but let me tell you there wouldn't have been enough room on the Titanic for all the people who say they were there at the time.

Like any great rock 'n' roll record, the story behind The Undertones coming to Good Vibrations is one of hardship, bad luck, good luck, and most importantly, humour. There are a lot of rumours circulating about my relationship with the band – apparently I didn't like them, apparently Feargal didn't like me – but it is all a load of bollocks!

The story really started when, in 1978, I received a demo the band had recorded. I can't remember exactly how I came by it – it was either given to me by Malcolm 'Maniac Mal' Stewart, a mad dancer down at The Pound who used to buy records from me, or the band may have just sent it in to Good Vibrations in the hope of getting signed. Either way, 'Kicks' was just one of the many songs the lads had recorded on what was, admittedly, a pretty rough demo. But there was something about the music that held my attention and kept me coming back.

I remember sitting in one night, getting stoned and drinking poteen with a couple of mates – Ricky Flanagan and a guy called Jimmy Kirk who, in the sixties, had played in a band called The Set, a mod outfit like The Who. Anyway we were listening to some music and I decided to put on The Undertones' demo. By this stage I'd been listening to them for a few weeks and a few of the tracks had begun to grow on me. Jimmy decided to leave because he didn't like the sound of them but by 3.30 a.m., drunk on poteen, Ricky looked at me and said, 'I think that band's got something.' I thought it was the poteen talking, and remained undecided, I guess I needed a little push to force me to make a decision.

A few weeks later, as I was shutting up the shop, that push came in the form of Bernie McAnaney, a friend of mine from Derry who was studying at the Art College in Belfast. He knew The Undertones by way of several mutual friends and that Friday he came into the store to tell me that the band were on the verge of splitting up, and needed to know right away if I was going to sign them.

I didn't really know what to do, I had just been about to head up to Lavery's to sign a band I'd had my eye on, and Good Vibrations just didn't have enough money to sign both, though in an ideal world that's exactly what I would have done. But Bernie continued to hassle me as we walked up Great Victoria Street towards the pub and so, when we reached a set of traffic lights, I told him I would have an answer for him by the time we crossed the road. He kept his mouth closed for the amount of time it took for the lights to change colour and for us to walk across the road, before I eventually caved. 'OK,' I told him, 'they're on the label.' And that's how we got The Undertones.

I went into Lavery's feeling pretty sorry for the other band. They were well organised, had a manager, some good songs and, most importantly, a van – I had been genuinely keen to sign them up. But when I told them we couldn't sign them, they weren't too disheartened. They had set their sights on London and I guess my turning them down helped them make the decision to go there instead. We never heard from them again. And you know what? I couldn't tell you who they were. It used to be that I deliberately kept it a secret, but now I simply can't remember!

The Undertones, L-R: Feargal Sharkey, Michael Bradley, John O'Neill, Damian O'Neill and Billy Doherty

The Undertones were vocalist Feargal Sharkey, bassist Michael Bradley, drummer Billy Doherty and brothers John and Damian O'Neill, both guitarists. Formed in Derry in 1975, the band spent countless hours practising and getting the odd gig in their home city. I think that's why I liked the band so much, unlike many guys of their age in Derry at that time, they weren't out rioting every night. These boys would rehearse whenever they could and that was one of the secrets of their success, they practised and practised and it ultimately paid off.

What I didn't know at the time of signing them was that The Undertones had already been turned down by three English record labels – Stiff, Radar and Chiswick – and that was the reason they were on the brink of splitting up. Good Vibrations was really their last roll of the dice – had we not offered them a deal they were out of options and if Bernie hadn't told me they were splitting up I might not have signed them at all. Fuck me! Then

RUDi
OUTCASTS
DETONATORS
UNDERTONES

plus surprise bands

McMORDIE HALL Q.U

Wed. 14th. June, 8 pm

Admission by ticket 80p from JustBooks
7 Winetavern Street

& GOOD VIBRATIONS
102 GT. VICTORIA ST.

the world wouldn't have got 'Teenage Kicks'. But thankfully The Undertones became part of the Good Vibrations family, and the rest is history.

Around this time Dave Hyndman – with whom I'd set up the building on Great Victoria Street – wanted to set up an anarchist bookshop called Just Books. He'd secured premises on Winetavern Street and we decided to put on a big punk gig in Belfast to raise some money for him. There were still very few punk gigs in Belfast, particularly any involving local talent – The Clash had visited, and Elvis Costello had played but we wanted to do a home grown thing. So we decided to bring The Undertones down from Derry and have them perform in a Battle of the Bands show alongside RUDI and The Outcasts. They would also be joined by several other local bands, The Idiots, Ruefrex (who were 'Roofwrecks' at the time), Rhesus Negative, and The Detonators. It was going to be incredible, and all we needed now was a venue.

So I got all dressed up, went to Queen's University and told them that I was from the Belfast Music Society and wanted to book the McMordie Hall for a concert. 'That will be £5, Mr Hooley,' they said, and gave me a receipt. 'Is that it?' I asked. 'Yes, it's in the book. Wednesday 14 June 1978, it's all yours.'

I knew it had been too easy, and sure enough it turned out they had thought I was from Queen's Classical Society. When they found out I had hired the hall for a major punk gig they freaked out.

I always knew universities were seats of learning and I can tell you I learned a few dirty tricks over the next few days as Queen's tried everything in their power to disrupt the gig. But this was too big an opportunity to allow them to succeed – the bands were determined to have their chance to stand on a stage and perform in front of a real audience on their own home ground – so the more the university fought it, the more determined I was that the gig should go ahead.

On the night of the event, Queen's were still fighting us. They tried to stop us getting lights, PA and other equipment into the building, but they hadn't counted on the ace up my sleeve – the Hell's Angels! During my time as an activist in the seventies I had become great friends with the Chosen Few, a Hell's Angels chapter in Belfast, and so I asked them to act as security for the night – the university didn't stand a chance!

Hundreds and hundreds of kids turned up from all over the country that night, making it one of the best gigs of my life. All my old hippy friends, the bikers, the punks, they were all there – it was a mad mixture of mad people. But most surprising of all, we actually received a telegram from John Lennon and Yoko Ono wishing us luck in our brave new venture! To receive something like that was surprising to say the least, considering our last encounter had ended in a slight disagreement! I can't honestly say what prompted it either, except that a few of my friends had stayed in touch with the loonies from London who surrounded Lennon at that party. But I read it out at the start of the evening, and it seemed to give the bands a real boost.

Seven bands in total played that night, so every act was permitted a twenty-five minute set, but Ruefrex figured they were never going to get a bigger audience than this so they tried to play on. No chance! I snapped my fingers and the Hell's Angels came on and physically lifted them off the stage. The biggest cheer of the night was given to my heavy metal friends!

Apart from that, we had no real trouble inside the gig, but because the kids were so upset about the way Queen's had treated me, they went outside and put stones through the windows of the Students' Union. A few days later I got a letter from the university saying I had been barred from the Union for life. Well fuck 'em! Quite honestly,

The vinyl sleeve for
'Teenage Kicks'

by that stage I just didn't give a fuck. Our Battle of the Bands had been a huge success and I was proud of all the acts. The fans had enjoyed themselves and we had shown, especially to the stuffed shirts watching from the staffroom across the road, that young people could put on a great gig. It had also been the first time any of the Belfast bands had seen The Undertones and they were very, very good.

So it was time to make things with The Undertones official. On the morning after the Queen's gig we took them into Belfast city centre to record their EP, which would feature four of their songs, 'Teenage Kicks', 'Smarter Than You', 'True Confessions' and 'Emergency Cases'.

I had booked them into Wizard Studios, a small recording studio located behind the Duke of York pub, and set up by Davy Smyth and his wife Valerie. They were in a band themselves, and they had wanted somewhere to record. They'd even set up a record label called Okey Dokey, though probably nobody remembers it. Dave was a nice enough guy but I don't think he had that much enthusiasm for punk in general, or for any of the local punk bands in particular. He often let mistakes go that should have been corrected, and so most of the Northern Ireland punk records – most of which were recorded in Wizard – can sound a little weedy and embarrassing today. Granted, a lot of the bands themselves were to blame for this as none of them really had a clue about recording, but that's why an experienced and enthusiastic producer would have made the difference.

Anyway, my mate Ricky and I gathered up a few cans of beer, and a few bags of crisps and sandwiches, and headed down to the studio where The Undertones were already at work with producer, Davy Shannon. It was then that I truly realised what we were dealing with – this band was something special. The song had been so well-rehearsed that the lads basically went in and did it all in one take.

We pressed two thousand copies of the EP at EMI in Dublin, and I immediately put three hundred copies on the bus to Derry for The Undertones. The whole thing cost £200 plus VAT.

I remember speaking to Mrs Sharkey on the phone later, and telling her what a wonderful song it was. She said, with typical motherly indulgence, 'Isn't it great the boys have made a wee record.' But I knew that this was more than just 'a wee record' – this was going to change everything.

But, before that could happen, there was still work to be done. The band made a standard record sleeve out of a large sheet of paper which was designed to wrap around the record itself. This sleeve folded out to reveal a poster of the band, and on the outside we had a photograph of a door in a derelict house upon which someone had written, 'The Undertones are shit'! The wee lad responsible for the graffiti actually turned up one day and apologised to the band for doing it. We enlisted the help of RUDI and The Outcasts, went to the store, and all got to work folding the sleeves.

I really believed in this record and so I decided that the best way to get it out there was to go straight to the lion's den – to London, the world capital of music, the theatre of dreams. I thought that if I personally did the rounds at the major labels and distributors, that they would have to listen and they would see just how amazing this record was. And so, with a bag full of 'Teenage Kicks', I was off to London. How could anyone turn this record down?

I should have known better. The record business has never ceased to stun me with its double standards and sharp practice, so I have never really had any love for the industry. In fact, I still hate it and the bastards who run it. They can be ruthless and money-grabbing, and it's the unknown bands and the small labels who suffer as a result. My one thought on that journey to London was, 'Fuck, I've got six days of being nice to these dickheads.'

But I was determined, and when I arrived, I made Rough Trade Records my first port of call. Rough Trade was, at the time, the biggest independent record distributor in the country. It had just signed up Stiff Little Fingers, another great band from Belfast, so I was full of enthusiasm. SLF were really starting to make waves beyond Northern Ireland, and I always see them as the ones that got away. I know I have always said I never rated them, but that was probably jealousy on my part. I actually think they are a great band and deserve their success. When their first album, *Inflammable Material*, was due to be released, I knew it was going to be big so I went over to Rough Trade and asked them for five hundred advance copies to make sure I got it before anyone else in Ireland – we sold out in days.

Anyway, I had a meeting with Geoff Travis and Richard Scott who ran Rough Trade, and wasted no time in playing 'Teenage Kicks' for them. When they told me it was a pile of shit and called it the worst record they had ever heard, I couldn't believe my ears! They had been my big hope. I thought that they, above everybody else, would surely understand what we were trying to achieve. But it was not to be. Instead, they agreed to take five hundred copies – due to the fact that the record was on Good Vibrations, and our label sold records in England – but I came away thinking that they didn't really understand what Good Vibrations or the Northern Ireland music scene was all about.

Despite the setback I took 'Kicks' to EMI and CBS, two of the giants of world music, and hoped that I would fare a little better with them. But after I played the record to the guys at EMI I was told that it was not the kind of music they wanted to put out. I begged them to play it again, which they did, but I was pissing in the wind. They had made up their minds after the first three chords – they were just so dismissive.

So off I went to CBS. Looking back, I suppose I went there with the intention of giving them a lesson on the world according to Terri Hooley and, to a large extent, I like to think I succeeded. I played the record to this guy who was sitting in an office with hundreds of singles stacked on his desk. I was in the middle of telling him that it cost only £200 to record and, without any attempt to soften the blow, he just said, 'No.'

Was that it? 'No'? He just pointed at the pile of records in front of him and said, 'Look at all this wonderful music,' so I picked up a record by Neil Diamond – who has never been one of my favourite artists, but who was discovered by one of my favourite songwriters, Ellie Greenwich – and asked him how much CBS had spent recording it. When he told me, I just lost it. I lifted the records off the desk and dumped them on the floor. 'These records are crap,' I spat at him, 'compared to this.' Seconds later I was physically removed from his offices.

After a few minutes of feeling triumphant, depression started to set in. I felt very alone standing on a London street with only my bag of records for comfort. I didn't believe we could improve on 'Teenage Kicks' and if the record companies were turning it down, what chance did we have? As a last resort I decided to take the time to drop a few copies of the single in at the BBC Radio offices for John Peel.

I had first met John Peel in the early seventies when I was in London looking into ways to set up a Belfast branch of Release – a charity which had been set up in London to help people who had been busted on drugs charges to get legal representation. They had lists of lawyers who were very sympathetic to the plight of those who were on the wrong end of the draconian sentences that were handed out in those days. Anyway, I was standing in their offices when John Peel walked in with boxes full of records and promotional discs from record companies that he wouldn't play on his show. He was donating them to the charity.

John had once been part of the pirate radio movement with a show on Radio London called *The Perfumed Garden*, and he played music that would have been very alternative for the day. While we obviously couldn't pick up that show in Belfast, I was aware of him and what sort of music he was playing.

In 1967, in a bid to take on the pirate radio stations, the BBC set up Radio One and, in a radical change in policy, recruited many of the pirate radio DJs – people like Tony Blackburn, Johnny Walker and of course Peely. Nobody could have predicted then that Peel would be the one to outlast all the others. He was a survivor. Over the years numerous heads of programming wanted to get rid of him, but each time he survived the cull. His nightly show was essential listening for generations of young (and not so young!) people, turning them on to every type of music.

For thousands of people in Northern Ireland – who had no choice but to remain indoors when the city shut down at 5.30 every evening – a social life was built around the John Peel show which aired between 10 p.m. and midnight. It was a nightly ritual and, without over-romanticising it, I like to think that Peely gave us all a two-hour break from the grim reality of life in Belfast. In fact, one of the big inspirations for me in establishing the Good Vibrations label was listening to John Peel and what was going on with the punk movement in the rest of the UK.

There were only three of us in the Release office when John dropped in with the records, so he and I exchanged hellos and talked about music for a while, but that was it. At that time he was a DJ for Radio One but he hadn't yet moved to the late-night slot that was to make him a hero to dozens of aspiring bands. And so, it was for all these reasons, and due to my enormous affinity with John Peel, that I found myself crossing my fingers and leaving several copies of 'Teenage Kicks' in the pigeon hole at his office door. I had no idea then just how important he would become in the Good Vibrations story.

I spent the rest of my time in London in a haze, getting hammered and trying not to think too much about those bastards at the record companies. But reality is never too far away and it wasn't long before I was back in Belfast, hung over, strung out and skint. I was devastated. Good Vibrations had become my life, and I had been so sure that 'Kicks' was going to put Belfast back in the headlines for the right reasons. I broke down in tears in front of Ruth. 'I don't understand,' I said, 'these people say they are in the music industry, but they don't get it. I'm never going back to London to put myself through that again, never.'

What could she say? I was broken, and I knew that I had no answers for The Undertones, or the other bands on Good Vibrations. But Ruth wouldn't let me give up, she said, 'Maybe John Peel will play it tonight.' We both knew it was a long shot. It was 12 September 1978.

We sat and listened to Peel's show, and then it happened. One song finished, another began and I instantly recognised those first glorious notes – he was playing 'Teenage Kicks'. And, as if that wasn't incredible enough, no sooner had the song ended than he said, 'Isn't that the most wonderful record you've ever heard in the world? In fact, I'm going to play it again.'

It was the first time in the history of the BBC that a record had been played twice in a row. It felt so good, it wiped out all the disappointment I had been feeling since my trip to London, and all of a sudden I could feel my energy coming back. 'We were right!' I

John Peel and Good Vibrations – a match made in heaven. Thanks John, I'll never forget you.

thought, and that meant that CBS, EMI, Rough Trade and the rest of them were wrong. And that's when the phone started ringing …

It seemed as though everybody in Northern Ireland had been listening to the John Peel show! All the bands I worked with at Good Vibrations were on the phone offering their congratulations – they couldn't have been happier if it had been their record that had just been played twice, back-to-back on national radio. I think that says a lot about the camaraderie that existed back then, and the wonderful people we worked with. From that moment on, my world, and that of the band, changed forever.

That night Seymour Stein, CEO of Sire Records was on his way to catch his flight back to New York when he heard 'Teenage Kicks' on the radio. He turned to his London chief Paul McNally and told him that he wanted to license the record for release in the United States. Sire had a big stable of American punk acts like Richard Hell & The Voidoids and the legendary Ramones, so it seemed like a great fit. We were now in with a real fighting chance!

Paul somehow managed to get my home phone number and told me they wanted the record. He asked me if I would do a deal. I told him that I didn't have a contract with the band and that, if he wanted to sign them, he would have to come over. They were playing in a club called The Casbah in Derry that week, and he agreed to come and see them.

I must admit to getting quite excited at this point – not only were Sire chasing us, but all of a sudden my old friends at Rough Trade were on the phone, wanting the record. The music press were all over us, while I was being wined and dined and taken to gigs. The Good Vibrations label had finally struck a chord.

Paul McNally did, of course, come over and we all went to The Casbah for the gig, an experience I'm sure he hasn't forgotten. If we thought The Harp was bad, it was nothing compared to this place. I think it was once a bar that had been bombed, and in its place were two temporary cabins nailed together to make a pub/rock venue.

I remember asking one of the kids where the toilets were and he took me outside onto the street and said, 'You can piss on that wall, that wall or that wall.' The windows were painted pink and blue, and the house rule was that you couldn't pogo, because when you did all the bottles fell off the shelves! Unfortunately nobody told me this! I soon learned that the bar staff had a stack of wet towels that they used to hit anyone who dared to pogo, and after four damp clothes in the face I got the message.

McNally had an expense account with Sire so he looked after us that night, and he had a great time. I had all the best intentions of heading back to Belfast, but they soon went out the window and I ended up staying in the spare room at Feargal Sharkey's mum's house.

I went to bed that night feeling very merry, and very content, at least I was until I saw the 3D picture of the Last Supper which had pride of place on the wall – when you moved, it moved, it was pretty surreal! There were also a few pictures of Bishop Edward Daly, and one of Feargal as a boy soprano. I always wanted to blackmail him with that, but The Undertones went on to use it on the cover of 'Jimmy Jimmy' and that was another moneymaking scheme gone.

The next morning Feargal came up to the room with a big fry, which I could barely face due to a raging hangover, and I said to him, 'I never thought I'd ever say this, but I'm proud to be a Prod.' Feargal seemed taken aback and replied, 'What are you talking about Terri? I've never heard you talk like that.' 'Take a look around,' I said, 'how could you have a wank in a room like this?'

Needless to say, it was clear that Sire wanted to sign up The Undertones, and so the boys asked me to become their manager, but I wasn't particularly interested. I didn't want to leave Belfast and I believed that there would be other bands like The Undertones who might need me.

The band went into talks with Sire the next day and, although I wasn't their manager, I was there while the talks were going on. With me was Ian Birch, Deputy Editor of *Melody Maker*. He was in Northern Ireland to do a piece on the punk scene here and had come with us to Derry to see The Undertones. As luck would have it, he just happened to be there on the most important day of The Undertones' lives.

Sire offered them a contract and I told them not to take it because it was shit, and Ian agreed with me. I always say that artists shouldn't be afraid to refuse the first offer, because if they know they are worth more, there will be other, better, deals. But I think The Undertones were afraid they would miss out altogether and so they took the contract.

But this was not before CBS and EMI got back in touch – now they wanted to do something with the band. Peely had been playing the song every night and that must have made them realise just what they had missed out on when they had turned me down several weeks before. They were too late, of course, so CBS asked if I had any other bands. I took great pleasure in telling them, 'Plenty, but I wouldn't let them sign for you bastards.'

Unbelievably, Good Vibrations never made a penny out of The Undertones or 'Teenage Kicks'. I know I could have held on to the rights, or sold them for a bundle – I was once offered £5,000 for the song by Solomon and Peres, the Belfast-based record producers and distributors; and CBS offered me more than £22,000 – but I turned these and all other offers down, and I think that probably spoiled my relationship with The Undertones a little bit. When I signed the rights over to Sire, all I asked for was £500, an autographed picture of the Shangri-Las and a few albums. I remember a Hell's Angels friend of mine, Captain Pugwash, telling me, 'You're giving it away,' and I told him that was exactly what I wanted to do.

I really only wanted the money to buy a van for the bands to help them haul their equipment to gigs, but it was such a small amount of money that Sire never paid me.

SIRE

SIRE RECORDS, INC • 165 WEST 74TH STREET • NEW YORK, N.Y. 10023 • (212) 595-5500
Telex Number: 62622 • Cable: BLUHORIZON

August 13, 1979

MR. Terry Hooley
Good Vibrations Records
102 Great Victoria Street
Belfast, N. Ireland

Dear Sirs:

In consideration of payment by us to you on signature hereof of the sum of 1,000 pounds, receipt of which you hereby acknowledge, you hereby grant and assign to us the full and exclusive world-wide and perpetual rights in the master recordings specified below embodying the performances of the artists professionally known as "the Undertones". You further acknowledge that this sum will include full reimbursement by us to you of any costs incurred by you in the production of these recordings. You further indemnify us against any claims that may be brought by any party against us in respect of the recordings specified below.

The rights assigned to us shall include the sole, exclusive and perpetual right throughout the world to sell, release and distribute such recordings.

"Teenage Kicks"
"True Confessions"

Please sign below to signify your agreement with the above.

Very truly yours,

ACCEPTED AND AGREED   SIRE RECORDS COMPANY

Terry Hooley

GOOD VIBRATIONS RECORDS

That is, until I forced their hand. During a trip to London a few weeks after 'Kicks' was released I went to visit an old friend of mine, David McCullough, who had once worked for *Alternative Ulster*. David now worked for *Sounds*, a magazine that ran the 'Fair Deal' column, and I asked him to introduce me to the girl that wrote that particular feature. 'Fair Deal' usually dealt with people who hadn't received goods they had ordered by post

– shirts, records, tickets and so on – so mine was the biggest story she had covered. When Sire found out, they went into a panic and offered me a bundle to kill the story, but in the end I settled for £1,000, which I used to buy the van. Though I never did get my photos or my albums!

The truth is I didn't want to stand in the The Undertones' way, I'm not a businessman, and never really have been. All I wanted was to put Northern Ireland onto the music map of the world. Bands from Northern Ireland didn't often get the chance to sign to a national label and I knew it was a delicate process, so I was concerned that if I drove a harder bargain, I would blow the whole deal. We had done our bit by giving the band a platform to get to where they deserved to be, and I loved them so much that I just wanted them to do well.

Within a month of the Casbah gig, Sire had re-released 'Teenage Kicks' and the song managed to make it to number thirty-one in the UK singles charts. It was a high enough ranking that it led to the boys performing on *Top of the Pops* in October 1978.

They followed their debut single with 'Get Over You', which charted in January 1979, proving they were no one-hit wonder. Over the years they would release classics such as 'Jimmy Jimmy', 'Here Comes The Summer', 'My Perfect Cousin' and 'Wednesday Week', which just showed we knew what we were doing when we signed them up. But by that stage, I was merely an interested spectator sitting on the sidelines in Belfast.

In June 1983, the band decided to split up. Feargal went on to have some success with The Assembly, and as a solo artist, getting to number one in the charts in 1985 with 'A Good Heart', before becoming one of those dreaded record company A&R (Artists and Repertoire) men! Damian and John O'Neill went on to form That Petrol Emotion, and put out a couple of critically acclaimed albums – *Rolling Stone* described them as 'The Clash crossed with Creedence' – but sadly their critical success was not matched commercially, and they eventually split up in 1994.

The other boys returned to Derry. Mickey Bradley worked as a producer with BBC Radio Foyle and Billy Doherty played in several local bands. In 1999, The Undertones got back together – minus Feargal, and with new lead singer, Paul McLoone – and have recorded two albums of new material since. They are still playing gigs across Europe and further afield, including sets at Glastonbury in 2005 and the Electric Picnic Festival in County Laois in 2007.

But 'Teenage Kicks' will always be the signature tune for the band, and for Good Vibrations. It has been a continuous seller over the years, having been covered by the likes of Green Day, The Raconteurs, The Coral, Razorlight, Snow Patrol and others too numerous to mention. I even read about a Europe-wide poll taken recently in which radio stations listed their top one hundred most-requested songs, and 'Teenage Kicks' had come in at number ten.

I'm immensely proud of what we did back then. 'Kicks' was the most important record to come out of Northern Ireland since 'Gloria' – which brought Them, my favourite band in the world, to the world stage – and it proved what I have always believed, that for such a small population, we have more talent per head of poets, painters and performers than anywhere else in Europe.

It's always been very difficult for artists here, there is an edge about the music, because of our in-between status: we're not English and we're not Irish. Even Paul Brady – another of our great singer songwriters – once said to me that he felt that he never fitted in anywhere because he was from Northern Ireland.

But the success of The Undertones gave people in Northern Ireland something to be proud of at a very difficult time in our history. It proved to every kid here that they could achieve something in their lives, and have a bloody good laugh doing it.

Musicians may still have had to leave Northern Ireland to get a contract, but the Good Vibrations label allowed bands to have some success, hone their sound and get a sense of the industry before they went to England to make their mark, and of that I will always be very proud.

I remember, not long after The Undertones got their deal with Sire, John Peel decided it was time he made the pilgrimage to the home of 'Teenage Kicks', and brought another Radio One DJ, David 'Kid' Jensen along with him. Peel couldn't believe that our tiny operation, working from what he called 'a Dinky Toy telephone booth', could have produced such a polished product.

We were in the tiny back room of the shop at the time, and Getty from The Outcasts was there too. Now, as anyone who knew him then can testify, Getty was a fairly scary looking individual, with spiked bleached hair and a studded leather jacket, but he was the one who offered to make the tea. However, it was only after Peel and Kid had left that Getty realised he had forgotten to boil the kettle! Both DJ's were obviously so intimidated by him that they sat in silence, drinking cold tea, rather than say anything.

John Peel and Good Vibes had a fantastic relationship. Many of our bands would travel to London, do sessions for his show and go on to better things. Thanks to him, Good Vibrations soon became a world name – and that's not being arrogant or overstating the matter – because Peely was playing our records all the time. He once told me he reckoned twenty per cent of his mailbag was filled with letters from Northern Ireland. He also did a show for the BBC World Service, and this is why the label became popular outside of the UK and Ireland.

When the label was in financial trouble a few years later, we threw a big concert in the Ulster Hall and John flew over to be with us. He got a standing ovation that night. He stayed with my mother-in-law Beryl and brought her a bunch of flowers as thanks. Beryl was delighted to have him – he was a much quieter and more polite houseguest than me! If he heard I was coming over to England, he would invite me down to Peel Acres – his country home – or round to the show. A few times he even changed the show to include a new record I had just discovered.

There weren't really any wild times with Peely, he was simply a dedicated fan with three loves in his life: music, Liverpool Football Club and his lovely family. He always said that 'Teenage Kicks' reduced him to tears and indeed many of us shed a tear when he died of a heart attack in 2004 while on holiday in Peru. The ultimate and final tribute he made to his favourite song was to have the lyrics, 'Teenage dreams, so hard to beat' engraved on his headstone.

John Peel was the only honest man I've ever met in the music industry and I have learnt nothing since that has altered that opinion.

Session Music/Good Vibrations
OUTCASTS
MOONDOGS
RUEFREX
RUDI
BIG SELF
Ulster Hall
Thursday 24 April 7·30
Tickets £1·50 Door £2

from   Session Music   93 York St.
Good Vibrations 102 Gt. Victoria St.

THE UNDERTONES
JOHN O'NEILL

Back in 1978 our only ambition was to make a record as some kind of tangible proof that we existed. We had been playing The Casbah and the Rock Club in Derry for at least a year, which is a long time when you're seventeen or eighteen. We lacked opportunity from every direction, but we instinctively knew we were doing something right because there just wasn't another band like us in Derry.

We were like a new car without the wheels – everything worked, we just couldn't go anywhere. Also, there was definitely something in the air, a connection that started in New York and which eventually spread all around the world. Punk wasn't simply a music trend, it was an attitude, it was getting the basics right first, and you either got it or you didn't, it was that definitive, and it felt great to be a part of it.

Anyway, it was Spring 1978 and we were ready to make a record. We demoed some songs and sent them off to various record companies in England, but they turned us down.

However one of the tapes managed to find its way into the hands of a man called Bernie McAnaney – the brother of Sammy McAnaney, one of Feargal's Radio Rentals workmates – who was at college in Belfast, and who knew Terri Hooley, owner of the Good Vibrations record shop.

Terri had been making records with some Belfast punk bands and so Bernie gave him the tape, though I think Terri attributes this to a guy called Malcolm Stewart. Either way, the tape was understandably raw, so it was possibly the novelty of having a band from Derry on his label rather than the quality of the music that convinced Terri to let us make a record. Whatever the reason, he agreed and it was our chance.

So, it's 14 June 1978 and it has been arranged for us to play a Battle of the Bands show in the McMordie Hall in Belfast, then record the songs for our single in Wizard Studios the next day. I can't remember how we took our gear up, possibly loaded it into Feargal's Radio Rentals van, but we had small combo amps in those days which wouldn't have taken up much space anyway, and some of us probably took the train up. We had played Dublin a couple of times but this was our first time playing

John O'Neill with Michael Bradley
at the Ulster Hall, 1980

in Belfast and we curious to hear, and compare ourselves to, the other bands playing that night.

Up to this point we hadn't met or talked to Terri, so we had arranged to call into the Good Vibrations shop to say hello that afternoon. It was a really cool shop, from the life-size 1955 Elvis effigy outside, to the great selection of music on sale inside. And then there was Terri! I remember feeling slightly intimidated by him at first. He was like Neal Cassady without the amphetamines – he had the energy of a speeding train about to go off the rails, and at first I found it quite overwhelming. However, as we discussed music, you could tell straight away he knew what he was talking about and how much passion he felt about it.

The Battle of the Bands show that night was a great success. We were on near the end, just between RUDI and The Outcasts. Terri acted as compere, even reading out a telegram from John and Yoko wishing everybody the best, which was very impressive. Playing the night before recording was a good idea too. At the very least, we could see that we were as good as any band on the night and that gave us a nice confidence boost going into the studio.

The recording itself was fairly straightforward. We had decided to copy The Buzzcocks' idea of recording an EP and, with most of us being sixties aficionados, we were aware of the history of early classic EPs by the Rolling Stones and The Kinks and so on, so it seemed a good idea. Also it was better value for money. Davy Shannon, the engineer, was very accommodating and pretty much let us do what we wanted.

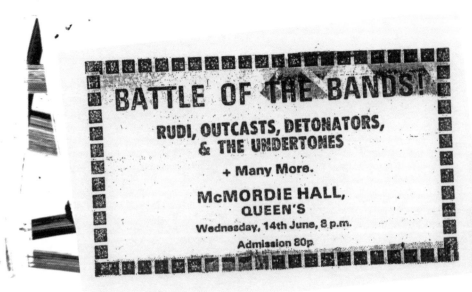

We came back up to Belfast a couple of days later to do the mixing with Terri present. He had obviously been on the tear the night before because he was unusually subdued. I think he even fell asleep at some point during the mixing which, when you consider the volume it was being played at, is some feat in itself! I do remember him being sceptical about us doing handclaps in the middle parts of 'Teenage Kicks' but he let us have our way after a bit of persuasion.

We then went back to Derry and, in the months that followed, proceeded to break up, then get back together again a couple of times. Despite our new relationship with Good Vibrations, the rejection by the English labels had taken its toll and, even then, the relationship between Feargal and the rest of the band was a little uneasy. But we managed to work through it in time for the now-famous playing of 'Teenage Kicks' on John Peel's radio show.

Amazingly, our drummer Billy Doherty had been in contact with John Peel a couple of times during that summer so, when Terri sent him a copy of the record, he had actually heard of us, though no one expected the reaction it got when he did play it. After that, it was fantasyland for us. As the years went by, we did meet Terri a few times and I always felt a bit guilty that I never properly thanked him. After all, he was the one who gave us a chance when no one else would. It's not inconceivable to think that we never would have made a record at all; we were always in a constant state of flux.

In my experience, the music industry is generally filled with two types of people, those that are in it for their own gratification at any expense, and those, like Terri, who have a genuine love and passion for music and see it as a relevant form of expression that has the potential to change the way we think and behave for the better. It was pleasure then.

HITTING THE ROAD

GOOD VIBRATIONS

GOOD VIBRATIONS SINGLES'

RUDI................BIG TIME
VICTIM.............STRANGE THING BY NIGHT
OUTCASTS.......JUSTA NOTHER TEENAGE REBEL
PROTEX...........DON'T RING ME UP
XDREAMYSTS .....RIGHT WAY HOME
RUEFREX ....ONE BY ONE
TEARJERKERS.....LOVE AFFAIR
THE TEE VEES......DR. HEADLOVE
RUDI.....................I SPY E P
OUTCASTS....SELF CONSCIOUS OVER YOU
BEARS.................INSANE
JETS.....................ORIGINAL TERMINAL
GOT
STATIC ROUTINES..ROCK'N'ROLL CLONES

12" REGGAE SINGLE.
ZEBRA...........REPRESSION

2 SINGLE E.P.
BATTLE OF THE BANDS.
RUDI/OUTCASTS/SPIDER/IDIOTS

THE OUTCASTS L.P.
SELF CONSCIOUS OVER YOU

ENERGY RECORDS
ROOM TO MOVE E.P.
OUTCASTS/BIG SELF/SHOCK TREATMENT/VIPERS

POLYDOR SINGLES'
PROTEX.........I CAN'T COPE
PROTEX ....A PLACE IN YOUR HEART
XDREAMYSTS ......MONEY TALKS
XDREAMYSTS......I DON'T WANNA GO
XDREAMYSTS......STAY THE WAY YOU ARE

IGGY POP PICTURE DISC
FIVE FOOT ONE £1.00

ALL SINGLES £1.00 inc posta
12" SINGLE £1.40 inc postage
L.P. £3.70 inc postage

GOOD VIBRATIONS RECOR
102 GREAT VICTORIA STRE
BELFAST. BT2 7BE. (29152)

With the success of The Undertones fresh in people's minds, the Good Vibrations label became more popular than ever. We were fast becoming a production-line of bands.

In late 1978, we signed both XDreamysts and Protex, releasing their respective singles, 'Right Way Home' and 'Don't Ring Me Up'. In Easter 1979, both bands played together at a gig held in Chester's, Portrush, where they were seen by A & R men from Polydor, London, and it was with great excitement that we learnt that Polydor had decided to sign them both to the label – at long last the big record companies had woken up to the fact that there was talent in Northern Ireland! But we would all soon learn, through Protex and XDreamysts, just how the music industry monster can chew you up and spit you out.

XDreamysts were a four-piece from the Coleraine/Portrush area and while I thought their music was fantastic, they weren't really ever a punk band, being influenced more by the likes of The Beatles and the Stones. In fact, they were good enough to earn a gig supporting Thin Lizzy on their 1979 UK tour. But after releasing three singles and an album, Polydor made the decision to drop them in 1981. The band split up not long after.

XDreamysts – the only hippies on the Good Vibes label. L-R: Uel Walls, Roe Butcher, John Doherty and Brian Moffatt

111

DON'T RING ME UP

ANNOUNCING THE FIRST NEW SINGLE FROM

PROTEX

FIRST 10,000 COPIES IN SPECIAL BAGS

FROM GOOD VIBRATIONS
102 GT. VICTORIA ST
BELFAST

Protex, L-R: Owen McFadden, Paul Maxwell,
Aidan Murtagh and David McMaster

Protex, I'm sorry to say, didn't fare much better. All four of them – Aidan Murtagh, David McMaster, Paul Maxwell and Owen McFadden – were still at school and studying for A levels when they were signed to Polydor, but they headed off to London where they packed more into two years than most people do into a lifetime. They released two singles, recorded an album (which was never released), performed two tours of the USA and landed a gig supporting the Boomtown Rats on their 1979 tour, but by the end of 1981, Polydor had made the decision to drop them too – they were all still in their teens.

Ruefrex, L-R: Paul Burgess, Jackie Forgie,
Tom Coulter and Allan Clarke

In 1979, I approached local punk band Ruefrex and asked them if they too would be interested in putting something out on the Good Vibrations label.

The band had first come to my attention in mid-1978, and I knew that they had a great sound. They had played at our Battle of the Bands event in McMordie Hall that June, but the guys had been playing gigs for a year or so before that. They played their first gig in The Trident in Bangor in 1977, supporting SLF, but by the time they signed with us, their name had changed from Roofwrecks to the current spelling, and the line-up had also changed slightly, with Allan Clarke as their new lead singer alongside Paul Burgess, Tom Coulter and Jackie Forgie. I remember seeing them play The Harp and Clarke was an absolute lunatic, a ball of energy. The audience loved them.

Good Vibrations put out their single 'One By One' in 1979. It was the only single they did with us, but they continued to make a huge mark on the local scene anyway. They never turned down a gig no matter where it was, or how dodgy the area. Shankill, Ardoyne, Falls, Turf Lodge, any religious enclave you care to mention, they played it. Their message was way ahead of its time and I liked that about them.

That being said – and I can look back now and say they were a great band – at the time we didn't exactly see eye to eye, if you can forgive the pun! To say they were angry boys is an understatement, and that often led to some heated arguments. Drummer Paul Burgess once claimed that I tried to hit him with a chair, but if I did, it's an incident that I truly can't recall. He seemed to think that I was making money off the back of his band, which would have been quite a feat since they only released one single with us!

They did last longer than most of the bands from here though. They took part in TV documentary *Cross The Line* in 1980 – on the so-called 'peace' walls that divide Belfast

– and after that split up, getting back together in 1983 to record on London indie label, Kabuki. Their message was so strong that a journalist from *New Musical Express* labelled them as 'the most important band in Britain'! They put out two albums, *Flowers for All Occasions* (1985) and *Political Wings* (1987), and finally split in 1987.

But I think that they left an impact on Northern Ireland and, indeed, on me and two things about their career stand out. In 1985, they released a single called 'Wild Colonial Boy', which was a savage attack on those tossers in America who donated huge amounts of money for the IRA to buy guns; and later that same year, they held a fundraising concert for Lagan College, Northern Ireland's first integrated school for Catholic and Protestant children. I have a lot of respect for them for doing that.

I've already mentioned that my music tastes are wide and varied, and that was why, in 1979, we also signed The Tearjerkers to Good Vibes, despite the fact that they were influenced by the likes of the Beach Boys and were not a punk band at all! Drummer Nigel Hamilton and lead guitarist Paul 'Groover' McIlwaine wrote the music, while lead singer Paul Maxwell wrote the lyrics. On bass was Howard Ingram, while Brian Rawson played guitar. They made their debut at the Rockin' Chair in Derry in February 1979. They looked and sounded much different to the other bands coming from Northern Ireland and I suppose that was why I liked them really. Lord knows it wasn't because of their personalities! They always thought they should have been more famous than they were and so they weren't really the most popular band around. In fact, the one and only time they played The Harp Bar, a few of them ended up in hospital after the dyed-in-the-wool punk fans took exception to their poppy style, pelted the lads with bottles and cans, and beat them up as they fled the stage. Those were the good old days!

That didn't deter them though, and they came to me with a demo tape, which featured their songs 'Love Affair' and 'Bus Stop'. They sounded good and I reckoned they were worth a punt, so in March 1979 they laid down four tracks at Keystone studios in Dublin, and we released 'Love Affair' later that year – it turned out to be their only release with us.

In April that year they became the first Good Vibes band to perform on the telly when they played live on UTV's *Good Evening Ulster*. I think they were the only band we had who promised not to swear on air! But their big claim to fame came in mid-1979 when they were given the chance to support Thin Lizzy on tour. U2 – at that time only beginning their own career – was also Thin Lizzy's support act, and it was even rumoured that Tearjerkers drummer, Nigel Hamilton, was asked if he would be interested

The Tearjerkers, L-R: Howard Ingram, Nigel Hamilton, Brian Rawson, Paul Maxwell and Paul McIlwaine

in becoming their drummer instead. He reputedly turned them down because he thought The Tearjerkers had a better chance of success – good call Nigel! – but in my opinion it may have been more a case of U2 giving drummer Larry Mullen a boot up the arse, and reminding him he could be replaced.

Most importantly, it was around this time when The Tearjerkers were signed up by Back Door Records, a subsidiary of Phonogram Records. They did a couple of sessions for the John Peel Show, supported Dexys Midnight Runners on tour, and while they recorded several singles for them, Back Door released only one. The lads began to feel as though the record bosses wanted them to be something they weren't – to be more of a punk band – but The Tearjerkers had more of a pop feel and so probably suffered by association with the Northern Ireland punk scene.

Two years after they had formed, The Tearjerkers broke up when Nigel Hamilton decided to leave the group. A few of the lads reappeared in bands Radio City and The

115

Dingo Babies but it was another case of promise unfulfilled. I'll always believe it was because the record companies weren't giving new bands like them the chance to show what they could do, nor were they giving them the right advice, so bands were being dumped from their labels and shipped home very quickly.

1979 was a very productive year for Good Vibrations, though admittedly I was a little concerned that losing The Undertones had left a big hole in our list. I needn't have worried – not long after the 'Tones signed with Sire, a Derry band called The Moondogs came to my attention. I knew very little about them, except that they had formed the year before and had only just given themselves a name! They were regular performers in the famous Derry punk venue The Casbah, so it was really only a matter of time before they would be noticed. I had been told a lot about them – like how they had once played a gig from the back of a lorry in Derry's Bull Park – but it wasn't until they recorded a session at Downtown Radio that I heard them properly and I liked them immediately. Like XDreamysts and The Tearjerkers, their music had a slightly poppy edge, which I thought would make them very popular.

I made contact and in April 1979 Good Vibes released their first double A-side single,

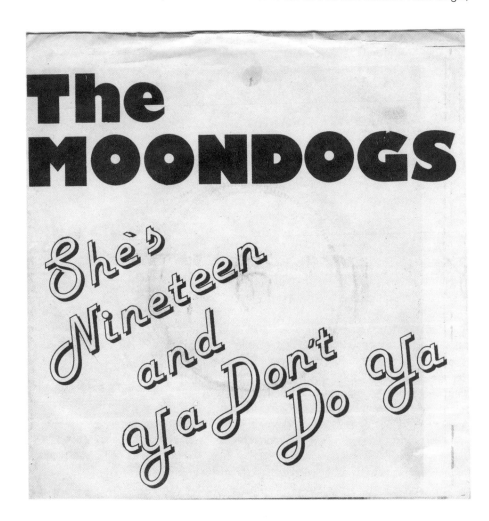

'She's 19'/'Ya Don't Do Ya'. It was to be their only release on Good Vibrations as John Peel took to it immediately and began playing it on his show. The publicity this generated for them meant that they were able to secure a gig supporting The Undertones on their debut tour of the UK. After that, things moved very quickly and barely three months after they had released their debut single, they signed a deal with Real Records, a subsidiary of Sire.

From playing to a crowd from the back of a lorry to working in a recording studio with the likes of Pete Waterman and Ray Davies of The Kinks, the boys were riding high. In 1981, they were even given their own teatime TV show, *Moondogs Matinee*, by Granada TV, rehearsing and filming on the *Coronation Street* set of all places! So when they were invited to New York to work on their album with the legendary Todd Rundgren – producer of Meat Loaf's epic *Bat Out Of Hell* album – it seemed they had the world at their feet.

But at this stage they were still only a bunch of kids – bassist Jackie Hamilton was only seventeen – and things were happening too quickly for them. A long stint in the Big Apple is a big ask for a bunch of teenagers from Derry, and a mixture of homesickness and incompatibility with Rundgren drove them home where they broke up, declared bankruptcy and signed on the dole. Jackie would go on to become a very successful TV producer, lead singer Gerry McCandless forged a career in computers, and drummer Austin Barrett stayed in the music business playing with blues band, Double Trouble.

Amazingly Rundgren finished the album with the material the boys had already recorded and in 1981 it was released by Sire … but only in Germany. The boys didn't know a thing about it until 1985, when a bloke came into my shop and said he had a copy. Jackie tells me he hadn't ever clapped eyes on his band's album before that and it took him years to get his own copy – and he had to stump up £85 for a copy someone was selling on eBay!

Of course, in 1979, we didn't know about all the record company drama that lay ahead for us. All we were concerned with was the music and wanting to get that music heard by as many people as possible.

At that time, many people outside the bigger cities had never seen live punk bands before – the most exciting live gigs would have been a night at the local boozer listening to cover versions of Elton John or Simon & Garfunkel songs. The very few concerts that took place in Northern Ireland were put on at the Ulster Hall or King's Hall in Belfast, so if you lived in the sticks you never got to see an original band. Kids from all over the country would have travelled to Belfast to see live acts, so we decided it was time to return the favour – we were going to tour Northern Ireland.

In April 1979, packed into a white van, RUDI, The Outcasts and The Tearjerkers took the inaugural Good Vibrations Tour to the highways and by-ways of Northern Ireland. We had one mission: to spread the gospel of punk.

There were ten dates in all, including one in Dublin. Nigel Hamilton from The Tearjerkers, in a very democratic manner, suggested that the bands would alternate running order, all coming on to jam together briefly at the end. It was supposed to be like one of the old fifties/sixties package tours and it was all great fun. The bands really tried hard to outdo each other, and the gigs were mostly packed.

Our first stop was on 9 April 1979, in the tiny village of Glenarm in the stunning Glens of Antrim. Davy Miller – who worked with me in the shop – and I set off in his car, heading for the venue which was just a small pub in the village. The rest of the guys were following behind in a van and, just as we came out of Larne, we spotted a girl hitch-hiking. It was a horrible night so the van stopped to offer her a lift. It turned out she had just arrived on

the ferry from Scotland and was heading to Glenarm to see her favourite bands.

We didn't tell her she was actually being driven to the gig by her heroes, just that we were heading that way. When we arrived she got out and thanked us, it was only then we declared our hand. You'd have thought she'd won the lottery, and her reward was to help the lads haul the gear into the venue! For the first time, I realised we were making a mark beyond our own shores. I don't remember a hell of a lot about the gig itself, except that there was no trouble and everybody went home happy.

I'd had a few drinks by the end of the night and once the van was packed up, I nipped down a laneway to have a pee, but being a little unsteady on my feet I ended up falling into a river. I spent the journey home completely naked, except for a rather smelly blanket from the back of the car. To make matters worse, on the way home we were stopped by a UDR patrol and asked to show our ID. I didn't have mine so I was told to get out of the car while it was searched. There I was, naked and freezing by the side of the road, surrounded by armed men – not an experience I'd care to repeat!

The night we took the tour to Armagh was, thankfully, a lot less eventful. The audience there was full of heavy metal fans – an endless sea of denim – but I got on-stage to warm them up, and after a while they seemed to accept us. They even took a real shine to The Tearjerkers.

We did, of course, include The Harp and The Pound on the Good Vibrations Tour

– well every good tour has to have a homecoming gig! But it was touch and go as to whether or not I was even going to be allowed into The Pound, as I had been barred the previous year for punching some bloke after an Undertones gig. It was like something out of a John Wayne movie actually, this guy had been a bit of stalker and at every opportunity would turn up at the shop, or accost me in the pub, to slag off the bands. On this particular night though, I'd had enough and chinned him. The bouncers descended, but before they could lay their hands on me the kids in the audience lifted their beer bottles and made it clear nobody was going to touch me. The bouncers were no match for them!

But that's how it was back then, at least in Northern Ireland. We were family, and we looked out for each other. Every band, and at times it seemed every fan, would do whatever they could to help another band out, even if they hated each other! Whether that meant lending them some gear, or folding their record sleeves, there was a real sense of solidarity that we just didn't seem to get from visiting bands.

XTC, for example, came over to play a gig at Queen's the day after the last date of the Good Vibrations tour, and RUDI and The Outcasts played support. But, in contrast to the experience we had on our own tour dates, which were hectic but fun, and with everyone doing their part, XTC turned out to be incredibly pretentious, acting as though they were big boys who were lowering themselves by visiting the regions. As Brian Young of RUDI pointed out, a pattern was emerging in that, almost without exception, the bands visiting from England or further abroad acted like spoilt pampered rock stars, treating the local support acts with contempt. Belfast people are not too impressed by celebrity so when some band tries to act big then we don't take kindly to it.

But our guys knew that they had as much talent, if not more, than those posers. The likes of RUDI, The Outcasts, Protex and The Undertones weren't concerned about how they would sound on-stage, they had complete faith in their own ability and their fans believed in them. They had raw, unrefined talent and there is no doubt in my mind that this set the Northern Ireland punk bands apart from all the others – there were no boundaries, just unlimited enthusiasm and determination.

Anybody who was at any one of their gigs back then will remember nights of barely contained exuberance – it was like sex! Well maybe not quite, but it was exciting all the same and the only way to come down from a climactic evening like that was to roll a joint, lie back and slowly relive it. Because it was clear that touring and performing for their fans was what all the Good Vibes bands cared about most. A recording contract would be great, of course, but I think if you ask any of the bands they would say that they were never in it for the money – which was just as well really! – they weren't even in it for the fame – they were just hooked on music.

So, having successfully taken our music to the people of Northern Ireland, we decided to turn our attention to Dublin, which eventually became an incredibly important market for us. In the early days there were very few outlets for punk bands in the south so it was very difficult for new bands to get their music heard. The only real vehicle was Dave Fanning's *Rock Show* on RTÉ. Dave was a fantastic supporter of our bands and often spoke about how important Good Vibes was for the wider music scene in Ireland. He was a regular visitor to Belfast and bands like Ruefrex, The Outcasts and The Tearjerkers all recorded sessions for his show.

I loved taking the bands down to Dublin to play. The Belfast music scene seemed to be years ahead of what was going on down there, so the audiences were appreciative of what we were trying to do. The bands loved playing there too, as they had built up a

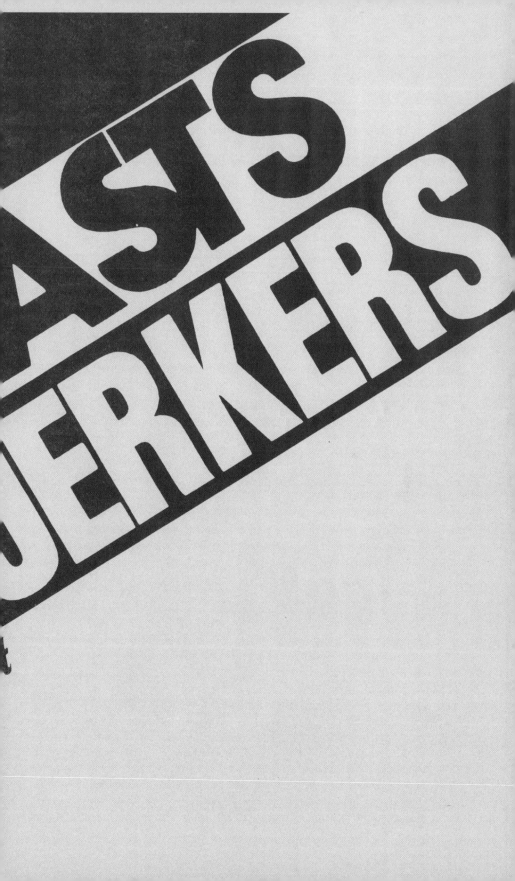

good following. So, in May 1979, we all headed to Dublin for the twenty-four-hour Dark Space Festival at the Project Arts Centre, where U2, the Boomtown Rats, Virgin Prunes and a whole lot of Dublin bands were playing.

John Peel was with us, having visited The Harp the night before, as were Protex, RUDI and The Outcasts who, at one stage, formed the Good Vibrations All Stars, with yours truly on mic. To this day I can't understand how U2 hit the big time and the All Stars missed out! But we saw a reggae band called Zebra that night, and Peel recommended that we sign them.

Zebra had the privilege of being Ireland's only homegrown reggae band and we put out a 12" single called 'Repression' on the Good Vibes label, which did surprisingly well. We pressed 1,200 copies and for a while it was very popular on the Irish indie scene. I hear that copies of this are worth about £300 these days, so I'm delighted to say that I was given a copy one Christmas! If I'm honest, I'd have to say I didn't think that much of them – I had only signed them on John Peel's recommendation – and I have no idea what happened to them, but it goes to show that Peely didn't always get it right!

As other new bands emerged in Dublin we often invited them to play The Harp, but none of them ever came. I guess they were scared shitless of coming to Belfast. I knew that they would have been safe, but I suppose I don't really blame them for their reluctance as the memory of the Miami Showband Massacre on 31 July 1975 – when three members of the band were shot dead by the UVF – would have still been very fresh in the minds of many Irish performers. How could anyone expect bands from the south to cross the border after that?

That was part of the battle for Good Vibrations; we had only ourselves to rely on when it came to making music. The Troubles discouraged not only bands from across the border from playing here, but also bands from across the water. We were so isolated musically that a group of friends and myself, under the name The Tribe, had launched the Music For Belfast Campaign in an attempt to convince English bands and artists not to leave Northern Ireland off their tours. The campaign succeeded in winning us some attention across the water and, in the late seventies, we were invited to bring some bands over to play a festival at Action Space in London. We took RUDI, The Moondogs and The Outcasts over, but received a threat from the IRA warning us not to take to the stage. We ignored it of course and the resulting press conference caused a bit of a stir. It seemed that the paramilitaries didn't want the outside world to see that there was something relatively normal going on in Belfast, that it was not a total war zone. But we wanted to show that most young people were not involved in the paramilitaries, preferring to carry guitars instead of chucking stones at the cops.

It was this desire to show what our music scene really was that had inspired John T. Davis to put together the 1979 punk documentary *Shellshock Rock* which was, in my opinion, one of the most important pieces of work to come out of Northern Ireland for a generation. It was produced on a really low budget – made more with enthusiasm than money really – but it succeeded in accurately reflecting the attitudes of the punks in Northern Ireland at that time. It contained interviews with bands and fans alike, alongside live performances by the likes of Stiff Little Fingers, The Outcasts, RUDI and Protex.

It was due to premiere at the 1979 Cork Film Festival, so a group of us decided to make the journey down to show our support. I was also due to appear on Dave Fanning's *Rock Show* to talk about the film. But the night before we were due to set off, John T. rang me with news that the festival had made a decision not to show the film, saying that it was 'technically not up to standard'. It's my personal opinion, but I maintain that this was not the case at all, that actually there was a snobbery about the 'black north' and about punk – they didn't want to acknowledge what was going on up here. John was gutted of course, and asked me not to mention it on the radio, but I knew that we needed to make people aware of what had happened so I said, 'John, fuck off, of course I'm going to mention it.'

We drummed up as much media attention as we could and word began to spread. A few weeks later it even took a silver medal at the New York Film Festival. Banned in Cork, feted in New York – I know what I'd rather have on my CV!

The film is raw and uncompromising, and in my opinion, a genuine piece of social history. I grew up in the sixties and it is sad that there is nothing from that time to record what was happening in Belfast or the great bands that played here, but *Shellshock* is a lasting record of what it was like to be in Northern Ireland in the late seventies. As John T. put it at the time, 'The music is rough and reactionary and is all punk, but contains a certain quality that speaks volumes on contemporary life in Northern Ireland.'

123

SHELLSHOCK ROCK
JOHN T. DAVIS

It's hard to believe the story I'm telling you has its origins some thirty years ago, in 1978–9, the dawn of time for me as a young filmmaker as I searched for the diamond, the golden trail, the canvas to cast off into life's great illusions. I'm talking about *Shellshock Rock* and the subsequent mythology surrounding the film, which has attained such a cult status as to be recognised by the British Film Institute, in whose vaults it now resides for all time.

There is of course the even more murky mythology that precedes *Shellshock* days, concerning how Mr Hooley and I may have met. My strongest memory is of the Folk Club Terri had just off the Dublin Road in Belfast. This was one of those places in the late sixties where folk had gone well beyond the idea of the Kingston Trio. It was hip, and the higher you got while in that three storey building, the hipper it got.

I can remember one particular night when all manor of music and relevant consumables had been consumed, and the festivities were winding down, that I found myself experiencing one of the most enduringly inspirational moments of all time: myself, Terri, Charlie Whisker and Van Morrison, all relieving ourselves out in the back alley – a stream of hot, steaming, creative urine running together, flowing into the Dublin Road and beyond.

I wonder if Van remembers this event.

It was really when *Shellshock* started to happen that my friendship with Terri was rekindled. One day whilst crossing the Queen's Bridge I saw this figure, complete with cycle clips, cycling towards me. It was Terri, who I hadn't seen for a long time. We quickly caught up amidst the rush-hour traffic. He told me to come on down to the shop, and that's how it all got started. I had already filmed Stiff Little Fingers for the film and was beginning to understand a little of what was happening with music in Belfast during Northern Ireland's darkest days. Kids were coming from both sides of the divide – punk was bringing them together – and they were rejecting traditional ideas. There was a little chink of light flickering in the blackness, and Terri Hooley's record shop, Good Vibrations, was Punk HQ. I could hardly believe what I had stumbled upon.

Terri and John T. Davis
outside the Oh Yeah! centre, 2008

Terri was, and still is, the punk guru of Belfast and possibly the world. He never sold out and was responsible for creating an environment that nurtured and developed the hopes and dreams of kids from war-torn Belfast. The fact that I had known him years before opened the door for me – he gave me a seal of approval with the bands and their fans, so they welcomed me into their world. It was wonderful and it totally revitalised me. I had been out on the prairie too long.

I can't go into the whole tale of *Shellshock* here in this piece, there are just too many good stories to do them all justice. All I will say is that *Shellshock* would not be the film it has become without Terri's help: he is a master of promotion and publicity.

When the film was finally finished, and our little diamond in the rough was ready for the world, great celebrations were planned for the premiere at the 1979 Cork Film Festival. Terri, myself, RUDI, The Outcasts and Ross Graham – who worked on the film with me – together with our own respective entourages, were to arrive en masse in Cork on the day of the premiere like a band of punk gypsies. There was a great feeling of excitement and jubilation in the air.

Then, out of the blue, the day before our departure for Cork, I got a phone call from the festival organisers ... We had been axed, banned, rejected – call it what you will, Cork didn't want us. The festival selection committee had issued a statement declaring our film, 'technically not up to standard'. They had effectively banned *Shellshock Rock* and all it stood for.

Well, you can imagine how I felt; I won't even attempt to describe the mood. I called Terri to break the bad news and he said, 'John, it's the best thing that could possibly have happened.' A master at work, he knew that this would be a great opportunity for some excellent publicity, so we all decided to go to Cork anyway. We were angry and ready for battle.

By the time we got to Cork, however, our bedraggled group of gypsy punks – now bemused and confused after hours of travel – wondered, 'what do we do now?' We were all standing on a street corner with Terri, as leader, pacing the sidewalk, deep in thought and clutching a can of Coke. As I watched, two American tourists approached, deposited a 50p coin into the can of Coke ... and walked off. I couldn't believe my eyes, what must we have looked like? Terri turned to me and said, 'John, we've got to clean up our act.'

Terri had already been on Dave Fanning's RTÉ radio *Rock Show* expressing his outrage at *Shellshock* being dropped from the festival, so the news was out. The battle plan was now to collar as many of the journalists who had flocked to Cork as we could, and to literally press-gang the festival into issuing an explanation as to the ban.

With indemonstrable style, Mr Hooley swung into action. Reporters swarmed around, each wanting an exclusive story from me and, with the help of local film-makers, Joe Comerford, Cathal Black, and Tiernan MacBride, a special press screening was hastily organised. *Shellshock* blew the press away, and we were in every major newspaper by sundown. At an extraordinary press conference held shortly after the screening, Festival Director Robin O'Sullivan squirmed his way through a barrage of pertinent criticisms, and was eventually forced to retract the original statement – 'technically not up to standard' – though he would not offer up any plausible reason for pulling the film hours before its premiere. This raised serious questions about their political views and brought the values of the very festival itself into question.

But we had won the battle, and now everyone wanted to see *Shellshock*.

OMAGH COMMUNITY ARTS GROUP
PRESENTS A

SATURDAY AFTERNOON POP CONCERT

In the TOWN HALL, OMAGH
SATURDAY, 6th OCTOBER
First showing in the North-West —
A film you must see

SHELL SHOCKROCK

Featuring bands like The Undertones, Stiff Little Fingers, Rudi, etc.

Plus live on stage — RUDI and OUTCASTS

Doors open 2.00. Two concerts, 3.00 to 6.00 and 7.30 to 10.30

DON'T FORGET THIS SATURDAY, 29th SEPT.

THE OPENING CONCERT

Featuring from Derry — The Moondogs, Crafty Jack and Rock Tonic. From
Omagh — Casper, R-U-1-2 and Control Zone.
One concert 3.00 to 6.00. Doors open 2.00
You can pay at door but to secure your seat buying tickets in advance is
advisable. For tickets call at Community Development Research Centre, 34
High Street, Omagh (above Smarti Pants, top floor). Phone 44712

All concerts, admission £1

The only problem now was where and how to show it. In stepped Elvera Butler – Entertainments Officer at UCC at the time – with an offer to help. She gave us the old Arcadia ballroom, which was UCC's 'Downtown Kampus', as a venue and that night *Shellshock Rock*, along with RUDI and The Outcasts, played to a crowd of two thousand ecstatic kids. Can you imagine how we all felt? That night has gone down in history.

Thanks, in many ways, to the Cork Festival and their inflexible attitudes of the time, *Shellshock Rock* came of age, even winning an award at the 1979 New York International Film and Television Festival. That same year, it got a distribution deal in America and took its simple message out into the world for all to see. I am totally indebted to Terri for his part in all of this.

Thank you, bless you Terri.

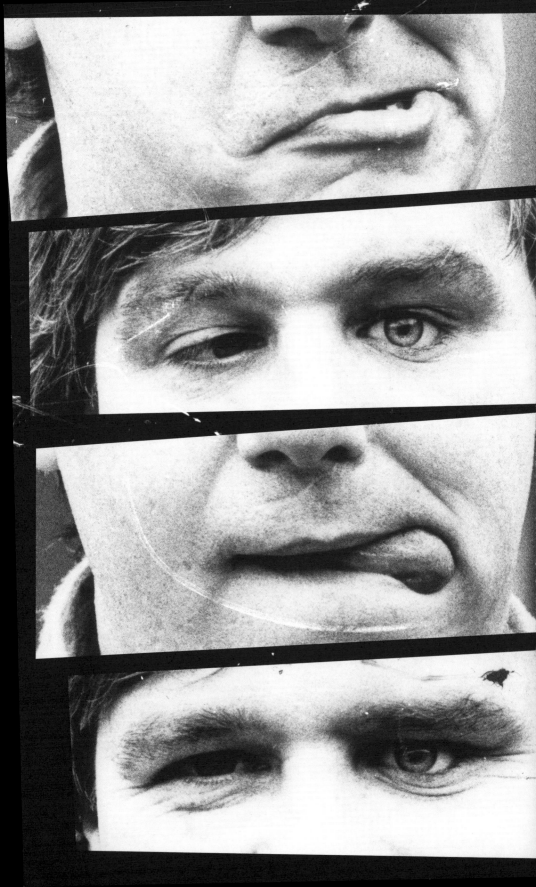

LAUGH AT ME !

By late 1979, I was riding high. The Good Vibrations tour had gone off without a hitch, most of our bands were being signed up to the big leagues and life was a constant party. I had reason to celebrate!

Most importantly, on 6 September 1979 I became a father when Ruth gave birth to our beautiful baby daughter, Anna. Sadly, in those days it wasn't customary for dads to be there for the actual birth but, true to form, when she was born I had the party of all time. My wife and newborn daughter were in hospital and I was out partying like a madman!

Anna, aged 2

I remember that at this time The Outcasts' bass player Greg Cowan had been injured in a road accident and was brought to the same hospital as my wife. All these punks would arrive to see him and then come down the corridor to see Ruth and the new baby. You can just imagine the look on the faces of the staff as dozens of punks invaded the maternity unit to coo over the new arrival!

But they were all great lads at heart, despite their tough exterior, and the more time I spent with them, watching them on-stage and helping them develop their careers, the more I knew I wanted to experience the thrill of performing myself. Being around those young, energetic, anarchic bands really got me going, and they would often coax me on-stage to do a turn – not that I needed much encouragement to get up and do my thing!

My song of choice was always 'Laugh at Me', an old Sonny Bono number that nobody ever really remembers, but when I first heard the song in the mid-sixties, the lyrics struck a chord with me:

Why can't I be like any guy?
What do they care about the clothes I wear?
Why get their kicks from making fun?

I had only ever considered myself to be a warm-up act for the bands, it was just a laugh really, but the audience always seemed to love me and I really enjoyed being up in front of so many people. I had performed a few times before during the sixties, though it was always just for fun. When I went to parties people would sing and play guitar and, since I didn't have a note in my head, I would get up and recite some revolutionary poetry or something! I have always been a bit of an exhibitionist and I loved getting up in front of a crowd, so I would do it any chance I got, though I think the most memorable occasion was on my thirtieth birthday in December 1978.

The big day had coincided with a punk gig at The Harp Bar, so I basically turned it into a birthday party for me. I wanted to put on a performance for all my friends, so I had approached people who I used to play with in the sixties to put together a band. I had even thought of a name for us, we could be The Geriatrics. However, getting those guys out of the pub proved difficult, so RUDI and Protex agreed to back me instead. I got up on-stage and sang 'Laugh at Me'. The audience loved it, and someone even suggested I put it out as a record. This reaction stuck with me and so I performed the song as a party piece for a while afterwards. It always went down well so I thought, why not record it and see what sort of reaction it gets?

LAUGH AT ME

By *TERRI HOOLEY*

A SMASH HIT

FROM **Fresh Records**

So, around Easter 1979, I booked a slot at the Chicken Shack recording studio in Ahoghill and, with the help of the late Geoff Harden – an old friend of mine, and an engineer at the BBC – we recorded my spoof record under the name Terri and the Terrors. Several members of The Outcasts and RUDI provided the instrumental, even recording an orchestral version for the B-side.

At that time, my good friends Stan Brennan and Phil Gaston – whom I had known from my days in the Queen's Esoteric Society – ran a stall in London's Soho Market which, by the way, is where I first met a certain Shane MacGowan, before he became the world's most famous drinker! Anyway, thanks to Stan and Phil I was in contact with a bloke called Alex Howe, who ran the Wretched Records stall at the market. Alex was a big Good Vibes fan and regularly sold our stuff on his stall. He even ran a regular ad in *NME* and *Melody Maker* advertising the fact he had our products. But even more importantly, I had discovered that he was setting up his own record label, Fresh Records, and so I decided to send him a copy of 'Laugh at Me', just to see how it would be received.

Alex called me up a few weeks later and told me that he was interested in putting 'Laugh at Me' out. He had no idea that I was the singer and when I told him he couldn't believe it! But I agreed to let him put the song out and the record was released in October 1979.

I remember going to London around that time to meet up with Alex. It was around then that XDreamysts were signing with Polydor, and they were performing at The Venue in New Cross (which was owned by Virgin boss Richard Branson) so they invited me to come along. When I arrived, they asked me to take to the stage and, as there were a lot of record company and

Performing at The Empire, Belfast – much to the annoyance of the audience!

music press people there, I obliged. I knew that this was my chance to tell them all what I really thought of them, so I got up, grabbed the mic and then got stuck in.

I told them they knew fuck all about rock 'n' roll, and fuck all about bands and how they operated. I said, 'This one's for you' and sang 'Laugh at Me'. At the end, I took out my glass eye and shouted, 'Go, laugh at me now you fuckers.' Trade magazine, *Music Week* said I was a genius for taking on the music press and then went on to report: 'After taking on the press he took out his glass eye! What does he do for an encore? Unscrew his wooden leg?' So in the end, 'Laugh at Me' got a London launch and review, and it didn't even cost me a penny!

Six months later, I received a phone call from an old friend of mine, Walter Coote, who was from Belfast originally but had been living in London for a few years. He told me that he had picked up a copy of *Sounds* magazine, that he had taken a look at the Alternative Chart and that his eyes had nearly popped out on stalks when he saw that my song had reached number one – I couldn't believe it, I thought it was a joke. I ran out as soon as I could to buy my own copy of *Sounds* and there I was at number one, ahead of all these great bands like the Dead Kennedys and The Damned.

That's when it really hit me: I had made it to number one! I said to myself, 'I'm never going to let anyone in Belfast forget this,' and I haven't! Terri and the Terrors earned £3,000 in royalties from 'Laugh at Me' and we used the money to buy presents for kids at Barnardo's, so we never felt guilty about making money from a rip-off record. If anything, this song had managed to expose the double standards of the music industry. I mean, there was nothing polished about the record, yet 'Laugh at Me' was a hit, while so many bands and performers who deserved to record for a big label were passed over.

There was no denying that I had caught the performing bug and I went into the studio a number of times after that. My particular favourites were 'Falling In Love With The Monster Man' and 'I'm In Love With Dracula's Daughter' which I recorded the following Halloween in one of those record-yourself booths for a couple of quid. I gave copies to friends whether they wanted it or not. After recording those songs I put together a band called The Rocking Humdingers and we landed a gig at the Halloween Ball at Queen's where I was carried on-stage in a coffin. When we first came on-stage the crowd chanted, 'Fuck off, Hooley!' but I got an extra £100 for the extraordinary performance. Carlene Carter, Johnny Cash's stepdaughter was also on the bill that night and the whole thing was bonkers.

ALTERNATIVE

1 LAUGH AT ME, Terry Hooley, Fresh
2 ETON RIFLES, Jam, Polydor
3 UK '79, Crisis, Ardkor
4 BURGLAR, Damned, Chiswick
5 CAST OF THOUSANDS, Adverts, RCA
6 BEATLE JACKET, Atoms, Rinka
7 KILLING JOKE 10" EP, Malicious Damage
8 BLOOD AND LIPSTICK, Pink Military, Eric's
9 WE LOVE YOU, Psychedelic Furs, Epic
10 KISS THE MIRROR, The Wall, Small Wonder
11 TIME TUNNEL, The English Subtitles, Small Wonder
12 SMK, The Proles, Small Wonder
13 CALIFORNIA UBER ALLES, Dead Kennedys, Fast
14 LET YOUR HEART DANCE, Secret Affair, I-Spy
15 MARGARET THATCHER, The Not Sensibles, Redball
16 FIRST AND LAST, Art Attax, Fresh
17 MAP REFERENCE, Wire, Harvest
18 MY NUMBER, Girl, Jet
19 CID, UK Subs, Pinnacle
20 SUMMER OF HATE, Chaos UK, Chaotic
21 ROWCHE RUMBLE, Fall, Step Forward

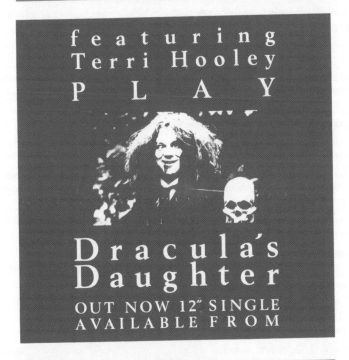

THE ROCKING HUMDINGERS

featuring Terri Hooley

PLAY

Dracula's Daughter

OUT NOW 12" SINGLE
AVAILABLE FROM

GOOD »VIBRATIONS«

But the best bit about my whole recording experience was when I received a telegram from Thin Lizzy's Phil Lynott. He had heard about my alternative-chart success with 'Laugh at Me' and had wanted to congratulate me in his own unique way: 'You one-eyed Protestant bastard,' the telegram read, 'I've always wanted to be number one in the alternative chart!' Luckily, I had been good friends with Phil for years so I knew he was happy for me.

135

Phil was one of the true pioneers of modern Irish music. He had started his career in the mid-sixties with a band called The Black Eagles and, after flirting with a few other outfits, formed Thin Lizzy in 1969 with guitarist Eric Bell, keyboardist Eric Wrixon – both former Them stalwarts – and drummer Brian Downey. He also did a lot of work down the years with a sensational guitarist from Belfast called Gary Moore with whom I had gone to school.

I first met Phil in The Pound in 1973 – that place has a lot to answer for! – when Thin Lizzy's breakthrough hit, a rocked-up version of traditional Irish ballad 'Whiskey In The Jar', was in the charts. I can't remember who was playing that night but Phil and I got talking and struck up a good friendship. We didn't swap numbers or anything like that but we often bumped into each other on the music scene. I'd like to think we were kindred spirits, only he had all the talent and I had the good looks!

I certainly had some really great times with Phil. We used to meet up in Dublin, in a pub just off Grafton Street called The Bailey – a great spot that was frequented by musicians and other luvvies – and I recall going to see him one particular night in London while he was working in the studio.

It was 1979 and Thin Lizzy were putting the finishing touches to their *Black Rose* album with legendary producer Tony Visconti – best known for his work with David Bowie and T-Rex. When I arrived, Phil told me that he'd had a tip off that the Drug Squad was going to raid the place, so he had ensured it was completely clean. However, not everyone seemed to have received the message as, no sooner had we arrived, than someone produced some Nepalese Temple Balls, which essentially were balls of hashish. The fear of a drugs raid went out the window, and soon we were smoking away. Gary Moore was Thin Lizzy's guitarist at this time, so he was there that night and, after a few hours smoking that stuff, we both felt sufficiently moved to sing 'The Sash' for Phil!

That night they were mixing 'Sarah', a song about Phil's newborn daughter, and I said to Visconti, 'I think you should move some of your faders.' Imagine that, Terri Hooley giving one of the greatest producers of all time advice on how to mix a track! But I was so stoned and was feeling super-confident so I told Phil that if they ever released the track as a single it would be a hit. They did, and it was. Now, I'm not saying it had anything to do with me, but you have to wonder ...

In 1981, I met up with Phil again. This time, one of the new Good Vibes bands, The Nerves, had won the Northern Ireland heat of a Battle of the Bands competition and were through to the national final. Ricky Flanagan and I went over to England to support them, but, rather predictably, didn't make the gig and instead ended up smoking dope with a couple of girls we met from County Down. I rang the band to see how they had done – they hadn't won, but had done very well – and arranged to meet them at a nightclub in Park Lane for the after party. It was only when I arrived that I discovered that Lynott had been one of the judges! Inevitably, we both got stuck into the drink and the rest of the night is a blur. The only thing I remember is that he gave me a great piece of advice which I, unfortunately, couldn't remember when I woke up the next morning! That was a night out with Phil.

Thin Lizzy were huge at that stage, and Phil's partying lifestyle had become the stuff of legend, as had his capacity to drink and take ridiculous amount of drugs. Most of us took drugs back then, but for Phil it became a way of coping with his celebrity status – he found it hard to deal with all the attention he was receiving and I got the feeling that he would have been content playing in a wee pub band and enjoying his music without all the hassle fame brought. Sadly, in January 1986 his drug dependency resulted in multiple organ failure and Phil passed away. It was a terrible loss of a great talent.

Phil Lynott, when Thin Lizzy performed at
Belfast's King's Hall in June 1980

THE HARP
BRIAN YOUNG

To paraphrase an old cliché, 'if everybody who now claims to have been a regular at The Harp Bar back in the day was lined up end-to-end (though face-to-face would be more fun!) you could probably reach the moon and back!' Such is the notoriety of this seedy, run-down watering hole in Ulster punk lore!

Unlike The Pound – where initially we always seemed to be regarded with suspicion, if not hostility – The Harp actively welcomed the punky waver hordes through its doors, at least, as soon as they realised that there was a substantial amount of cash money to be made from these strangely attired youngsters!

AN EVENING OF ALTERNATIVE ENTERTAINMENT

RUDI
☆ ☞ ☆ & DISCO

BY THE LEGENDARY TERRI HOOLEY
THURSDAY 4th FEB at the HARP BAR 8p.m.
Tickets £1 admission strictly ticket only

Like The Pound, The Harp had a less than salubrious reputation – though, while The Pound had a certain notoriety as a den of iniquity, it was never regarded as a dangerous place to go. The Harp, on the other hand, had a very bad reputation indeed. Not only was it staunchly nationalist – hardly welcoming to us folks hailing from loyalist east Belfast in those far-off days – but it had also achieved some local infamy as one of the few venues in town that staged regular strip/sex shows, and believe you me this was the real deal, with shoddily projected XXX films and hard-faced strippers who would often perform group hand jobs in the toilets for a few quid! Charming, huh?

Still, necessity is the mother of invention, and with venue after venue refusing to allow anything remotely punky-flavoured to darken their doors and more and more local punk bands looking desperately for places to play, a couple of enterprising bands approached The Harp asking if they could play in the old upstairs function room, 'The Harp Lounge', which lay disused and empty most nights of the week. With little to lose and much to gain Pat Lennon, the owner of the bar, agreed.

RUDI playing at The Harp Bar, 1979

And though the initial gigs weren't packed, they were financially successful enough for him to allow other punk bands in to play on a more regular basis.

RUDI was one of the first bands to get in on the act, making our Harp debut in May 1978. Sure, we were kinda apprehensive at first but, as soon as the punters started arriving, we breathed a huge sigh of relief and just got on with what we were good at – knocking out our own particular brand of no-holds-barred, two-fisted punk rock! By then, we had already amassed a following who would come and see us whenever and wherever we played, but what soon became noticeable was the amount of new faces in the audience – people that we'd never seen before and didn't know at all – and once we all got talking, we discovered that these fellow punky wavers hailed from all over the place. Not only did they come from parts of Belfast we'd never set foot in, but also from Antrim, Newtownabbey, Carrickfergus, Portrush and further afield.

We played The Harp several times before leaving for London in August 1978 and it was there that we played a particularly memorable farewell gig with Protex playing a smashing support slot. After we'd finished the main set our pal Henry Cluney from SLF got up to run through some spirited, if shambolic, cover versions as we all got wasted!

Living in London we missed the entire Punk Workshop episode, though I do remember having to reassure one of our acquaintances there, a guitarist with The Nips, that he'd not get shot in Belfast once he opened his mouth and everyone realised he was a 'Brit' – at least not while he was in The Harp!

We came home from London at the end of December 1978 after a run-in with the dreaded Special Patrol Group in Clapham. Though it had been positively surreal living there when The Undertones Good Vibes EP took off and media attention focused briefly on Northern Ireland, it taught us many important lessons, allowed us to make several invaluable contacts who would prove vital later in our career and also enabled us to write a heap of far better quality material. We debuted much of this in The Harp on 22 December in front of a jam-packed and rabid audience and breathed a huge sigh of relief that we hadn't been forgotten when we were away! Amazingly, dozens of people had to be turned away at the door and even *NME* noted that this was the biggest crowd at The Harp ever!

From that point on we played The Harp at least once or twice a month, until it closed its doors to punk midway through 1981. We always regularly pulled the biggest crowds and I've many fond memories of that period, from the sublime to the utterly ridiculous. How could I forget having to squeeze past the strippers getting changed as we lugged our gear up the back stairs and tried not to stare too much?! Or filling up

Grimmy's hollow drum seat with as many bottles of beer as we could stash in it when were supposed to be sound checking! Or our pal Mr Puke regularly spending most of the set lying on-stage with his head stuffed into the bass drum! Or always having to turn Big Gordy's bass amp down behind his back when he wasn't looking! Or Halloween night 1979, when Terri Hooley joined us on-stage to be presented with a gold disc for his indie-chart-topping smash 'Laugh at Me', which we'd played on. The record had been recorded in a converted henhouse outside Randalstown when we were all half-cut, and the 'gold disc' was a Lurkers freebie flexi-disc with a 'Laugh at Me' label stuck on top!

If you wanted, you could hang out in The Harp seven nights a week just playing pool or listening to the jukebox without any real hassle from the bar staff Maureen and Tony, even if you never bought a drink! Many of the regular punters preferred the more economical option of knocking back their beverage of choice in the nearby subway prior to setting foot in The Harp! Sure, it was dilapidated, grimy and the toilets had to be seen to be believed, but it also had a decent-sized stage, was easy enough to fill sound-wise, had proper seats, tables, and even some booths. Best of all, it had a biggish dance floor right in front of the stage with plenty of room to pogo to your heart's content. The bands were usually pretty hot – but even if they weren't the DJs always played a first-rate selection of primo punky wax. And did I already mention that they also sold alcohol and didn't ask too many questions about your age? What more could you ask for!

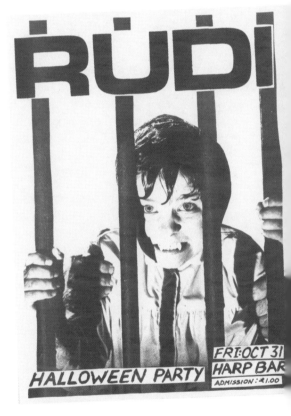

A lot has been said about The Harp over the years, and it's pretty obvious in hindsight that a relatively accessible, quasi-neutral, punk-friendly venue in the centre of Northern Ireland's largest city would encourage young people to venture outside their own enclaves to participate in the whole glorious punk explosion first-hand. But it really was the first time I can remember that significant numbers of young people from all sections and classes of the community, and from both sides of the sectarian divide were able to meet up and get to know each other, initially drawn together by their enthusiasm for this new music and lifestyle. Perhaps unsurprisingly, many lifelong friendships and long-term relationships resulted.

Personally too, I reckon it's not too wide of the mark to say that for most people at The Harp what really mattered was the music you liked – not where you were from, or what foot you kicked with. You were a punk rocker first and foremost and everything else was secondary. At least that's what it felt like to me, others may beg to differ.

Don't get me wrong, it most certainly wasn't all sweetness and light, not all punks were non-sectarian by any means and there were always the usual heated arguments and fights you'd get in any large group of high-spirited teens, but in all honesty there really never was that much trouble inside The Harp – certainly nothing like we would have experienced at our previous haunts the Glenmachan and Girton Lodge. It's also worth noting that any actual fisticuffs were generally more to do with your allegiance to a particular band or crowd, rather than along more usual sectarian lines. Though, believe you me, the rivalry between some of the bands could, and did, get pretty damn intense (no names, no pack-drill as we were all guilty of this to a greater or lesser degree!).

Outside The Harp, it was a very different story and you definitely had to be wary of marauding 'Spidermen'/predators looking to pick off unwary stragglers on your way there and home. So, relying on safety in numbers, everybody used to walk round to the City Hall en masse to get the last bus home at 11 p.m.! In those distant times nobody had their own transport. That feeling of intimidation is what the RUDI song 'Tigerland' is about:

> I'll meet you when the clock strikes eight, we'll
> walk into the darkness.
> I'll see you there, all dressed in red at the end
> of the day.
> At the end of the day, they stalk their prey.

For Ulster's budding punk musicians The Harp truly was a godsend! Realising that if chancers like us could do it, then anyone could and now – with a readily accessible venue in which to strut their stuff – zillions of local hopefuls took their first faltering steps on-stage. Amazingly, most of 'em weren't half bad, more than making up in enthusiasm and sheer panache for what they may have been lacking in musical ability.

This was the real DIY punk ethic put into practice and was much more important than the haircuts and funny clothes – though that was fun too! And it didn't just apply to musicians either. The Harp provided both focus and catalyst for an emerging network of writers, DJs, artists and activists, unleashing a wave of creativity in all sorts of unlikely areas, and planting the seeds for all sorts of weird 'n' wonderful things to come in many impressionable young minds too!

For more experienced acts The Harp provided the perfect opportunity to hone your stagecraft in front of a fiercely partisan audience. You had to put up or shut up – simple as that! But it encouraged many local bands to sharpen up their act and it's no accident that most of the bands that played there benefited hugely from the experience. Admittedly, it wasn't all plain sailing, as several hapless acts found to their cost when they incurred the audience's wrath and were bottled off!

There was never any time for complacency either – the competition was fierce and kept you on your toes. You were always only ever as good as your last gig and there was always somebody snapping at your heels. I guess the bottom line was that if you could cut it at The Harp you could cut it anywhere – as we proved time and time again when we were signed to the Jamming! label and got to tour the length and breadth of the UK and Ireland. But, home is where the heart is and I guess I always looked forward to playing The Harp more than anywhere else! Certainly many of the wildest, most memorable and most fun gigs RUDI ever played took place within those walls – when everything clicked into place and the band was firing on all cylinders, the audience was going totally apeshit and sweat was running down the walls, there really was nowhere like it!

Sadly, all good things must come to an end and as punk became less popular The Harp decided to cut its losses, metamorphosing almost overnight into a country and western club in mid-1981. We did actually play there again in February 1982 as a one-off, but whether or not it was the fault of the surreal backdrop of painted cacti and rustic fencing I'm not sure, but the magic had gone and it had become just another venue. Sadly, the anticipated C&W boom The Harp was hoping for never materialised and it gradually slipped back into obscurity, finally shutting its doors for good a few years later.

WHAT
GOES
UP

From humble beginnings, Good Vibrations had grown into something very special. The Undertones may have been our biggest success but we helped a host of bands realise their dreams. And I'll let you into a secret – many of these bands were signed up, not because I had some great insight into their musical prowess, but simply because I knew and liked the people involved. Sometimes people would ask me, 'Why on earth are you signing them up?' and I'd say, 'Well, one night he bought me a pint in The Pound.' A proper business plan just wouldn't have worked for me.

By this stage I was being tortured with demos – I even had prisoners in the Maze sending me their songs – and we were signing up scores of new bands to the label.

In 1980, we signed The Shapes, a band who had been signed to EMI, but left when the label tried to force them in another direction. This worked out well for us though, as it turned out they were huge Good Vibrations fans and had wanted to record with us. My friend Willie Richardson, who worked for Virgin, had heard about this and suggested that I go and see them, so Getty (from The Outcasts) and I travelled to their hometown of Leamington Spa, and met them in the local pub. After a great evening, during which I managed to beat the local pool hustler, we went to one of the lads' flats, only to find the walls covered with the sleeves of every record that Good Vibrations had put out. It was no surprise then when they told me they were keen to put something out on the label. I agreed to release their song 'Blast Off'.

Despite these successes, money was starting to run a little low and so, in August 1980, I put together Belfast's 'First Punk and New Wave Festival', a two-night Good Vibes showcase /fundraiser to be held in the Ulster Hall. We wanted to show people that it was possible for local talent to fill the venue and I'm happy to say that we packed the place on both nights – stories of me letting in hundreds of punks free of charge are wide of the mark, there were only a few dozen!

Over the course of the two nights all the bands currently on the label played a set, and while people have since asked me why RUDI didn't headline the festival, the truth is that by this stage they had split from the label. They had been a huge success for Good Vibes but we wanted to give new and upcoming bands the chance to shine. I'd hoped that this event would make the industry across the water sit up and take notice.

I was doing my best to get as much exposure as possible for the label, so the following year I took a number of bands over to Newcastle upon Tyne for an Irish music festival. Unfortunately it turned out to be total shite, and just as I began to regret coming over at all, the trip was redeemed when I found out that The Pogues were playing the Town Hall that same weekend.

I was quite friendly with lead singer Shane MacGowan, having met him several years previously when he was working on a market stall in Soho. Good Vibes had supplied some stalls at that market with records and, once we got to chatting, it turned out that we had a lot of things in common. He and his punk band, The Nipple Erectors, were just starting to make their mark, so we would often go drinking at the local pub, The

147

Shaftsbury Inn in Soho, and talk about music. We always had a great time. I invited him to bring the band over for a gig in The Harp in 1978 and was amazed to learn that, despite his strong interest in all things Irish, it was to be the band's first visit to Ireland.

When the band, who later changed their name to The Nips, put out a single called 'Gabrielle' in 1979, I agreed to stock it in the shop but, only a few years after its release, Shane decided to leave the band, joining celtic rock group, Pogue Mahone – or The Pogues as they would come to be known – instead.

As such, he turned out to be in Newcastle upon Tyne the same weekend I was, so I made sure to head round to the gig. I managed to blag my way in and had an absolutely brilliant night, and not just because the band were on top form. I remember The Pogues' tour manager Joey Cashman grabbing me after the show and asking me, for whatever reason, to look after the bar. 'Not a problem,' I thought, and proceeded to swipe a few bottles of wine for later. Shane was supposedly off the drink – which just meant he wasn't drinking spirits! – but whenever he came over to chat to me he managed, within seconds, to suss where I had hidden the wine. The man has an unerring nose for alcohol! We spent that night in a hotel bar enjoying a sensational sing-song round the piano. I still keep in touch with Shane and whenever he's in town I try to hook up with him. He doesn't drink as much as he used to, but he can still put on a sensational show.

In 1981, we wound up in the High Court for the sum of £2,700 which we owed to a wholesaler. That may not sound like much, but it was symptomatic of larger financial problems and those money difficulties had me pretty stressed out. Despite all our hard fundraising work, things were getting tougher all the time on the money front. I couldn't handle it, and threw myself even harder into partying. As a result, things became increasingly difficult at home.

Anna's arrival had been a blessing, but now Ruth and I were fighting all the time. She had outgrown all the frantic partying and needed a more settled life. I suppose she was tired of coming down the stairs in the morning to find several young punks sleeping on our living room floor. I'm sorry to say that I didn't make any real attempt to change my ways and one day she just said, 'That's it, it's over,' and she asked me to leave.

Looking back, I guess I was just so wrapped up in my own wee party world that I didn't see it coming. I knew that Ruth had put up with so much over the years we had been together and it's true when they say that you don't realise what you have until it's taken away from you. I knew I wasn't looking after her properly and I went to pieces. I moved into a house in Andersonstown in the west of the city for a few months, and began to party harder than ever. Outwardly it may have looked like 'same old Terri' and that I was just getting on with life, but inside I was devastated.

I threw myself into Good Vibrations and, in 1982, I signed a great band, Cruella de Ville, and we put out their double A-side single 'Drunken Uncle John'/'Those Two Dreadful Children'. They also recorded the single 'I'll Do The Talking' with Good Vibrations, which was licensed and released with Polydor. The band was brilliant, and so were signed up to EMI's CPL label in 1984, re-releasing 'I'll Do The Talking' to critical and commercial success – it was a great track and people still come into the shop and ask for it. They recorded an album too, though CPL never released it. The band – Colum and Philamena Muinzer, James Clenaghan and Mike Edgar – split up in 1985, but drummer Edgar went on to become a DJ for Radio Ulster, creating the show *Across the Line*, which, to this day, is a showcase for new and established local bands.

In 1982, I also worked with a great outfit called The Bankrobbers – John McDonald, Liam Carville, Joby Fox and Seamus O'Neill – releasing their single, 'On My Mind'. They were very talented and they too were quickly snapped up by EMI. They released a few things with them but, tired of continual gigging for no money and getting little support from a disinterested record label, they split in 1984. Joby Fox, along with some ex-members of 10 Past 7, went on to form the excellent Energy Orchard – another band that should have enjoyed greater success – before he formed The Blue Dolphins.

I really felt that The Bankrobbers should have had much more success than they did, although I must admit that they often made things difficult for themselves and had some colourful run-ins with the law. In 1979, they posed for a photo shoot in Newtownards wearing combat gear and were mistaken for paramilitaries, so when they got back to Belfast and went into Robinson's Bar for a pint they were greeted by armed police who

The Bankrobbers, L-R: Liam Carville, John McDonald, Joby Fox and Seamus O'Neill – they would've made more money robbing banks!

had tailed them home. Then, in 1982, they decided to mark the release of their debut EMI single, 'Jenny', by printing fake £50 notes embossed with the band's logo and were arrested on forgery charges – they just couldn't seem to catch a break!

My difficulty was that I loved the music and the bands, but I hated the industry. The big companies could afford to sign up new bands in the hope that they might turn into a success, but if they didn't it was no big deal. The bands needed support and help and, nine times out of ten, they didn't get it. But I did my best to support the bands in any way I could, making sure that the fans would always know about the band's next release. We sent records all over the world, and if you ordered a single from us you also got a Good Vibes newsletter with information on all our bands. We sold badges and other merchandise – it was a proper package. And our bands had fans all over the world. We would get invitations to play festivals in Australia, Japan, New Zealand and even Israel.

Of course, I made sure that we put on as many local events as possible too, and during the eighties the message also finally started to get through to Belfast City Council. On 14 May 1982, they let Good Vibrations put on a festival at Maysfield Leisure Centre. I arranged for English band, The Membranes – who weren't on our label, but whose manager came from Newtownards – to come over, along with The Shapes and, with other bands from the label, we put on a fantastic festival. The council put up the funding but didn't publicise the event which mystified me at the time, but I later found out that gangs of mods had been fighting with punks in Belfast city centre, and the council had thought that if they didn't tell anybody about the festival, the mods wouldn't turn up.

Sadly, the festival came to have a sombre and important overtone. It was staged the day after Colin Cowan from The Outcasts was killed in a road accident. The day became a tribute to him, and fans came from all over Northern Ireland to register their sadness. His funeral was huge – so many kids turned out to mourn in what I saw as a remarkable display of loyalty. It was then that I realised that these bands had become heroes to many people. Colin was a great person, a real character, and I miss him to this day, so this book gives me the opportunity to pay tribute to him and his role in the music revolution that was punk.

Although Ruth and I had separated, we had stayed friends. She was worried about me living on the other side of the city. Single again, I was partying far too much – the drink and drugs were flying. So with her help I moved into a rented house in Wolsey Street, just off Botanic Avenue in south Belfast, and one lovely Saturday afternoon in the summer of 1982 I, along with a few others, decided to throw a street party for my new neighbours.

We had Punch and Judy shows for the kids, street theatre, a huge barbecue and, of course, music. We didn't ask anyone's permission, we just blocked off the street and partied. The police seemed happy as the street wasn't a main thoroughfare, and there was no trouble. The next day, as we cleared up the mess and looked forward to going to the pub with the £80 I'd picked up from the street – coins that people had dropped as they

With some of The Shapes and The Membranes before the Maysfield gig, 14 May 1982

danced to 'La Bamba'! – I received a phonecall from Father Pat Buckley, a local priest who had heard about our mini-festival.

Buckley was an outspoken parish priest, based in west Belfast, and a constant thorn in the side of the Catholic Church, calling for an end to the vow of celibacy and campaigning for those who had been abused by members of the clergy. He also declared that, like him, as many as forty per cent of the Catholic clergy were gay, and even claimed that the Devil himself could be cleansed of his sins – so there's hope for me yet! Anyway, Father Pat told me that he helped to run a small community festival every year in the Divis Tower area of Belfast, and asked if I would help to get a few bands to play.

Divis Tower is a huge complex in the west of the city. Built in 1966, it had become a focus for sectarian tensions. In the early seventies the British Army installed a huge listening post on the roof of the tower in order to keep watch over the natives and so there was barbed wire everywhere, armed troops on every street corner and sporadic outbursts of gunfire. Young people growing up there really hadn't a chance – they were virtually unemployable because of their address, and quite often their only option was to join the paramilitaries. As a result, Divis Tower became a symbol of IRA resistance to the army throughout the Troubles, which were at their height when Father Pat called me about helping to run a festival at the heart of the complex.

We agreed to meet at the shop, and then myself and Mervyn Crawford – whose band Apartment had just released their record 'We'll Have A Holiday' on Good Vibrations – took him to lunch in Capers Restaurant on Great Victoria Street and then to Lavery's

bar for a couple of pints to talk about the festival. Pat was concerned that we wouldn't be able to convince anyone to play in Divis, but by the end of the day we had a great line-up including The Bankrobbers, Apartment and 10 Past 7 – a band featuring Brian and Bap Kennedy who, in 1983, would eventually release their single 'Cracking Up' with Good Vibrations.

The only thing left for us to do was sell the idea to the Divis Residents Committee, which wasn't as easy as it sounded. They wanted total control and were suspicious of someone from outside their area coming in and calling the shots, but Father Pat was right behind me and in the end we won them round. He agreed to get in touch with the police and army to ask them to stay out of the area, while I was to go to the IRA and tell them that we didn't want them to use this as an excuse to shift bombs and shooters. I met with IRA representatives and they agreed to our terms, assuring me that everything would go smoothly and that we would be able to get our gear in and out without it being damaged, burned or stolen.

Logistically it was difficult to get a sound system into Divis, because the tower blocks formed an amphitheatre, which could only be accessed by narrow passageways. On top of that, to get the sort of sound we wanted we needed a big system. I spoke to John Connolly at Queen's University who let us rent a huge fifty-thousand-amp system, which was actually paid for with money from Belfast City Council. It had been tough to persuade them to give Divis any money, let alone enough for them to stage a festival, but we succeeded. With tower blocks on all sides a huge sound stage was generated and it was a truly momentous event.

10 Past 7 at the Divis Festival, 1982

It's hard to say how many people were there in total. People watched from their balconies and from the ground – there must have been at least two thousand – and as far I could see, everybody enjoyed themselves. We called the festival 'Have a Holiday For a Day' as there was no trouble from 'the boys' and for once the kids in the area could play without the sound of army helicopters hovering overhead.

Sadly, things were not going as well for Good Vibrations. The store and the label were experiencing some real financial difficulty – we were owed at least £5,000 from distributors in England who had failed to pay us for goods we had already supplied. I also remember getting an order from Italy for five hundred Outcasts' albums and I was so pleased that there was such demand for the record that I didn't think twice. I just packed up the records, sent them over and we never got paid. At one stage the shop was doing phenomenal business but we just didn't seem to have the money to show for it. Looking back I suppose what I really needed was a good accountant to look after the money side of things.

I never really made any money from sales of records on the label either. There was never a formal arrangement with the bands' though they sometimes made a few quid doing gigs – we operated like a collective and pretty much all profits made were centralised and ploughed back into buying equipment, or putting petrol in the van and so on. It was the same for everybody, we were in it together.

I turned up to sign on and they were closed – typical!

I tried everything to keep the business afloat, but in late 1982 our creditors filed a bankruptcy petition, and that was the beginning of the end. After five hectic years, it looked like Good Vibes was going to go under.

It was a very difficult period for me but my friends rallied round and did what they could to cheer me up. A great friend of mine, Francis McCartney, had just come home from Canada where she had been living for a few years, and she convinced me to accompany her to a party in the Royal Avenue Hotel. On the way in I met another old friend, Mina Wilson, and she invited us to join them at their table. We hadn't been sitting there long when Francis pointed out a girl who had been up dancing, 'Isn't that the most beautiful woman you have ever seen?' she asked me. But I had already spotted the woman of my dreams, and it wasn't the girl on the dance floor. I didn't even know her name, but at that moment I knew she was the one and that somehow I was going to end up with her.

I said as much to Francis, who couldn't believe it. 'Her?' she said, 'she looks like someone from the sixties!' To which I replied, 'Francis, I am someone from the sixties!' But I wasn't brave enough to approach my mystery woman, and before I knew it, the party was over and the crowds were leaving. Luckily though, as I was sitting in the taxi rank waiting to go home, she walked in and I offered to share my cab. That was the start of it.

She told me her name was Eithne McIlroy, and when the taxi dropped her off, we arranged to meet up some days later. Over the following weeks I met up with her a couple of times and one night I took her to see a band called The Zen Alligators in Queen's University. The band featured Eamon Carr from Horslips – one of the greatest bands Ireland has ever produced – and Eithne was a big fan of his, so I think she just wanted to see him rather than having any real interest in me. I don't think I made a particularly good impression but I really liked her, so I rang her a couple of times and soon we started seeing each other. It wasn't long before I was really serious about this girl.

With Eithne

I wanted to spend time with Eithne away from the pressure cooker of Belfast and the reality of my business going under, but with the bankruptcy proceedings, I had no money of my own. So I went to my mum and asked if I could borrow £300 to take Eithne to Paris – she gave it to me without question, she knew I needed a break. If anything, I think she was just so pleased that her son could still come to her and ask for help.

Eithne agreed to come away with me and within a few days we flew to London. I had arranged for us to stay overnight with a friend of mine, Bob Johnston, the manager of a band called The Gas who Good Vibes had worked with in the past. Bob was also managing Frankie Goes To Hollywood, who were a new band at the time, and he showed us a video in which they were performing 'Relax' in its rawest form. He asked me what I thought of them but before I could open my mouth Eithne said she thought they were brilliant, so I think she can legitimately claim to have had a helping hand in the success of the one of the biggest bands of the eighties. Mind you she never got a cheque!

It was a good start to the weekend and we headed to Paris where we stayed in a small hotel. We did all the predictable things: picnics in the park, sightseeing, shopping, drinking wine and, of course, partying – I was floating on air. I remember standing at the top of the Eiffel Tower with her when I saw a bit of grafitti: 'Even though you think that nobody in the world loves you, I do.' I thought that this was a wonderful sentiment and I was so happy. I was supposed to be in court to answer bankruptcy proceedings, but I was in Paris acting as if I hadn't a care in the world, while back in Belfast a judge was winding up my business.

But reality has a habit of creeping back and I felt in my heart that the relationship with Eithne couldn't continue while I had so much on my plate, so when we got home we broke up. I made my way to the shop where I was confronted by a bloke who identified himself as an officer of the court, before handing me a document telling me not to touch anything. He wouldn't even let me take a few quid out of the till to see me through the day, talk about kicking a man when he's down! It was a definite low point in my life. I bought a bunch of flowers for a friend of mine with the last money I had – I suppose I didn't see the point in keeping such a small amount of money – and that was it, it was all over. I'd lost everything.

I went to see my ex-wife Ruth, who had encouraged me to go out with Eithne in the first place, and she could see how down I was – more about the end of my relationship than the end of the business, I have to say. She encouraged me to call Eithne and tell her the truth about my situation, that I was penniless. I did and we moved in together pretty much straight away.

I was so grateful to Eithne for being there during such a difficult period in my life, though I had long since reconciled myself to the fact that it was time to bring the curtain down on Good Vibrations. I believe that we could have stayed open – many people owed us money – but I was tired. I had poured all my energy into the shop and the label, and it had all become too much. But at least I could take some satisfaction in knowing that we had proven to the world that it could be done – one tiny store in Belfast had made an impact on the music world. The Clash, Ian Dury, Jools Holland and many other visiting rock stars had all made pilgrimages to the shop, and countless stars had had their pictures taken with our beloved Elvis sign – we had made a difference.

When the shop closed, I decided to burn Elvis to mark the passing of something so important. I wanted to give him a decent farewell but Belfast's crematorium refused to let us use their ovens, so I put a match to him in my own hearth! We then collected the ashes in little bags and gave them to people, so Good Vibrations fans all over the world could have a wee reminder of the days Elvis pointed the way in Belfast.

ELVIS' ASHES

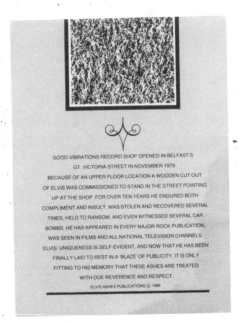

GOOD VIBRATIONS RECORD SHOP OPENED IN BELFAST'S GT. VICTORIA STREET IN NOVEMBER 1979. BECAUSE OF AN UPPER FLOOR LOCATION A WOODEN CUT OUT OF ELVIS WAS COMMISSIONED TO STAND IN THE STREET POINTING UP AT THE SHOP. FOR OVER TEN YEARS HE ENDURED BOTH COMPLIMENT AND INSULT, WAS STOLEN AND RECOVERED SEVERAL TIMES, HELD TO RANSOM, AND EVEN WITNESSED SEVERAL CAR BOMBS. HE HAS APPEARED IN EVERY MAJOR ROCK PUBLICATION, WAS SEEN IN FILMS AND ALL NATIONAL TELEVISION CHANNELS. ELVIS' UNIQUENESS IS SELF-EVIDENT, AND NOW THAT HE HAS BEEN FINALLY LAID TO REST IN A 'BLAZE' OF PUBLICITY, IT IS ONLY FITTING TO HIS MEMORY THAT THESE ASHES ARE TREATED WITH DUE REVERENCE AND RESPECT. ELVIS ASHES PUBLICATIONS © 1989

'TOO MUCH JUNKIE BIZ'
JOHNNY THUNDERS

In October 1984 the late, great Johnny Thunders – one-time lead singer of legendary American garage band the New York Dolls, and later The Heartbreakers – played the TV Club in Dublin before, at the behest of Terri Hooley, getting into a minibus and driving north for a memorable gig at McMordie Hall in Belfast.

It was his first-ever visit to Ireland and, upon arriving at the border, he was shocked to be asked to get out of the vehicle while soldiers searched every inch of it. They were then questioned by the police and army before being allowed to continue. It was an everyday occurrence for those of us who lived here, but it left Thunders unsettled. He was spooked even further by the sight of gun-toting soldiers on every street corner.

Terri and Liz Young with
Johnny Thunders

The band played to a packed McMordie Hall on 27 October, but his shock at what he'd seen was evident as he spoke from the stage:

> Hey kids, you've got a strange fuckin' city here, a strange fuckin' town. I don't know how you live with it, I couldn't live with it, but at least I have now seen what the rest of the world needs to see – it needs to see Ireland.

> I hear that if you are Irish you kick with the left foot and if you are English you kick with the right, but I know that's not true. You don't care what you are, you just wanna live. Speaking about livin', this one, 'Too Much Junkie Biz', is for that weird guy Terri. You know Terri the weird guy? The guy with only one nostril.

> There's a lot to sing about here, I tell you man, I don't know how you put up with it. What does it take to put up with something like this? But I'll tell you something kids, you're lucky to have a guy like this, real fuckin' lucky. All you need is The One, and he is The One for you.

When he got backstage, he had this to add:

> I dunno how anybody could actually live here, but the audience really appreciate you. When they get into it they really get into it, like Detroit used to be in '74. I get the same feeling from Belfast.

Johnny Thunders died on 23 April 1991, aged fifty. The official story was that his death was drug related, though family and friends remain convinced he died by foul means. New Orleans police have consistently resisted calls to re-open the investigation.

DOWN BUT
NOT OUT

When I lost Good Vibrations I thought that my music store days were over – I had been floating along in a bubble of denial for so long that, when it popped, I didn't know what to do. I knew that I wanted to stay in the business, I just didn't know how.

In stepped local businessmen Willie Richardson and Ken Donaldson, who recognised that Good Vibrations had the potential to be a successful venture. Willie came from Belfast and had worked for Virgin Records – for a time he was their head A&R man – later finding success as Van Morrison's manager, a job he held for more than fifteen years. He loved music almost as much as I did! Ken, on the other hand, was a businessman through and through. His family were the 'Donaldson' in the famous Donaldson & Lyttle high-end furniture store in Belfast, so I think he looked at Good Vibes as a moneymaking venture.

They approached the Official Receiver to inquire about buying stock, offered to buy the business and decided to keep it based in the original shop. They didn't, however, ask me to step in and help. At least not initially. It seems that they believed that the reason the original store had failed was because I was unable to run it properly. People had been amazed when I went bust as they had assumed the business was worth a fortune; an assumption, I think, that was probably due to all the media attention we got.

That attitude soon changed when it came to light that a lot of the stuff I had been ordering when I was owner hadn't even reached the shop floor. Instead, they had found boxes and boxes of records at the home of one of the employees. Once they realised the shop hadn't got into debt because of my mismanagement they came to me, told me what they had discovered and asked if I would be interested in managing the shop.

It seemed perfect. I was back behind the counter of the store I loved, without the stress and worry that came with actually running the business – it certainly took the pressure off me for a bit. Although, if I'm honest, I was never truly happy with the arrangement, as I don't think Ken and Willie really understood what Good Vibes was all about. To them it was simply a business venture – for me it was a way of life.

As time went on, and it became obvious that Good Vibrations was never going to pull in the sort of profits they were looking for, Ken and Willie made it clear that they wanted out. In 1984, a very dear friend of mine, Eamonn McWilliams, who had worked in his family's bakery business – Ed's Bread – came forward with a package to buy the business, and they accepted. I think they were glad to get shot of it, to be honest. The last I heard was that Ken was living on a boat in Spain, and I don't mean a small dinghy!

Thankfully, Eamonn understood what I was all about and agreed to become a silent partner, handing me control of the everyday running, while he looked after the books. Unfortunately, we had to relocate to premises on the other side of Great Victoria Street as there were plans to knock our original building down, but I didn't mind too much as things were going so well. Of course, we still had the Troubles to contend with, and on one occasion in 1992 we had to evacuate the store because a car bomb had been left down the street. All our windows were blown in and a lot of stock was damaged. Not wanting to make a crisis out of a drama, the insurance firm refused to pay out! But it was a good location and we had some great people working for us, so we ended up in that shop for almost ten years.

The label, I'm sorry to say, didn't do nearly so well. In fact, apart from a few bursts of activity, which were often years apart, the label was pretty much dormant. In 1983, to coincide with the Channel 4 show *The Tube* doing a special on the Belfast music scene,

Local musician Andy White performing outside the new
Great Victoria Street store in the early nineties

Good Vibrations released two singles – 'Jenny' by The
Bankrobbers and 'Cracking Up' by 10 Past 7 – but these
were self-financed, and really only used the label's name,
which still carried some weight in the music world.

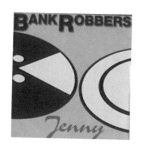

We just didn't have enough money to release singles on
our own, and for the next seven years the label didn't put
anything out. At that particular time I had felt that it was up to
someone else to pick up where I had left off, for other labels
to spring up and follow our example, but apart from a few
half-hearted attempts from other like-minded music fans, it
didn't happen.

Aside from my work in the shop, I had also taken up the mantle of pirate radio DJ
once more. I had become friendly with a guy called Miles Johnston, who worked for the
BBC, and who had also set up a string of pirate radio stations across the country. Miles
is best known now as the founder of the Energy 106 pirate station, which broadcast
from Alien Mountain in County Monaghan from 1998 to 2005, but the operation in which
I became involved – the appropriately named Radio Ganja –was a lot less grandiose.

Miles broadcast under the pseudonym, The Phantom, and I acted as guest host for
him on a number of occasions. Quite often we would just pre-record the shows – usually
in Miles' house in south Belfast, in a room covered in Samantha Fox posters! – because it
was so difficult to get a place from which to broadcast live. But one day in the summer of
1987 the *Irish Times* journalist Jim Cusack offered us his house as a venue.

At the very last moment however, Jim was called away and we lost the site, but
thankfully that turned out to be a blessing in disguise! In one of those great coincidences
that life throws our way my great friend, the late Anne Maguire, was throwing a party to
celebrate the end of her year as student president of Queen's University and she invited
me to come along. I told her I would be delighted to come to her party, but on one
condition, that we could broadcast Radio Ganja from the Students' Union – all we had
was a hi-fi system and an aerial to put on the roof. She agreed and we wound up with

Talking on the radio was
never a problem for me!

the best site we ever had. There we were; free dope, free food, free drink and free radio and that night they were picking us up in Sweden!

Both The Phantom and I were very grateful to Anne for letting us use the Union that night – she was a lovely, bright, intelligent, witty girl who, in other circumstances, could have become a future Mrs Hooley! After university she secured a position with the *News Letter*, where she worked for several years before joining the *Irish Times*, and was set to become one of the finest journalists this country has ever produced. Tragically, one night in 1992, when driving back from a visit to her family in Fermanagh, she was involved in a car accident and was fatally injured – her loss was an unspeakable tragedy.

But as a talented writer Anne had left a legacy. Along with her journalistic writings, she released a book in 1990 that covered the campaign to release the hostage Brian Keenan, who had been kidnapped by Islamic jihad while working as a teacher at the American University in Beirut. Brian is an old friend of mine, so the campaign to have him released was one I was very passionate about. I knew him from my anti-Vietnam war days and he had been as involved as I was in the protest. We had marched together on a number of occasions, including the march in 1966 to mark the fiftieth anniversary of the 1916 Rising. We were all young socialist republicans at that time, though none of us had been taught Irish history in school or anything like that. In my case, I think it was a reaction to being brought up in east Belfast where I was constantly exposed to loyalist prejudices and, as a result, when I learned about our political and social history, I was heavily influenced.

Brian and I hadn't seen an awful lot of each other over the years but our paths had crossed regularly until 1986, when I heard the news that he had been kidnapped. I remember bumping into a pal of mine, Dr Ian Banks, in the Crown Bar in Belfast some time after hearing the news and he suggested that I should get involved in the campaign to have Brian freed.

I arranged to meet up with Brian's sisters, Brenda Gillham and Elaine Spence, as they were leading the campaign. All they knew about me before then was that I had once jumped out of a coffin onstage dressed as Dracula, so I'm not sure how much confidence they had in me, but we got on really well and I promised to do what I could to help the campaign.

We wanted the press to keep the topic of Brian's captivity in the public eye, so I contacted Jim Cusack and asked him to help. Jim approached his news editor at the *Irish Times* and told him that he had spoken to people inside the campaign to free Brian, but, I'm sorry to say, his editor told him not to bother with the story, as he believed

Brian was already dead. Thankfully, Jim persisted and soon became deeply involved in the campaign himself. Through his own contacts in the Department of Foreign Affairs he discovered that the Irish government believed that Brian was very much alive and that they were working closely with the Iranian government in an effort to secure his release. The British government, by comparison, had no interest in doing anything for Brian – or the other hostages, Terry Waite and John McCarthy – but his friends in Belfast were not about to give up so easily.

In early 1988, I got in touch with a couple of people I knew who were involved in the Irish Arab Friendship Society and asked if they had any way of finding out how Brian was. I was given a message that Brian was still alive, although he was in a very bad way. I immediately contacted his sisters to pass on the news but their response took me aback. 'Of course he's alive,' they said. 'He's our brother and we would know if he was dead.' The strength of their belief that Brian was fine and that soon he would be allowed home was admirable.

In the meantime I did whatever I could to help. I protested outside the City Hall and the Dáil and I organised gigs to highlight the issue and to keep it in the forefront of people's minds. I'd also hoped that by organising concerts we could raise enough money for the sisters to fly anywhere in the world to talk to people who could help.

In early 1990 – which would turn out to be only a few weeks before Brian's release – we had been in London for the launch of the Korgis' hit 'Everybody's Got to Learn Sometime', which had been re-released to raise funds for International Hostage Relief, and it was there that I met John McCarthy's girlfriend Jill Morrell, who was a lovely girl. That event inspired me to plan a benefit in Belfast to raise funds for International Hostage Relief and, on 24 August 1990, a week before it was due to take place, it was announced that Brian had been released. Through an intermediary, a large sum of money had been paid to secure Brian's release, and the Irish Foreign Affairs Minister, Gerry Collins, was flying to the region to bring him home. We went ahead with the gig of course – we wanted to make it clear that we weren't going to forget the plight of the other hostages.

I was in the Limelight bar in Belfast a few days after Brian's return to Ireland, and it was there that I received a message from his sisters. Brian, it seemed, wanted to see me. So the following day Eithne and I went down to Dublin. When we went to check into our hotel – the Fairways in Dublin, where all the supporters were staying – we got a nice round of applause and a cheer. But of course the real hero of the time was Brian. He gave a press conference at the Mansion House where he spoke about his treatment at the hands of his captors. His voice was so weak that I had to strain to hear him and, even taking into account the years he spent in captivity, I was still shocked at his appearance. He was shockingly thin, but his eyes burned brightly and I knew his spirit was strong. What was most surprising, however, was what he had to say. He didn't condemn his captors, he just tried to explain that he understood why they did what they did. I'm not sure too many of us would have been so forgiving.

The following day I got a taxi out to Blackrock Clinic to visit Brian. When he saw me, he tried to get out of bed but it was clear that he was in considerable pain. His face was completely unmarked, though etched with the pain and suffering caused by more than four years in captivity, and his body was a mass of black, blue and green bruises. He told me that, before his release, his captors had given him one last 'treat' – they had put him in a sack and beat him so hard that he thought it was the end.

I told him to get back into bed, and he thanked me for my part in the campaign. I reminded him that the last time we had met he had said to me, quite out of the blue,

'Hooley, I'll never forgive you for what you did.' I didn't know what he had meant at the time and his comment had haunted me during the years he had been held captive, so I asked him if he could remember what it was I was supposed to have done. He told me that he had no idea so I said, jokingly, that if I'd known he was going to forget I wouldn't have bothered trying to get him out!

That same year Brian was presented with an RTÉ People of the Year award and I was invited to the reception in Dublin. It was there that he told me about the full extent of his treatment and it really shocked me – his captors had even been putting cyanide in his food. But when Anne Maguire released her book about Brian's sisters and their campaign, I saw how quickly we can all settle back into normality. I went along to the launch, and afterwards we all went to the pub and I remember the two sisters were having a row. Brian went to sort it out but they both turned on him – it was like he had never been away!

In 1990, things began to pick up for the Good Vibrations record label – several bands had come forward who were willing to finance their own records, but who wanted to have our name attached. As I used to say back then, the label would often 'rear its ugly head from time to time.' We were still in no position to finance the recordings but I was happy to let bands use the label. It kept the name alive and gave them a vehicle for releasing their material. I would let them use the contacts I had made in the music industry over the years, and agreed to help them in any way possible.

It was in this way that Good Vibrations came to release material from Tyrone band, tiBeriuS' minnoWs. In 1989, the band had won the 'Smithwicks Band of the Year' competition which had been held in the Errigle Inn, a smashing music venue on the Ormeau Road in south Belfast. It was a big win for them and it led to a strong fan following. Within a year, hundreds of people were queuing outside the Errigle – the band's new spiritual home – to gain entry to one of their numerous sell-out shows.

The lads became regular customers in the shop and, as so many people were coming into the shop, raving about how good the band was, I got them to play me one of their songs. They played 'Time Flies' and I loved it straight away. I could see they were serious about their music and, with such a strong following in Belfast, I knew they deserved a proper release. It was then that I suggested they put it out on Good Vibes.

This was greeted with general approval, but I was told that we had to get the band's manager, John Henry, on board too. So one night, not long after, I found myself in a meeting in the cramped living room of a house in Collingwood Avenue, a street in Belfast's infamous Holylands area. In an effort to help seal the deal, I had turned up with a case of beer – much to the band's delight – and my 'company secretary', Albert Fusciardi, who was actually just a mate of mine that worked in the shop and who I'd asked along to take notes. The decision to bring him along however, was one I soon came to regret.

I had had a sort of mini-presentation in mind to help convince the band's manager and, while I knew we should have rehearsed before going in, I really didn't foresee what a bollocks Bert would make of it.

'Bert,' I said, 'what band did I tell you was the best I'd heard since The Undertones?' Failing to take my lead, Bert stared at me in silence, so I repeated the question, this time a little more impatiently. This time Bert was ready … with the wrong answer, 'Uh … The Airmen?' By which he had meant Ghost of an American Airman. He had fucked up. 'No!' I shouted, a little panicked now, 'It was tiBeriuS' minnoWs. Didn't I tell you that?' 'Erm, yes,' Bert quietly agreed, head down and obviously embarrassed by the whole situation. Ploughing on ahead, I moved on to talking about the song. 'The minute I heard it I said to myself, "That song could be a hit".' And, giving Bert a chance to redeem himself, I turned round and said, 'Bert, what song did I say would be a hit as soon as I heard it?' 'Uh … "Teenage Kicks"?' an uncertain Bert replied. Well, that was it! I lunged at Bert, grabbed his notebook and threw it in the fire, destroying the minutes of our catastrophic meeting. Although by that stage it still hadn't reached its colourful conclusion.

By the end of the night, with the beers all finished and spirits high, we had all pretty much agreed that 'Time Flies' would be the minnoWs' first single, and that it would be released on the Good Vibes label. It was then, full of beer and not satisfied with having bitten the head off Bert, that I turned my attention to the band's manager John.

TIME FLIES

'John,' I said, slowly and deliberately, 'can I tell you something?' There was a silence as he nodded. 'John, you're a cunt.' Now, in my defence, I did follow that statement straight away with what I had intended to be a back-handed compliment – 'But there are a million bigger cunts over there than you' – but it was lost in the melee that ensued. In my own way, I had been trying to say that while most people who manage bands are just in it for one thing, the money, I had admired that John was prepared to give his band the chance to record a single with no strings attached. So much for my compliment-giving ability! The band was pissing themselves laughing, John was demanding an apology, and I was doing my best to calm the situation down, which I managed to do … eventually.

'Time Flies' was released in March 1991, and to promote it I went to London armed with a batch of singles and handed them into various radio stations in person. When Radio One played it on their prime-time programmes every day for a week, the band was delighted. DJ Dave Lee Travis even went so far as to say that if the minnoWs weren't signed by a major label, there was something seriously wrong with the music industry in Britain.

As it turned out, there must have been something seriously wrong with the music industry in Britain, as the guys weren't signed, but 'Time Flies' was a huge success in Ireland nonetheless. *Hot Press* magazine said it was a 'bona fide pop classic'.

A second single 'Oh June' followed that same year with similar success, and in 1992 they released *The Love* EP. I thought it got a great reception, even making it into the Top Twenty, but the band were disappointed as they felt it was somewhat lightweight.

Good Vibes enjoyed a fantastic couple of years working with the minnoWs, but there is one particular incident that sets my time with them apart. It was 1991 and we had just returned to Belfast having watched the band play the Rock Garden in Dublin as part of the Belfast Rocks Again tour (which, incidentally, also saw them play the legendary Mean Fiddler in London). We had been drinking all the way from Dublin and weren't quite ready to call it a night, so the band, a number of friends and I headed to Lawrence Street, an eight-bedroom house in the Holylands to continue the party.

At around 4.30 a.m., as lead singer Michael Rafferty, bassist Kevin Carson, John Henry and I sat in the living room still drinking, there were a few loud knocks on the front

Oh June

door. John went out to answer it but as soon as he opened the door, two men forcefully pushed their way in. John fled upstairs while one of the men slammed the living room door shut and held it closed by the handle, leaving me, Kevin and Raff locked in the room. We tried the handle.

'Get away from the fuckin' door or we'll shoot you through it,' the voice on the other side shouted. Naturally we obeyed. There had been a lot of sectarian shootings in Northern Ireland around this time so we weren't going to take any chances. Besides, we were totally out of our collective trees and hadn't a clue what was happening. It was then that we heard a commotion upstairs. The band's drummer Stephen O'Sullivan had been coming back downstairs when John had fled past him and locked himself in a bedroom. One of the thugs had followed but, meeting Stevie on the stairs, attacked him instead. Stevie, with the advantage of being on a higher stair, kicked him off but the bastard dusted himself down and started coming back at him.

Stevie ran back upstairs, and started banging on the door of the bedroom John was hiding in, shouting, 'John! John, let me in, let me in! Let me in for fuck's sake!' but the door was locked and by all accounts John was hiding behind the bed. The guy was still attacking Stevie, and he was kicking him back, banging the door and shouting to get into the bedroom.

The shouting became louder, until it was almost screaming, and the banging was deafening. Meanwhile, downstairs, we were in a real state. 'What the fuck is happening up there? What the fuck will we do?' There were no mobile phones so we couldn't call the police from where we were. The house phone was in the hall, but our friend was still guarding the door and threatening to shoot us if we came near it. I decided to take the lead – it's amazing how brave you get after a skinfull of booze and some serious drugs.

'Your friend is getting killed up there!' I shouted to Michael and Kevin, 'Are you going to sit back and let your best friend get killed?' I grabbed a guitar and rallied the troops, 'Are you with me?' I shouted, and smashed my way through the bay window at the front of the house.

Once it was demolished we three intrepid heroes, armed with an upside down electric guitar, slowly stepped out into the street, being careful not to cut ourselves to pieces on the jagged shards of glass that surrounded our exit. As we straightened

On-stage during the Belfast Rocks Again tour, 1991

ourselves in the street and made for the front door, we were greeted by the welcome sight of our two assailants running up the street, away from the house. The police arrived shortly afterwards, undoubtedly notified by the neighbours. If only they had arrived earlier, it would have saved us a lot of stress, but then we wouldn't have this story to tell.

To this day I have no idea what it was all about – I suspect they were opportunists looking for drink or drugs, or else money to buy drink or drugs – but I think John Henry is still hiding behind the bed. When the band released their first album in 1996 and entitled it *Holyland*, I thought it was a fitting tribute.

We continued to record music, and over the next few years Good Vibes released material from other bands such as Four Idle Hands, The Mighty Fall – with a certain Jonny Quinn, now of Snow Patrol, on drums – and PBR Streetgang. There were a lot of good bands out there during the nineties and I'm proud of the great records that came out on the label at the time.

By the nineties the process of recording a record was a little different to when we first started out. Then we hadn't a clue how to do it properly, the bands would just go into the studio and belt out the songs as they would have done on-stage – they simply played the song. During the nineties, we had access to better producers who knew how to maximise the sound, and they got the bands to lay down tracks in layers – vocals, harmony, guitar, drums were all recorded separately and set down on top of each other. It made for a richer production, rather than the slightly tinny, shallow sound of the early Good Vibrations records – although in many ways, I believe this is what makes the early stuff so special.

Of course, the format had 'evolved' from those days of vinyl records and bands were now putting their stuff out on CDs instead. Now, I like CDs … I sell CDs … but I have always lamented the demise of vinyl. For me there is nothing quite like getting a new album, sliding it out of its sleeve, sticking it onto the record player and sitting back to read the sleeve notes. Thankfully, the format has made a bit of a comeback in recent years, but at the same time, we now have downloads to contend with. Nowadays people know the songs they listen to, but not the bands performing them, it's a real shame.

Of course, by this stage, the punk era was well and truly over. The world had moved on and, while the influence of that time still resonates to this day, we had entered a new age for music. The sound had changed but, I'm sorry to say, the industry had not – we still had the same problem of getting our bands seen by record company A&R men. We could never entice them to come to Belfast and so, more often than not, we had to bring our music to them. This was pretty frustrating for us, especially as I remember hearing that seventy talent scouts flew over for the Cork Music Festival in 1989 just to see The Cranberries, while we could barely get one to come to Belfast. I decided to take action, and in 1990 I set up the three-day Belfast Rocks Again Festival at the Limelight. We did this for three years in a row and, during that time, we showcased bands like Four Idle Hands – whose single '99 Streets' was released on Good Vibrations in 1990 – alongside other Irish acts like The Divine Comedy, Therapy?, Ghost of an American Airman and Ashanti, but even then we couldn't attract the attention of the big record companies. It was pretty disappointing. Thankfully, many of the acts on the bill did eventually get signed up by major labels. I'm quite proud to think that, however small, we had a hand in that.

THURSDAY, I
THINK

In early 1993, Warner Brothers, in their wisdom, approached me to ask if I would be interested in writing a poetry album for them. The idea was for me to recite songs as poems – the sung word spoken! – a bit like Bob Dylan. There would be a musical accompaniment and I would read original material that they wanted to commission from me. I accepted, pitched them the title, *Belfast, Beirut and Berlin: Three Divided Cities* and, for that little gem, they gave me an advance of £5,000.

I had developed a good relationship with Warner Brothers over the years, having met a guy called John Gustaffson in London during the 1960s. We were both hippies and he was part of the London scene so our paths crossed a few times. I remember that he had a house full of records, but he didn't own a record player so had nothing to play them on. I don't know why that was but I always thought it a little strange. He wasn't involved in the music industry then, but in the seventies he got a job with Warner Brothers and was tasked with setting up a panel of people – some in America, others in Europe and the UK – to give advice on tracks that would make good single releases.

John approached me to be a part of this panel and Warner Brothers frequently sent me album tracks by some of their recording artists to select the ones I thought would make good singles. I remember in 1982 recommending Laura Branigan's 'Gloria' – which would go on to become a worldwide smash – but they probably already had their eyes on that one! I wasn't paid for it, but every now and then they would fly me to London and wine and dine me for a couple of days, which suited me.

Anyway, I decided that I would use the advance money they had given me to get away from Belfast and work on the album. I was given carte blanche to choose anywhere in the world, and believe it or not, initially I thought of Donegal! I had spent a few days in Ramelton in Donegal just after hearing about the album, and while there I had bumped into Arty McGlynn, a fantastic traditional Irish musician from Omagh. I told him about the album and I was delighted when he offered to play on it. I came back to Belfast where I happened to meet Liam Ó Maonlaí from Hothouse Flowers, a fantastic rock band from Dublin who were doing a gig in Belfast's Duke of York bar. When he too offered to play on the album I was over the moon. I thought Warner Brothers would be really impressed with my networking skills. But it was the exact opposite. They said they wanted the album to be made with the help of my mates, not established stars, that it would be too much hassle to get them released from their record labels to work with me.

After all that I realised that, if I went back to Donegal, I would get no work done – I knew too many people there and there were too many pubs! – and so, in the end, I chose St Lucia as my destination. Warner Brothers will never know just what they did for me by enabling me to go there – I had the time of my life! The music was astonishing and, before I saw it for myself, I could never have imagined that there was a place as beautiful as Rodney Bay on this planet. There was a lot of beer, hash and parties of course, but what I remember most is the people.

I got chatting to a man called Carlton who insisted that he had met me before. He told me that he had been a student in Dublin, but had been going out with a girl from the Falls Road. Apparently, they used to go to a bar in town called The Spanish Rooms and he swore blind that it was there that we met and that I used to ply him with cider. I have no recollection of plying anybody with cider in The Spanish Rooms – apart from the odd lady of course – so I had to take his word for it. I asked him if he could get any grass and when he came back he had three big silver balls, each about the size of a football, and

Chillin' in St Lucia

all full of grass. 'They're all for you,' he said, 'that's for the cider in The Spanish Rooms.'

When I got back to the room, Eithne looked at me and said, 'You're stoned!' –she couldn't believe her eyes when I showed her what I had. I didn't know what to do with them, there was too much even for me, and in the end I actually stashed a couple of them outside the hotel! I even had to pay the maid in the hotel not to come and clean the room. So instead of sitting in my room writing all this stuff for Warner Brothers, I sat there watching TV and getting stoned instead!

But I did get chatting to quite a few of the locals who recommended that I make a trip to Kastisse, the capital, and visit a club where Gregory Isaacs and Denis Brown had played. It was incredible.

And word of my interest in the old music was getting around. The next day I got a call from reception to tell me there were people in the lobby asking for me, wanting to take me on a tour of the island. I agreed of course, and soon earned the nickname, 'Belfast Terri'. I had a wonderful day, which ended with me being brought to a festival in the hills. There were guys playing dominoes, gallons of Red Stripe beer to be drunk and, of course, tonnes of hash to be smoked. I was coming to the end of my trip and I still had two balls full of the stuff Carlton had given me, so I was dishing it out hand over fist! By the end of my trip there was even a woman selling 'I've partied with Belfast Terri' t-shirts! By the time I left the island I felt more St Lucian than the St Lucians. In an ideal world I would like to retire there, it is the only place on earth I would leave Belfast for.

Not surprisingly, when I returned from the Caribbean I did so empty-handed – I had been far too busy enjoying myself to do any real work! – and the only writing Warner Brothers ever got for their £5,000 was a postcard from Rodney Bay with the words 'Thursday, I think' scrawled on it. The words are taken from J.D. Salinger's novel *Franny and Zooey*, but I have no idea what I was thinking when I wrote them. To be fair to Warner Brothers, they never actually asked me to repay the money, though I was summoned to a meeting in a plush Park Lane hotel in London to discuss the project. In the end we just agreed – over a few bottles of wine – that we would write the whole thing off, which was just as well as there wasn't a snowball's chance in hell of them getting that money back!

But it was back to reality for me, back to working round the clock at Good Vibrations. What a downer after St Lucia. I felt so low. I tried to get back into some sort of routine, and whenever I wasn't at the shop I headed to the pub or to a party to try to cheer myself up. One evening in particular, I went down to the Rotterdam Bar in the docks area of Belfast and stayed late into the night.

The next morning I got up and didn't really feel the best but, putting it down to a hangover, I caught the bus to the city centre and headed for the shop. I had only travelled a short distance when I started to feel pains in my arms and chest, it was then that I figured I should go home. When I got through the door I made myself a cup of tea to help settle my nerves a bit, but instead of diminishing, the pain was getting steadily worse. Then it hit me – I was having a heart attack.

I managed to stay on my feet but the pain was incredible. I knew I needed to call the hospital. I picked up the phone, rang Belfast City Hospital and said, 'I'm having a heart attack here.' I expected them to leap into action, to tell me an ambulance was on its way and that I would be OK. Instead they replied, 'You have to phone the Royal!' I couldn't believe my ears – hadn't they understood me? I tried again, 'Listen, I'm having a fuckin' heart attack,' but they only responded by offering to give me the Royal Victoria Hospital's phone number! I hung up and dialled 999.

As I waited for the ambulance to arrive I began to assess my life – I wasn't scared, I felt ready to go. I don't mean to be flippant, but I can genuinely say that, at forty-five, I really thought I had done it all. I would have had no complaints if the Big Man in the sky had called me home right then. I remember thinking at the time that if there is a God there was still a good chance I would get into heaven – I've done more good things than bad over the years. Maybe I was still stoned from St Lucia.

My only regret would have been that I'd never got the chance to tell the people in my life how I felt about them. Though when I say 'the people in my life', I don't mean the people I loved, they already knew how I felt about them, but rather the people who had let me down in my life. I won't mention any names, but I remember thinking that I might not get the chance to speak to those bastards again. So I called a few people and told them I was having a heart attack and that I was in no mood to forgive them for what they had done to me during my life! I was very calm and I must admit it felt very liberating to be able to say those things. Of course, the very people I rang were among those who flew over from London and further afield to visit me in hospital.

Once that was done, I suddenly felt very composed and knew I needed to call Eithne and tell her what was happening. I hadn't wanted to scare her, and I think I sounded reasonably calm, despite being in incredible pain – I'd experienced nothing like it ever before. The ambulance seemed to take an age to come, and by the time I eventually arrived at the hospital to be met by Eithne – who actually worked in the Royal at the time

A comic strip by Peter Johnson and Frankie Quinn
which appeared in *DV8* magazine in 1993

– she looked more worried than I was, so I put out my hand and asked if she was OK.

When they got me settled on the ward they were able to tell me that I had suffered a massive heart attack, that I was lucky to have survived and that I should consider it a warning that I couldn't continue living the sort of lifestyle I had enjoyed for so many years. And looking back I can see the strain I was putting on my body – I was drinking too much, smoking like a train, taking drugs and I never did any exercise – but we all think we are invincible and I was no different. It was a warning that went in one ear and straight out the other.

My arrival at the Royal sparked ten days of fun and madness and I had a lot of visitors. Jim Cusack and Mervyn Crawford, who were great friends of mine, and Joby Fox from The Bankrobbers came most days and there were always people standing at my bed. It got so loud at times that staff had to warn me that unless my visitors calmed down and toned down their language they would be refused entry. One day the lads suggested I put on my Dracula cloak and run screaming through the ward at about three in the morning and then we would see who really had a bad heart! It was just a really funny time.

In the bed next to me was a really big man, a loyalist with 'I hate fenians' tattooed on his arm. He assumed I was a Prod and we sort of got on all right until one day a nun arrived at my bedside, got the holy water out and started blessing me. I thought he was going to have another heart attack! He hardly spoke to me after that, which suited me as I didn't have much in common with him.

The day I got out of hospital, with warnings about no drinking or smoking still ringing in my ears, we called in to see friends of ours who lived close to the hospital. Within ten minutes I was smoking a joint – so much for a new lifestyle. They say that coming so close to death should be a life-changing experience, but not for me. If anything it made me more determined to live life to the full and I haven't looked back. Of course, I recognise what a trauma it was for my family but I really just put it down to another little obstacle on the path of life, you get over it and move on. It's funny, Nigel Martin who used to be my guitarist suffered a stroke a while back and he got the same warnings about changing his behaviour, but he said he wanted to recover the Hooley way!

The one positive thing the heart attack did for me was to light a fire under me work-wise. When I got back on my feet I decided that I wanted something bigger than working for someone else. By that stage Eamonn McWilliams no longer owned the business,

having sold it all to an accountant called Abraham Titus a few years before. It had seemed to me at the time that an accountant for an owner would be no bad thing – it was what I had been lacking all those years – but Titus was all wrong for Good Vibrations. I had very little contact with him – at times I felt that he was completely ignoring me. It was clear that there were problems and my heart attack only served as an excuse to pull the shutters down, and shut up shop. I don't really know what happened to Mr Titus after that.

Naturally, I came up with the idea of opening another record shop of my own – the fact that I was an undischarged bankrupt was a minor detail. The most important thing for me was having my own store, it didn't matter if it was making money or not and, to be honest, it was the only way people could ever find me! So Eamonn McWilliams

Leaving Vintage for the night and
heading to my 'office' – The Crown Bar!

stepped in to help me once more. Together we sourced the premises and he was a great practical help in getting me to a position where we could move in. Finally I owned my own store again!

I took over premises on 54 Howard Street in the centre of Belfast, and it turned out to be the best premises I ever had. It had once been a big fabric shop so I had plenty of space to work with, and I sold every genre of music there was to sell. I had a great sixties section and a great country section, I even decided to put in an old maple dance floor. It was just brilliant – Vintage Records was born!

I chose the name in homage to the Vintage Record Shop in central London, my first big customer in the sixties. I would buy rare singles from the Gramophone Shop in Deptford for a pittance – they hadn't a clue what they had – and I would knock them on to Vintage for a couple of quid.

I can't tell you how pleased I was with that shop. We were in a prime location in the city centre, just round the corner from the Grand Opera House and, of course, The Crown Bar! We had all sorts of famous customers too. Jools Holland once commented that we had a great blues section, and the Mavericks were regular visitors. Any of the stars appearing at the Opera House would also make a point of coming in. The Krankies even came in once, but I don't brag to many people about that!

But I'm sorry to say that Vintage had quite a sinister start. We had just opened the store to the public when I was approached by a couple of guys who said they were from the Ulster Defence Association, a loyalist paramilitary organisation, and they wanted £500 in 'protection money'. Well, they may as well have taken the keys to the shop. I didn't have that sort of money, but they warned they would be coming back that Thursday night to collect.

It was, and still is, a fact of life in Northern Ireland that when you open a business here you are susceptible to pressure and extortion from the paramilitaries. You are expected to pay out hundreds of pounds every week in so-called protection money. In return for these 'donations' you are supposedly immune from attack from other organisations. Great in theory, but there were quite a few key holders in town who didn't get much protection for their money!

Over the years, and in all the stores I had worked in, we would regularly get people coming into the shop looking for money. Sometimes it would be under the guise of collecting for prisoner welfare groups, and if they were carrying a collection box or bucket I would throw in a few coins. Quite often there would be veiled threats if we refused to pay, so I would say we were already paying someone else.

When we first opened Good Vibrations in 1976, for example, I was approached for protection money, but since I had no money to give it wasn't really an option. Instead I arranged a meeting with the paramilitaries in question and I said I would give them the pick of my record collection, on the condition they left me alone. It's amazing the crap I got rid of in that meeting – paramilitaries have very dodgy taste in music.

In reality I refused to pay protection money to any of those bastards, so that first Thursday in Vintage was a pretty tense day. Around teatime this fella came in and said, 'You're Hooley aren't you?' I nodded and he put a down a box of beer, making several return journeys until the place looked more like an off-licence than a record shop. Before leaving he said that the boys would be down later.

It turned out he was from the Ulster Volunteer Force, another loyalist paramilitary organisation – so no doubt the beer was stolen! – and they weren't about to let the UDA muscle in front of them. I guess they wanted to mark their territory. So later that evening they all arrived down and started a party! It was bizarre, there were people walking up and down outside the shop, terrified to come in because the place was now full of paramilitaries! In the end, I called up some friends who came down and we all partied together into the small hours. The UDA didn't turn up that night at all and the Thursday Club was born – we decided to make Thursday our weekly party night.

After a while though, the club inevitably began to attract a bit of attention from the Drug Squad. One night we were raided while I had a stash of drugs upstairs in the office, but I managed to flush it all down the loo as a policewoman was banging on the toilet door. I told her I was taking medication for my heart – feasible enough as I was meant to be taking four tablets a day!

But it wasn't all just parties, a lot of hard work and effort went into trying to get Vintage Records off the ground. I was spending all my time at the shop, often working till two in the morning and I had some great customers. I would also regularly get tourists in looking for very specific stuff – you know bodhráns, turf and penny whistles – but I'm not an expert in traditional Irish music, so when a friend of mine who worked for Gael Linn, one of Ireland's biggest distribution companies, told me they had pressed two CDs of traditional Irish music for record shop HMV, my ears pricked up. HMV had been selling them at £7.99 and they weren't shifting terribly well so I managed to get a load of them for a pound each. I then decided to sell them two for £5 and was still making a profit.

But the arrival of US President Bill Clinton in Belfast in 1995 gave me the chance to make a real killing. I heard from Michael Macy –the Assistant Cultural Attaché at the US Embassy in London, and also a friend of mine – that the Americans didn't know what music to play when Hillary and Bill Clinton walked into the Europa Hotel so I gave him one of my Gael Linn CDs. Incredibly, that's what they used and it seemed that the whole Clinton entourage wanted a copy as a result. I ended up selling hundreds of them, though I'm not sure how pleased HMV were!

Things were also busy in the studio, as it was around that time that we were approached by Oliver's Army, a great wee band from Bangor who were obviously named

Hearts of Steel, L-R: Jimmy Symington,
Nick 'Loopy' Hamilton, yours truly and Jonny Quinn

after the Elvis Costello hit of the same name. They wanted to release their EP, *Too Much*, with Good Vibrations. I really liked these guys but my abiding memory is of lead singer Keith Lloyd, who was a right mouthy wee bastard! He really thought they were the best thing since sliced bread, and often told me they were the best band ever to record on Good Vibrations. He later got a top job at HMV, but fuck he was a lippy one!

It was through Oliver's Army that I paired up with Jimmy Symington, a fantastic guitar player who I met in The Crown Bar when I first signed the band, and he became a great friend of mine. Together, along with Jonny Quinn and Nick Hamilton, we formed a band called Hearts of Steel. We gigged around Belfast and had a strong environmental message, which was pretty radical in 1995.

We wanted people to think about the bigger issues, and we didn't care if they liked us or not, we just wanted to play. But my bandmates were too good, and soon people began to rave about us. We landed a gig supporting a great Northern Ireland band called Watercress, who were headed for greatness but who sadly broke up before that could happen. Anyway, as we performed people started waving their lighters in the air – an action which is more at home at an Elton John concert! – and I remember thinking, 'That's the end of it, they like us.' Hearts of Steel never played again, though the lads and I remain very close friends.

When I turned fifty I took stock of my life – I'd been partying for over thirty years and I needed something to calm me down. Eithne and I had been talking for a while about having a kid, we wanted to have a family before it was too late and, once we'd decided, it happened very quickly. The birth of my son Michael on 13 November 1999 was one of the most joyous occasions in my life. I hadn't been allowed to be at Anna's birth twenty years earlier, but this time I was involved from the start. I even went to parenting classes, which I loved, even if I was a pest, constantly asking questions. When the penultimate week of the classes arrived I sat talking to a nurse over a cup of coffee, and I lamented the fact that once the classes were finished my life was going to be completely messed up – what was I going to do on a Wednesday night?

Of course, the night Michael arrived everything I had learned at the parenting classes

I wish Michael had stuck to the guitar – he plays the drums now!

went out the window. I had been told the first thing to do when a baby is born is to put them on their mother's stomach, but I grabbed Michael and wouldn't let go of him for about ten minutes. They had to practically force me to hand him over. I knew he was going to change my life, I was finally going to calm down. I decided to take two or three days off from the shop each week in order to spend time with him, and I stayed at home with him every Friday night watching the TV, while Eithne was off partying!

Things were looking bright, not only in my personal life, but in the world outside my front door – Northern Ireland was experiencing a period of hope and of peace. Though sadly, there are always some people who want to drag us all back to the dark ages. A man called Johnny Adair was one of those people, and somehow I found myself in the dangerous position of being in his bad books.

Adair was notorious, a real evil bastard. He was commander of an outfit called 'C' Company which was part of the Ulster Freedom Fighters – who in turn were aligned with the UDA – and his followers were responsible for countless murders of innocent Catholics. They killed people simply because of their religious affiliation. He was a gangster, a bigot and, as it turned out, a racist.

He had formed a skinhead band called Offensive Weapon which openly endorsed the National Front – in fact, it was believed that the National Front was funding the band and buying them instruments – and a rumour had spread around town that I had been planning to give them a record deal, but that when I found out about their less than savoury connections, I had pulled the plug. To be honest I have no clear recollection of making such a decision. I can say that I have always refused to stock music from race hate bands such as Screwdriver and No Remorse and I would never have put on a gig that included such bands. Maybe that was why Adair got it into his head that I was preventing Offensive Weapon from getting any gigs in town. It may have been true, however indirect my involvement may have been, but I didn't really think much of it and didn't see the warning signs.

Every week for several weeks, four guys from the Lower Shankill – Adair's patch – had been coming in at night and demanding money, and every week I would tell them to fuck off. It got to the stage where, when somebody came in, I would just show them a piece of cardboard I kept under the counter upon which I had written, 'We only give to reputable charities, please don't ask for donations.'

One night in 2000, I was there late because I had been at home during the day spending time with Michael and I took a tenner out of the till to nip round the corner for a packet of fags. They were on top of me before I knew it. I don't know how many there were of them, or what they looked like, but I remember going down, putting my hand over my good eye and then just curling into a ball trying to protect myself as best I could.

They were hitting me in places I had never been hit before – this time I really thought it was the end. My next memory is of being put in an ambulance and a policeman asking me my name.

I had been given a real good kicking and I'm convinced it was Adair's mob that did it. They didn't break any bones, but I suffered severe internal bruising and the doctors wanted to keep me in hospital. I was having none of it, and clambered out of bed, made my way to a phone and ordered a taxi to collect me from the Royal Victoria Hospital. Trouble was, I was in the City Hospital.

But I needn't have worried about getting a lift home. Word had got out that I had been beaten up, and when I came out of the building there was a row of cars waiting to take me home. I lay on the sofa for ten days, and was in so much pain that I couldn't walk. If I needed to get anywhere I just crawled on the floor on all fours. I remember when Johnny from punk band OOOPS – whose album *Social Scum* had been released on the Good Vibrations label that year – came to see me, he took one look at me and said, 'Christ! They were out to kill you', and I think he was right.

A few weeks later I was back on my feet, and back in the shop when a man I had never seen before came in and told me I wouldn't have any bother again. To this day I have no idea who he was. Maybe he was a UFF or UDA representative; maybe he was from a rival paramilitary group; or maybe he was just somebody delivering a message. What I do know is that, for the next few weeks, every time the door of the shop opened I shit myself!

In the meantime, my own music career was still going strong. Jimmy and I were still playing the odd show here and there – me reciting my poetry, and Jimmy playing his heart out – and in August 2002 we managed to secure a gig playing at the most 'happening' club in East Berlin, Kaffee Burger, thanks to my old friend Bert Papenfuss, the punk poet. Bert came from east Berlin and used to listen, illegally, to John Peel's show, resulting in a love for The Outcasts. When the Wall came down he came to stay in Belfast and lived for a while in Ireton Street, just off Botanic Avenue, before returning to Germany. I was looking forward to meeting him in his home city.

On the flight over I got talking to a girl, a punkette with bright pink hair who, believe it or not, worked as a film editor in the porn industry. She seemed really nice so, as we were getting off the plane, I invited her to the gig. We arrived in Berlin late that night, but as

On-stage at Kaffee Burger, Berlin, 2002

Jimmy had been celebrating his birthday – drinking for probably two days straight, and wanting to continue – we decided to carry on the party. After dropping off our bags in our hotel we came across an African restaurant in the basement of a local building. We went in to get some food, and were served by a beautiful woman who was around six-feet tall. We had some chicken, some drinks and, before long, we had scored some drugs. The party was definitely on!

We stayed until around 6 a.m. that night, and while Jimmy headed back to the hotel to crawl into bed, I hauled myself off to a meeting with film-maker Roy Wallace who had joined us on the trip in order to film *Big Time*, a documentary on the Belfast punk scene. Roy had had this idea of taking me away from the streets of Belfast to another divided city and, exhausted though I was, I spent all day shooting scenes in various locations in Berlin. In the end though, he didn't use any of the footage – so thanks for that Roy!

When filming had finished, I met up with Jimmy and we went back to our African bar for a little pick-me-up, despite having a gig that evening. We stayed so long that we wound up being late for our own show!

When we eventually showed up, I set out the pile of 'Laugh at Me' records I had brought with me, and got ready to hit the stage. I asked the man who had organised the gig, Jürgen Schneider, to play 'Belfast' by Joby Fox – one of my favourite songs – and 'Babylon's Burning' by The Ruts to help me warm up. By the time the songs were over I was off my rocker, but ready to perform.

I remember that during the break Jimmy and I headed to the loo, unfortunately not realising that our microphones were still on. So as we discussed the exceptional quality of the coke we had been snorting the previous evening, our every word was being broadcast to a very appreciative and amused audience!

After the gig I agreed to do a signing and so people began to line up. I was taking my time signing a record for Jürgen's girlfriend, when these two girls in the queue shouted, 'Would you hurry up? There's a fuckin' taxi waitin' outside.' They had clearly spent some time in Belfast, as they spoke with a really weird German-Belfast accent – quite frightening!

The next person in the queue was the gorgeous punkette I had met on the plane. She invited me back to her place for 'a party', but when I told her I wasn't fit for a party she told me, 'Well, there's only two going to this party.' I was gobsmacked. It was very flattering of course, but way beyond my capabilities, so I turned to Jimmy for help!

I've been a regular visitor to Berlin ever since, it's a second home to me. The experiences I have had there will stay with me for the rest of my life. The friends I have made there are some of the best people I've ever known. It's a truly special place.

As 2002 wore on it became apparent that Vintage – or 'Good Vibrations: The Greatest Little Record Shop in the World' as I'd renamed it – was heading for the wall. I was spending so many days away from the place to be with Michael that it had gone to the dogs. I was shocked that the shop was losing as much money as it was, so Eamonn McWilliams advised me to put in security cameras, including one hidden over the till, and I was stunned at what I discovered – there I was, borrowing money to keep the shop open because I couldn't pay the bills, but as soon as my back was turned, members of staff were emptying the tills. Unbelievable.

What with all pilfering the staff were doing, and the increase in shop rates which came as a result of Northern Ireland's peace time, Vintage went under in Oct 2002 and, for a second time, I was bankrupt. The official receiver took pity on me and bought a couple of CDs and gave me £20 to buy a drink in The Crown Bar. He knew it was a labour of love.

A FEW DAYS IN BERLIN
JIMMY SYMINGTON

FIRST REHEARSALS WITH TERRI

My good mate Keith Lloyd from the band Oliver's Army phoned me up one night in 1995 to tell me they had just been signed to the legendary Good Vibrations label. He asked me if I wanted to come down for a few beers in The Crown Bar and meet their new record label boss, Terri Hooley. We hit it off straight away! It even turned out that we had both grown up in the same street in Clarawood estate, albeit thirty years apart.

After too many drinks to remember, Keith was telling Terri how important his band were, how they were gonna take over the world and blow everything that has ever come out of Northern Ireland away. I think that I must have been pissing myself laughing at this a bit too much as Terri turned round and asked me what I did. When I told him I played a bit of guitar he stood up, chucked his glass eye into my pint and declared to everyone that he and I were, 'gonna be more punk than The Kinks'. After that he scooped his glass eye out of my pint, stuck it back in its socket and asked if I was up for it. Not to make a pun, but my answer was 'Aye'!

A few weeks later I had forgotten all about 'my new band' until I called into the shop and Terri told me that we had our first gig booked. It was going to be in Reading and we had better start practising. No pressure there then!

We arranged to hook up a few nights later back at the shop and when I got there, guitar in hand, we started to rehearse straight away. To my shock and surprise Terri had no timing, and was more the front man than the singer, but all that didn't matter. Never one to let the truth get in the way of a good story, Terri was more into telling me about his encounters with Them, Phil Spector, Neil Young, the Stones and so many other artists that I didn't think my brain could take much more information. This was more than just a mere practice session, for me it became an education. Terri just kept on playing his favourite records, while I tried to take in as much information as I could, though I was failing miserably. I think we might have rehearsed about two songs that night over a seven-hour period.

We carried on for a few weeks like this, with Terri spending his time playing more tunes on the record player than on the guitar; or else he would be at the mic with a brandy preaching to me, the converted, in a performance that Ian Paisley would have been proud of! But eventually we got to a point where we had six songs loosely put together.

Now, with any other band I had played in, this would have only meant a twenty minute set, but I was dealing with Terri now after all! Allowing for his stories in between the songs meant that this gig was gonna go on for well over an hour. I couldn't wait to get up on-stage with this mad one-eyed lunatic . . .

BERLIN

It was 19 August 2002, almost seven years after Terri and I had first met. I had been up partying all night as it was my birthday the day before and Terri turned up in a taxi at The Point bar to bring me to Aldergrove Airport for our flight to Stansted – I was in top form for sure!

It was there that I met the film-maker Roy Wallace for the first time, the legend that he is. He was coming with us to Berlin to shoot some footage for *Big Time*, his documentary on the Belfast punk scene. Also travelling with us was Rosie McMichael, who we had hired as a tour manager – I had only agreed to go to Berlin if we had someone there to keep Terri on his best behaviour. In the end, though, it was Roy who babysat us and got us all to Berlin in one piece!

We arrived at the hotel at 10 p.m. and Rosie and Roy headed straight to their rooms for some sleep. Terri and I were sharing a room and, rather than going to bed, he wanted to take me out for a birthday dinner. We left the hotel and conversation immediately turned to getting some food and drugs.

As Terri has always been 'to the left', so to speak, and since it was my birthday, I decided when we walked out of the hotel that we should go to the right for once. So, as soon as we came to a junction we turned right, then right, then right again and staring us straight in the puss was the most amazing African restaurant. Inside, we were met by a beautiful pregnant African woman and her husband. We both fell in love with the place immediately.

Terri turned on the old Hooley charms and the lady made us the most delicious chicken dish I had ever tasted. I turned on the old Symington charms and her husband went off to get us some recreationals – result on the old Hooley/Symington charm all round then. What is it they say about taking the boys out of Belfast and all that?

'Who are you lookin at?' – Terri and the other
Hearts of Steel guys were full of attitude

When the day of the gig came round we arrived at Kaffee Burger to
find the bar already crammed with Terri's followers. I knew that he had
always been a legend in Belfast but this was Berlin and he was getting
pawed left, right and centre – they were even pawing me simply because
I was with him! It was uncomfortable and I couldn't believe the love we
were being shown – talk about feeling out of your depth – but that night
we met some of the nicest and most beautiful people in the world.

I am the most privileged man in the world to be able to count Terri as a
true friend. He gave me a job when no one else would. He is the man with
the biggest heart and glass eye in the whole of Ireland, and I owe him
everything – he is my tutor, my mentor, my hero.

HEARTS OF STEEL
JONNY QUINN

For any music lover growing up in Northern Ireland, Terri Hooley is a bit of a legend. The man behind the Good Vibrations label, he's known to us all as the 'Godfather of Punk'. Not only that, but he seems to have been connected, in one way or another, to everything that's ever happened in Northern Ireland music – he set up his own pirate radio station, he started the Belfast Reggae Club, he was the first guy to bring The Pogues over to Northern Ireland ... he was always hugely passionate about music. During the seventies and eighties he fought hard to keep the Belfast music scene alive, facing down various paramilitary groups who'd demand protection money at gigs, because he always believed that music should cross all religious and political barriers. He had a shop in Belfast, also called Good Vibrations, and everyone would hang out there – punks, indie kids, bands – because this was when going to record shops was a social event.

I had been in several bands before Snow Patrol and I used to go into the shop and ask him if we could be on his Good Vibes label. Every time I did, he would just smile and say, 'I'll sign you if I fancy your girlfriend ...' Of course, even though he never did sign up any of the bands I was in, that didn't stop him from jumping up on-stage in the middle of our gigs, grabbing the mic and addressing the audience. He did this more times than I can count, and each time he had been completely uninvited.

One day however he asked me to join his band, Hearts Of Steel, and told me that our first rehearsal was to be held in the shop one particular night, after he'd closed up. I turned up on the evening in question, ready to begin, only to find that there was no drum kit there for me to play. Instead Terri pointed to a box in the corner and said, 'You can just play on that.'

Of course, anyone who has ever been present at one of Terri's 'rehearsals' will not be surprised to hear that we didn't actually do any rehearsing in the end: the evening consisted of Terri simply playing records for a few hours until we all gave up and headed to The Crown Bar – or, as Terri calls it, his 'office' – to talk about music.

He did book one recording session for the band though, at a little studio in the countryside, but for hours he just sat drinking brandy and telling stories as the studio filled with cigarette smoke. We'd already set up the gear and we knew that we'd have to make a start at some point, but as the night went on it became obvious that that just wasn't going to happen – instead Terri just got more and more hammered and reeled out more and more stories. At one point he even said, 'I don't know why I'm here ... I can't sing.' And we all thought, 'But, er, you booked the session ...'

We started again the next day, with more booze, more fags and more stories, and eventually we had to push him into the live room to record. All the while he was saying, 'I can't sing in front of you guys, I'd be too embarrassed, it'll be terrible.' But he did it in the end – he turned away from us and read the lyrics from sheets of paper stuck to the walls. Surprisingly, the songs still turned out really well ...

Years later, when Snow Patrol were signed to an indie label, we were given three months off, and I was pretty skint, so I walked into Terri's shop to ask if he needed anyone else to work there. 'No,' he said, 'to be honest I already have too many employees and I'm losing money.'

I was disappointed, but we carried on chatting about music anyway and, at the end of the conversation, as I was walking out the door, he turned around and said, 'You start on Monday.' Because that's the sort of character he is, a guy who will help someone out even when it makes no sense to do so.

And I can tell you, working in the shop was an experience. People would come from all over the world – England, Germany, America – just to chat to Terri. Famous people would also drop in when they were in Belfast, and they'd always leave clutching records. Terri would say to me, 'You should never meet your heroes ... but at the end of the day they're paying customers too.'

Not that Terri has ever been that impressed by celebrity – as he showed when he punched John Lennon – though he has had several brushes with fame himself, not least of which was his Number One indie charts single, 'Laugh at Me'. He always insisted that he only released that song to prove that anyone could have a Number One single, and it is pretty bad, to be honest – I have a copy of the single at home actually – but that's not really the point, the point was that he did it.

And that's Terri you know, always doing stuff he believes in, whether anyone else gets it or not ... When anybody else in his position would have left Belfast for greener pastures, he stuck it out. He always has and always will believe in Belfast and Northern Ireland. Punk was more than the hair and clothes, it was about attitude and no one has more attitude than Terri.

PHOENIX FROM THE FLAMES

North Street Arcade as it was
before the fire, c. 2002

Vintage Records was gone but I wasn't about to let that beat me. In November 2002, even as the shit was hitting the fan for Vintage, I was preparing my next shop, Cathedral Records. It was located in North Street Arcade, a fantastic old building situated in the Cathedral Quarter area of the city – hence the name!

The arcade was a listed, stylish building that had been built in 1936 during the Great Depression. Back then it had been the location of some of Belfast's most exclusive shops, but in later years, as the northern edge of the city centre grew ever more run down, it became a bit more bohemian, home to a motley crew of artists, second-hand book shops and tattoo parlours. It was perfect! Now all I needed was the money.

In stepped Andrew Thompson, a great friend of mine whom I had known from the seventies. He brought me to see the premises at North Street Arcade, and I had a good feeling about the place from the start. Andrew offered to help me with the rent in order to get me started and even bought me some stock. Without him I would never have been able to get back on my feet so soon.

I moved all my stock in and as time went by I could really feel the old arcade come back to life. It wasn't long before the other tenants and I began to build a wonderful community in that building. My friend Lesley Anderson asked if he could use the room I had upstairs to set up the Belfast Bohemian Collective, an art studio for performance artists, painters and other creative types. Bands would also often use the room upstairs to rehearse and some would even put on live music in the main arcade. My shop became a sort of commune – there were always people I knew hanging about – and all my mates from the days of the first shop in Great Victoria Street were still with me. As a result, we had some really excellent parties and some nights we didn't even go home.

I remember one night in particular when me, Lesley, and another friend of mine, DJ Death Darren, found ourselves sitting in the store at six in the morning after yet another evening of drug abuse and partying. Lesley was due in work at 9 a.m. so we knew there was no point in going home. Instead, we all bedded down and I slept behind the counter. A few hours later we were wakened by a customer banging on the door. Unfortunately for him, I had taken out my glass eye before going to sleep and couldn't find it! Instead, I had on a black eye patch – which I've always felt made me look a bit weird – and it was only when my glass eye was found jammed between a couple of albums that I returned to 'normal'.

There was no denying that the parties we had in our little arcade community were amazing, but unfortunately my business wasn't doing as well as I had hoped it would. I had an incredible record collection, don't get me wrong, but my store was just too far out of the way so we just weren't making any money. In business terms, Cathedral Records was probably the worst of all my shops to date – though the parties went a long way to make up for that!

My first store may have been long gone, but on 13 August 2003 the people of Belfast showed me that it had not been forgotten – I was asked by the Regional Development Board to plant a tree on Great Victoria Street, just in front of where the original building once stood. The board had used the press to ask the public who they thought deserved the honour and my name came out on top. They had previously asked people like Cliff Richard, Alex Higgins and Seamus Heaney to participate in the scheme, but I was the first person to be nominated by the public, and that meant a lot. I took Michael along that day – it was a very humbling experience. It touched me to see just how much people cared for Good Vibrations.

Sadly, things were not going so well in my private life. My hectic lifestyle had finally taken its toll on my relationship with Eithne and it was clear we weren't going to stick the pace. We had been a couple for more than twenty years, but we lived quite separate

No, it's not a giant marijuana plant, it's my
tree-planting ceremony, 13 August 2003

Me and Michael outside
Cathedral Records, c. 2003

lives. I had my music, and she loved her sports, devoting a lot of her time to camogie and football – she even played for the Northern Ireland Women's Football Team. In time, our relationship changed into a close friendship, and in some ways she has become the sister I never had. I still love that girl to bits.

We both decided that perhaps the best thing for me to do was to move out of the house. However, I needed time to sort out somewhere to live and while I was prepared to stay in the shop it was hardly a long-term solution. So we compromised – I would move my belongings into the shop and out of the house, but I would stay at Eithne's until I found somewhere else. So one weekend in March 2004, while Eithne was in Donegal I loaded up most of my possessions and brought them down to the arcade.

Three weeks later I was still at Eithne's but I wasn't worried, I knew I'd sort myself out eventually. It was Saturday 17 April 2004 and I was due to act as compere for the 'Maritime Reunion', an evening of music organised to commemorate 'The Maritime Session', a legendary event that used to take place every week in Belfast in the long-demolished Maritime Hotel. Throughout the sixties, many of the city's greatest talents – including Them, and the superb Sam Mahood – took to the stage there and the place was packed to the doors with people clamouring to hear some of our best bands. However, like almost everything else in this town, 'The Maritime Session' soon fell victim to the Troubles, as acts became ever more reluctant to travel to Belfast, while the hotel's location – close to the bottom of the Falls Road and a stone's throw from the Shankill – made customers even rarer than rock stars!

But times had changed since then, and some of the old artists, including showband stars like Frankie Connolly and ex-Them legend Billy Harrison, had decided to put on a night at the Empire bar in south Belfast to celebrate the Maritime and its musical history. It was a real honour for me to have been asked to compere as I had been barred all those years ago from the hotel for making political speeches and I was eager to do the old place proud.

I'd been off the drink for two weeks and before I went out that night I made a big bottle of orange cordial to see me through the night, though I remember that Eithne had little faith in my ability to stay dry. 'You will find an excuse to drink tonight,' she said, 'I know you will.' But I was determined not to drink and so, even when I saw that all my friends from the sixties were there, and even though people were smoking dope and offering to buy me drinks all night, I resisted. I can't think of any other occasion in my life when I turned down a free spliff or a glass of brandy!

Despite the lack of artificial stimulants however, I was thoroughly enjoying the night and I remember getting up shortly before 10 p.m. to introduce Billy Harrison on-stage. This done, I headed outside for a fag and swig of orange juice just as my mobile phone vibrated into life. It was my mate Biggy Bigmore – his real name is something of a mystery, even his family know him as Biggy! – who operated a recording studio and organised rehearsal sessions for bands in the arcade where I had my shop.

'The arcade's on fire,' he said, 'It's all gone.'

I couldn't quite take it in, 'What do you mean it's all gone?' I asked, 'What part of the arcade is on fire?'

The moment he replied, 'All of it,' my heart stopped. What if someone had been hurt? Bands would often use the soundproofed rehearsal rooms on a Saturday night and Lesley Anderson had a habit of bunking down in the shop after a day spent drinking – many a time I would pop over from The John Hewitt pub across the road to get some tobacco, only for Lesley to pop up from behind the counter and scare the shit out of me. And Anita, an artist who ran a business called The World Turned Round, would quite often spend all night working in her own shop – what if something had happened to them?

I made my way back inside where I met Frankie Connolly, who was due to go on-stage. I told him that the arcade was on fire and that my shop was gone – I was still in shock. But I still had a job to do, and in my confused state I thought it best to carry on.

Everything in my shop was destroyed, even the metal racks – it was like a scene from The Blitz.

I don't know why I didn't just leave straight away – I suppose I was thinking, 'What's the point? There's nothing I can do and the show must go on.' I'm proud to say that, before I left I gave Frankie the best introduction he ever had.

I called myself a taxi soon after, but even before I made my way round to the arcade, I knew I had lost everything.

When we got there, the taxi driver wouldn't take any money. 'Good luck Terri,' he said. I barely heard him – the sight that greeted me when I turned into Donegall Street left me breathless. I headed straight to The John Hewitt bar, keeping my head down and tripping over fire hoses the whole way. I marched up to the bar, ordered a pint of Guinness and a brandy – all the while thinking, 'sorry Eithne' – and it was only then that I dared look across the street. All I could see, past the fire engines lining the street, were flames climbing into the sky.

'Could anyone still be in there?' I wondered. I asked around and discovered that a band had left the building a mere twenty minutes before the fire started, but that no one else was suspected to be inside. My friends were safe, and now there was nothing else I could do but have a few more drinks and go home.

When it was safe enough to get into the building I couldn't believe the devastation that awaited me, even the metal racks that we used to hold the records had been damaged. There was melted plastic everywhere, but amazingly you could still read some of the labels on the records. I picked one up and it was 'I'll Be Back' by The Beatles. My records are like children to me and some of them were incredibly valuable – I reckon my stock alone was worth about £50,000, but I wasn't covered by insurance. I had singles worth about £200 each and, given a few years, the collection would have been worth £150,000.

As if that weren't bad enough, having moved all my personal possessions to the store meant that it wasn't just records that were lost in the fire. I lost the whole history of Good Vibrations that night – all the photographs and all the paraphernalia that I had collected, like ticket stubs and magazine articles. I lost the history of my life.

I also lost items of great financial, as well as sentimental, value. I had pictures, drawings and a book autographed by renowned German artist Joseph Beuys – a former Luftwaffe pilot who local artist Gerry Gleason had nicknamed 'Billy', joking that with a surname like that in Belfast there was no other nickname he could have had! Those items were even more precious because he had given them to me himself. I had befriended Billy when he brought his exhibition to Dublin and Belfast and he was one of the greatest men I ever met. His drawings were to be the children's pension fund but, thanks to the arsonists, they all went up in smoke. They must have been worth thousands.

Just as devastating was the loss of a collection of letters that I had exchanged with the legendary Bob Marley, a real hero of mine. I had had the incredible good fortune to have struck up a sort of 'friendship by correspondence' with Marley when I wrote to him in Kingston, Jamaica after hearing his song 'One Cup of Coffee', back in 1965. Nobody in Northern Ireland had ever really heard reggae music at that time, and it was only thanks to some musician friends of mine, who had left Northern Ireland, that I discovered Marley at all.

In those days most of the guest houses in London had the 'No blacks; No dogs; No Irish' rule, so a lot of Irish musicians lived in the same area as black musicians. A real trade of musical influences began, and a lot of my friends used to send me over the reggae records they were being introduced to, knowing I would appreciate them.

I remember playing 'One Cup of Coffee' one night in 1965 at our jazz club in Belfast, and it completely cleared the floor. The next time I put it on, about three people got up to dance. By the next week we had an almost full dance floor, and by that stage I was hooked. I can't say that I alone brought reggae to Belfast, but I was there at the beginning and it was the start of a lifelong passion.

In fact, I was the first person in Ireland to put on regular reggae discos, and I did so for many a year. I remember putting one on during the 1980s in the staunchly republican area of Ardoyne in north Belfast and, before the gig, an ex-IRA prisoner insisted on taking me to his house to show me his huge collection of reggae music and Bob Marley albums. Anyway, the gig itself went very well but, towards the end of the night, one guy asked me for a UB40 song. 'I don't do the white man's reggae,' I replied. 'You're not from round here,' he noted, with just a hint of a threat in his voice – I played the UB40 song!

So, anyway, Bob and I had developed this long-distance friendship without any real prospect of ever meeting, that is, until 1973, when he was touring the UK with his new album Catch A Fire and I was lucky enough to blag an invite to a party to mark his arrival in London. The party was in a flat in Balham, south London and, during the course of the evening, I finally found myself in the same room as the man himself. He came over to me and asked, since I was from Belfast, if I knew this guy Hooley who had been writing to him for years, and in my stewed state I said I'd never heard of him! I was used to smoking grass, but the spliffs I was being handed on that occasion were in a different league, and I guess they had affected me more than I thought they would. The morning afterwards I was kicking myself, I can tell you that.

Thankfully, I got a second chance to meet him because the next day I was down at Island Records with a couple of musician friends – helping myself to their free food and drink – and it turned out that Bob was in a neighbouring room arguing with Island founder Chris Blackwell. Apparently Bob was feeling homesick – the weather was getting him down and he missed his family – so he wanted to cancel a couple of dates and go home. It was then that we were introduced again. This time he said he wanted to go for a pint of Guinness so we went to a local pub. We spent the whole afternoon just talking about music, and by the end of the day I wanted to go and live in Jamaica!

After that we exchanged a few more letters but, as he became more and more famous, we gradually lost touch. He died in 1981, but I will always treasure that afternoon with the great man. Sadly, memories are all I have left, since the letters and pictures he sent me were all destroyed in the fire.

Even in the aftermath of the fire it had never occurred to me that someone could have done it deliberately, so I was gob smacked when I read in the paper that there had been six separate fires, started by blast incendiary devices – one report even suggested that the authorities knew the identity of one of the arsonists, a man they say was an expert.

I was devastated. The grief I felt soon turned to barely controlled anger, and I'm sorry to say as a pacifist, that had the person who ordered that fire been standing in front of me, I would have stabbed him in the heart. I'd happily do the jail time. Those people ruined so many lives that night. Not only had they destroyed a beautiful old building and a slice of Belfast history, but they had destroyed a community, and left a huge scar on the city and in the hearts of many good people.

Judging by the level of destruction caused, it was clear that there was only one intention – total devastation. Those people knew what they were doing, the building was to be left in such a state that there could be no going back for us tenants. The arcade could have been something special – people really cared about the place – but now it was gone. Very few of the key holders, including myself, even had insurance, and so we lost everything.

I descended into the worst depression imaginable. I veered between contemplating suicide and, for the first time in my life, resolving to leave Belfast and all its problems to start a new life in America. I was just so furious that those fuckers could get away with it and there was nothing I could do.

It was then, when I had sunk to my lowest point, that things began to turn around. I was DJ'ing in The Parlour, a local Belfast pub, when I met a journalist from the *Guardian* called Sarah. I was talking to her about the fire and told her that I had really thought about just ending it all. But Sarah and I had a long chat about the whole thing and, somehow, she made me realise that I still had some fight left in me, and that I needed to do something, or go crazy. So a short time later I organised a 'Solidarity With The People Who Were Burnt Out' night for key holders in an effort to boost morale.

We had held a 'Burnt Out But Still Smoking' night just after the fire as a way for us all to raise a glass to the old place. It was a sixties and seventies music night and we sent out hundreds of invitations, all of which said 'No arsonists or property developers allowed in.' But on the night of the 'Solidarity' event, I took a spray can of paint and wrote 'Thank You Sarah' on the shutters of the arcade, just to let her know what she had done for me.

The other traders and I decided that we would keep the fire in the forefront of the public's mind – we would not let anyone forget. I was nominated as spokesman and I made regular appearances on the BBC and in the local press. I lost count of the amount of people I gave my phone number to. I was determined not to be silenced.

But things turned really ugly after one appearance on BBC Radio Ulster's current affairs programme *Talkback*. When I answered a call on my mobile I was told, 'Don't ever go on *Talkback* again. Don't mention the arcade.' Then they hung up. But that was only the start. I started to receive similar phone calls on a regular basis, but I never told anyone about it. This went on for almost a year until it all came to a head the Christmas after the fire. I was walking across Writers' Square, which is just up the street from the arcade, when I got another call, 'Terri, you've got a son, and you wouldn't like anything to happen to him.' That was when I snapped. 'Hold on a moment,' I said, 'while this has been fun, taking your phone calls up to now, you tell me where and when, face to face,

and I will have three hundred people there with me. Tell me to my face to keep quiet about the arcade, 'cos I won't.'

I told them that if they knew anything about me then they would know that I had friends from both sides of the community. 'I'm standing in Writers' Square now,' I said, trying to keep the anger from my voice, 'and if you ever phone me again I'll get The Undertones, Snow Patrol and everybody else I know to play here. We'll stage the

The fire caused a lot of outrage
among the people of Belfast

biggest open-air concert Belfast has ever seen. Go and tell your masters that.'

I hung up the phone, walked into The John Hewitt and spoke to bar manager Pedro Donald about the calls. He was the first person I had told, and it was a relief to finally get it out, but thankfully my defiant words seemed to have done the trick and I never received any more calls like that.

To this day, the bastards responsible have not been caught and it makes me so angry to think that they may have gotten away with it. I try to ensure that people don't forget what happened though – I regularly post comments on Facebook about it, and if any graffiti is covered up I make a point of putting it back! The burned-out shell of the arcade is still there, a blot on the city, and I walk past it nearly every day as I go to The John Hewitt for a pint. It has become a symbol of everything that is bad about Belfast – the institutionalised vandalism and the wanton destruction of our heritage and history.

URNT OUT BUT STILL SMOKING

TERRI HOOLEY: A MEMORY
CHRIS MOORE

Terri Hooley was propped up against the counter in The Crown Bar in Belfast. It was a football day, a Sunday I think.

I don't know why he was there, it certainly wasn't for the football. Must have been for the drink. It was the summer of 1996 and I'd been watching some Euro '96 game transmitted live on television.

Whatever, the important thing is that Terri Hooley was propping up the bar so I moved over to speak to him. We'd known each other for many years – way back to the seventies when I worked in the *News Letter*.

Back then I had a weekly column aimed at young people called, 'Young Moore's Almanac'. I reviewed records and movies, wrote about teenage trends, and managed to upset Van Morrison and his family with remarks about his failure to play Belfast, even though he had returned to Ireland to play Dublin. He wasn't happy. Nor was his 'Aunt' Violet! She wrote to me and we met in Belfast city centre one day during her lunch break. She was a lovely woman and it wasn't until years later, during a Morrison show at Killinchy Castle, that I discovered 'Aunt' Violet was actually his mum! But she said my column and criticism made her glum.

And now, twenty years on, and I was facing someone else in a glum mood. Terri said there'd been a fire and he'd lost a lot of his record stock. What really upset him though was the loss of his copy of the first single The Undertones produced on his own label – Good Vibrations. I was shocked and obviously feeling a bit sorry for him. But not sorry enough at that stage to own up to having a copy at home.

By 1978 'Young Moore's Almanac' had long gone but I still had an interest in music, and consequently I attended some kind of news conference that Terri had organised to promote The Undertones. Can't remember the date of that either. Drink no doubt to blame.

And alcohol was about to impinge again. I bought Terri a drink. Then more drink. And more. His mood remained decidedly despondent. The more drink that went down, the guiltier I began to feel that I had the one thing this man craved. At home it was carefully hidden away among the few remaining vinyl singles I had.

Even as we stood there I could visualise the record at home. It came wrapped in a large sheet of plain white paper that was folded over into a sleeve for the single. It was an EP actually – that's 'extended play' for those unfamiliar with the language of the sixties generation – the *True Confessions* EP. I could also see the notes I had scribbled all over the sleeve – names of the individuals in The Undertones; name and details of Good Vibrations; and, of course, quotes from Terri.

Now, back in The Crown Bar, Terri and I discussed the joys of 'Teenage Kicks'. He recalled the difficulty he had in getting the band signed up to labels in England. That is until a certain John Peel took an instant liking to 'Teenage Kicks'. So much so that he played it over and over again. He was so impressed with the EP that he even paid for the band to record a session in a Belfast studio and played it on his show. To him 'Teenage Kicks' was the perfect pop track.

Soon there was a demand for the single across the water and soon The Undertones would be international stars. Terri was delighted of course.

But now he was standing in front of me getting pissed, (with me matching him drink for drink), and a little piece of his life had been taken from him.

The pressure mounted inside me. Should I? Should I? It might be worth a small fortune in years to come, but this was, after all, the man who had helped make The Undertones.

In the end my conscience was totally eroded – not by any issue of morality or decency, but by the intake of alcohol. I owned up. I told him I had what he wanted. Suddenly his eyes lit up (well eye actually!) and he bought a round. He promised me a copy of a CD which featured The Undertones singing 'Teenage Kicks'. It was a compilation of Good Vibrations' greatest punk band hits.

A few days later, we met and exchanged our packages. He got the original vinyl of The Undertones. I got the *Greatest Hits* from Terri's record label. We went our separate ways, though I was certain I could hear him sniggering uncontrollably as we moved away.

But it was meant to be, of that I was in no doubt. Burglars had come into my home a few weeks before my encounter with Terri and removed every CD I owned except for one – some ghastly African-American female singer!

They didn't touch the vinyl thankfully; so all my 45s were still in one piece and exactly where I left them. So I am glad Terri got the original Good Vibrations recording of The Undertones. That way I know it went to a good home for sure – unlike my CDs!

A BRUSH WITH FATE

Things were very difficult for me after the fire – I was homeless, penniless and for one of the very few times in my life, I felt beaten. Eithne was wonderful though, and she offered to let me stay in her house for as long as I needed – she knew that I was no longer in a position to move out fully. We may have been over as a couple, but we had managed to maintain a great friendship and we thought that, above all, it would be good for Michael to have me around. Now all I needed was a job.

Thankfully a friend of mine, Lawrence John – a well-known DJ whose claim to fame was that he was captured by aliens! – had just opened a vinyl shop in Smithfield Market, close to Belfast city centre, and he asked me to step in and run it for him a few days a week. He already owned a record shop in High Street, but he wanted a presence in Smithfield, which was once a thriving commercial area of the city, packed with every kind of shop imaginable. It has suffered with the advent of shopping centres, and has become a bit of a forgotten area but there are still lots of great shops and wonderful characters there, and it still attracts plenty of visitors.

The idea was that I would have one half of the shop to sell my second-hand vinyl – after the fire, friends had given me records out of their own collections to start building up my stock again – but, after a few months, Lawrence changed his mind about the store and stopped paying the rent. I had to find somewhere else to set up shop, and quickly, or I was back out on the street.

Once again, my friends came to the rescue. William Maxwell, a dear friend who has always been a big fan of Good Vibrations, got in touch with The Undertones, Ruefrex and a few other bands and suggested that they put on a fundraising gig for me. They were all more than willing, and the gig was held on 30 September 2005 at the Empire bar. It was a fantastic night and it meant the world to me to know that all these people were there, supporting me. I had been ready to get out of Belfast, but that night I knew I couldn't go. I realised that I couldn't turn my back on the place and that, more than anything, I wanted to open another store.

We identified premises in Haymarket Arcade, a small area just off Royal Avenue in the centre of Belfast, and Phoenix Records was born. Sadly, the arcade itself was dead – hardly anyone even knew it was there. The entrance was hidden between other stores, and we got next to no passing trade – it was a disaster. I took a little comfort in knowing that at least I had a record shop, but when the landlords said that there was no way we could have the Thursday Club, I knew it was on borrowed time!

A rare customer for Phoenix Records

I had been sub-letting and did not have the keys to the outside shutters, so I asked Raymond Giffen – whom I had known for years and whose father Patrick owned the Pancake House in the arcade – for my own set. He refused almost immediately, telling me that he knew I would be having the Thursday Club or some other wild parties. I guess he knew me too well!

In the three years we were there the shop never made a penny. It was then that I knew the vinyl record business was finished. I struggled on, thinking things might get better, but they never really did and Phoenix Records became the worst shop of them all.

Thankfully, things in my personal life had been going much better. I have always been fortunate enough to meet the right person at the right time and fate intervened for me once more when, just before the summer of

Me and my lovely girlfriend Claire

2006, my current partner, Claire Archibald, came into my life.

We met one night when Stuart Bailie, former Deputy Editor of *New Musical Express*, invited me to a photographic exhibition he was putting on in Belfast. I was already committed to doing a DJ set later that night in the Duke of York bar, in aid of the Rape Crisis Centre in Belfast – my daughter Anna works for the equivalent centre in Edinburgh – but I didn't want to miss the exhibition, so I went along early with my friend DJ Death Darren and had a few glasses of wine.

My friend Louise Gallagher, who worked for the BBC, arrived at that point with a colleague of hers – Claire. It was always a party when you met Louise, but Claire seemed totally unimpressed by my presence there – apparently she had never even heard of me! But we got talking and we seemed to get on really well. She told me that she worked for BBC Online but that she was taking three months off to work in a school in a small township in South Africa. She was also planning to spend some time working on the *Big Issue* magazine, writing and generally helping to run their office. I was impressed, and I must admit, was immediately taken with her. I wanted to stay and chat to her for longer, but I had the Rape Crisis gig to go to and had to leave.

Darren and I headed to the Duke of York where he opened the show with a soul set. I had a couple of pints in the downstairs bar and I found myself thinking about Claire – I knew I wanted to see her again. With a little help from Louise I managed to get in touch with her and it wasn't long before we started to see each other.

When she left for South Africa, it was difficult. We had only been seeing each other for a few months and I didn't know if, when she got back, we would be able to take up where we left off, but I missed her and I was determined to be there to meet her when she stepped off the plane. But the big reunion didn't exactly go according to plan. On the day of her arrival back in Belfast, I went to the airport to meet her. Two of her friends were already there holding big 'Welcome Home' banners, but as luck would have it, I ran into my old friend The Phantom – from my pirate radio days – and got so deep into conversation with him, that I missed the big reunion. Claire had arrived home, not to run into my arms, but to see me deep in conversation with someone else – I think she was a little miffed. But I told her how proud I was of her, and we managed to get things back on track.

I was still staying with Eithne at this stage. The set-up had worked well for us and, as our romantic relationship had been long over by then, we had become more like housemates. In fact, I lived there for a further two years after meeting Claire, but it was never a problem. Claire and I would spend Friday nights playing Scrabble – not very rock 'n' roll! – but she was a great calming influence on me and Michael thought the world of her. Almost every weekend she, Michael and I would take the dog for a walk along the beach at Holywood, or go together to get my parents their shopping. My mother was always glad to see Claire and she was pleased that I was in a relationship that worked well for everyone. I think that my parents were just happy to get regular visits from their son and grandson! Claire and I have a wonderful relationship and had it not been for her I would never have got over my shop going up in flames. She's an amazing woman.

But if things were looking up on the relationship front, they were also improving on the music front too. In 2007, nearly thirty years after the Good Vibrations label had first led the way, Belfast's struggling bands and musicians finally got the resource they deserved. On 5 May the Oh Yeah! music centre opened on Gordon Street – occupying a former whiskey warehouse in the heart of the up-and-coming Cathedral Quarter – with my old sparring partner Stuart Bailie at the helm. Co-founded by Martin Neill and Davy Matchett – both businessmen and music-lovers – and Gary Lightbody of Snow Patrol, the centre provides local artists with performing space, a privately-run recording studio, technical equipment, help and advice.

The likes of Elbow, Snow Patrol and Duke Special have all performed there, while Tim Wheeler from Ash, and former Radio One DJ Colin Murray are among the centre's many active supporters. Oh Yeah! has achieved more for Northern Ireland's music industry in three years than the government-funded Northern Ireland Music Industry Commission – which wound up in November 2009 due to 'irreconcilable differences' among board members – managed to in eight years.

I wish we'd had something like it back in the seventies when we were trying to find somewhere for bands to rehearse or put on gigs. I had tried to set up something similar in my days as a member of The Tribe – that motley crew of friends, activists and music fans. We had set up a small independent press that published

ohyeahbelfast.com

poetry magazines and, later, a newsletter called *Ego*, which was a platform for young people to write about the issues of the day. We needed a base of operations and a dream to set up the 'Belfast Arts Lab' was born. It was to be a central place from which we would generate our publications, and a rehearsal space for bands.

I remember on one occasion going to look at potential premises on the Oldpark Road in north Belfast with Colin McClelland – a journalist who became editor of the *Sunday World* newspaper, and who managed Stiff Little Fingers – when we were stopped by the police and asked what we were doing. This happened a couple of times, and Colin began to get a little spooked. I think the sight of Hooley with a respected journalist had raised a few suspicions, and so the visit ended with Colin heading for White's Tavern for a much needed drink!

We did eventually get premises off Donegall Street, but unfortunately it didn't work as well as we had hoped. The initial enthusiasm of others seemed to have waned, and there didn't seem to be the same appetite for enterprise as there had been in the beginning. It's a shame to say it, but looking back I wonder if perhaps Belfast wasn't ready for such a place. The onset of the Troubles meant that people had become ghettoised, and running something from Belfast's city centre was very difficult – people tended to stay in their own areas.

The Oh Yeah! Centre is long overdue and I'm very happy that the job of encouraging new acts is in the hands of someone like Stuart Bailie. We need to start shouting from the rooftops about the talent we have produced. Talent like Van Morrison, Paul Brady, Ash, Therapy?, The Undertones and Snow Patrol – the list is endless, and their success was achieved without there being a music industry here. For such a small area, we have produced some of the best poets and performers and their influence stretches around the world. Did you know, for example, that the famous McPeake Family have been a big influence on Bob Dylan? They also gave John Lennon uilleann pipes, although I'm not sure he knew how to play them. Did you also know that Kate Bush used a Lambeg drum made on Sandy Row on an album track? And of course, during their 1971 tour, Led Zeppelin performed 'Stairway To Heaven' for the very first time in Belfast's Ulster Hall.

One of the proudest moments in my own musical life took place on 22 February 2008 at the annual Fate Awards – a bash hosted by entertainment and listings magazine *Fate*. I had heard a rumour that, for the first and only time, the Oh Yeah! centre would be sponsoring the Legend Award and that it was to be presented to Van Morrison. 'No better man,' I thought. There are few artists anywhere who have had as much influence on others – every serious record collector has a copy of *Astral Weeks* in their collection – and while he might be a bit grumpy, he is fully deserving of the title 'legend'.

But, as it turned out, this rumour was wrong. As the award ceremony grew nearer, I was told that I should dust down the monkey suit as I was to be the star guest, the so-called legend. It was a huge surprise. Any recognition I had ever received had come from Dublin or further afield, I hadn't received a Northern Irish award in all my life. I don't consider myself a legend – well maybe I do after a few brandies and couple of spliffs! – so I think this honour was belated recognition for all the incredible things that everybody at Good Vibrations achieved over the years and a tribute to all the young talent that refused to get weighed down by the sectarian bigotry and conflict. We really did put Belfast back on the music map of the world.

It was with some nervousness that I got ready for my big moment to be held at Belfast's Waterfront Hall. My girlfriend Claire was out of town that night, so I did what any man would have done in such a situation – I took my ex!

Me, Michael and Eithne –
don't we clean up well?

Eithne and I took our seats and saw that at our table were Mike Edgar, once of Cruella de Ville, but now Executive Producer at the Beeb; Glenn Patterson, the celebrated Belfast author; John D'Arcy, Martin Neill and Davy Matchett from the Oh Yeah! Centre; and Gary Lightbody, with whom I had, by then, struck up a great friendship. He had insisted he would be there on the night, and I'll never forget him being interviewed on the red carpet when he refused to take any questions about Snow Patrol, who were busy conquering the world at that time. 'I'm not here for Snow Patrol,' he said, 'I'm here for Terri Hooley.' My mum saw that on the telly and it made her so proud.

Comedienne Ruby Wax was compere for the night and I thought she was brilliant. She told outrageous jokes and mispronounced everybody's name. Though she got mine right so she was all right by me. When she was finished I had to listen as Glenn and Gary told the room what a great guy I was – I thought I was dreaming! Then it was my turn.

Back at the table, everybody was a bit tense. I think that they had been anxious that the temptation of all the free wine and beer would have been too much for me and they were worried about my speech. I was really nervous but when I got up there, after having nursed one drink the whole night, and asked, 'Was Van Morrison not available tonight?' it broke the ice. I made a few comments about the bastards who burnt me out of the arcade, and then asked if anyone could put me up as Eithne needed her settee back!

That seemed to get Ruby going, and as soon as the speeches were over she walked straight over to Eithne and gave her a right tongue lashing, asking her why she was putting me on the settee and saying that I could come over to London and stay with her anytime.

It was a hell of a night, made even better by the news that a percentage of the profits made from the event were being donated to the Oh Yeah! Centre. From my own perspective though, it made me realise how far I had come in my life.

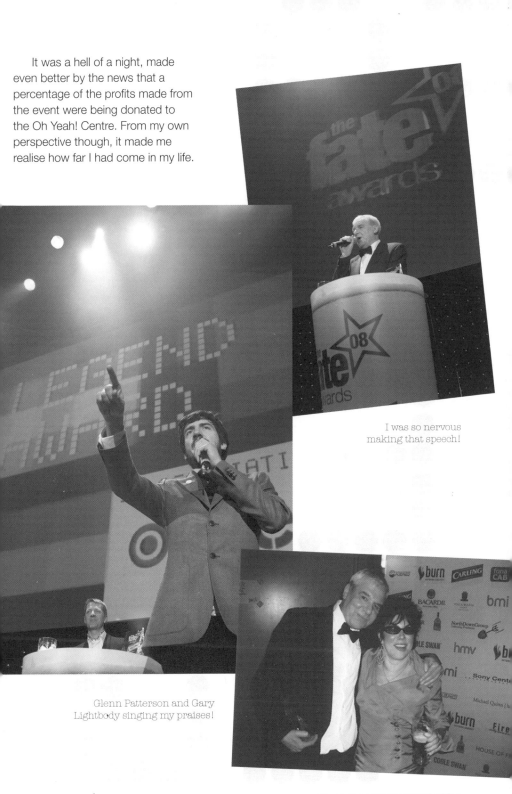

I was so nervous making that speech!

Glenn Patterson and Gary Lightbody singing my praises!

Me and the hilarious Ruby Wax

I FUCKING HATE SINGERS
GARY LIGHTBODY

I was introduced to Terri ten years ago at a party in Belfast by our mutual friend Jimmy Symington. I'd heard a lot about him and I was excited to meet the legend. Jimmy grabs him and says, 'Terri, this is Gary, he's a singer,' to which Terri spits, 'I fucking hate singers,' turns on his heel and stomps off to the bar leaving me standing dumbstruck and Jimmy stifling laughter. It was not clear to me straight away that Terri and I would be great friends. The first meeting with Terri can be hit, miss or disaster. It can take time to get on his good side – if you're a 'fucking singer' anyway – but we got there, him and I.

Once he's in your life he can be a cyclone of a man. He can crack thunder into your life and nothing is ever the same again, be they the tiny details or the grand scales. He can be by turns a drunken lunatic, a lucid guru, a hilarious storyteller, a cuddly bear, and many more things besides, but one thing is certain, hanging out with Terri is never dull. The other thing he always is, to those that get to know him well, is a fiercely loyal friend.

For all the stories of punching John Lennon, and putting his glass eye in your pint while you're not looking, it's the sweet man behind the chaos of his personal history and the carnage I think of first when I sit down to write about him. Don't get me wrong, he still can muster carnage, sometimes out of nowhere. Like magic. Crazy magic he's not in control of. Like a novice wizard playing with a spell book he found open at his master's table.

There is still this childlike wonder and abandon with which he throws himself at everything. Most men grow old when they succumb to the 'usual', consumerist way of things: job, car, house, things, blah. Even when dallying with these things, Terri never did anything conventionally, never really kept, or was tied down, by anything and therefore never really grew old. Behind his one good eye there always plays the spark of mischief. You've really got to watch out for that. On the same fateful night I met him, he fell drunk over a table and knocked all the drinks and food for the party over. Yes, you've really got to watch out for that. Yet, for so many other reasons (and to be honest the chaos too) he is always the first thought I have when I think of Belfast and its many modern heroes.

When we were shooting a short documentary for Channel 4 about what Belfast means to us, we called Terri for an interview. The film-makers were two guys from Manchester who'd never heard of him. After three hours of filming him in The John Hewitt bar drinking brandy and talking about everything except what he was actually being asked about, we were lucky we even made it into our own documentary. The two film-makers were awestruck at this man of a million words. He regaled us with story after story of a life lived at the same pace he tells a tale: rocket speed. We all sat and shut the fuck up. What else can you do? I really should get those interview tapes from those guys ...

One of my most treasured 'Hooley Memories' ™ was when, in early 2008, myself and Norn Irish novelist and screenwriter Glenn Patterson presented Terri with the 'Oh Yeah! Legend of the Year Award' at the Fate Awards in Belfast. All the Oh Yeah! team sat at Terri's table and we watched him nervously, and rather sweetly, nurse one drink all night while he waited for his award to come round. When the time came, and I rather drunkenly shouted the words, 'Ladies and gentlemen, Terri Fucking Hooley' (OK, maybe I should have nursed the one drink too that night), Glenn and I got to watch like proud sons as Terri took the public spotlight and was humble, poised and very funny. That night Belfast, finally, said thank you to Terri. It was long overdue.

We celebrated what Terri did for music in Belfast at a time when there was nothing. There was once no life on the streets of Belfast. The wind was all but out of the place and Terri was, at times, a lone bellows pumping some semblance of culture and defiance back into a city falling to pieces in the darkness. There is now life aplenty again in the city of Belfast, and in the music of Norn Iron, and we have people like Terri to thank for that.

Terri, Ruby Wax and Gary Lightbody
after the Fate Awards, 2008

Terri Hooley

13 - 8 - 2003

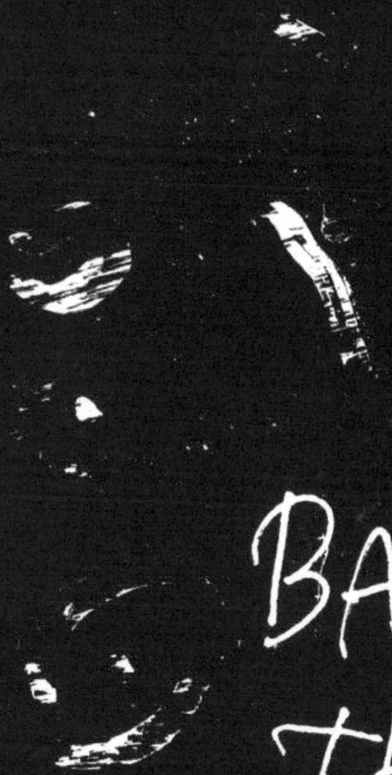

BACK TO THE FUTURE

After the Fate Awards it seemed like the good times just kept on coming. The Good Vibrations label had reached the ripe old age of thirty and, to celebrate, we decided to organise a massive gig, 'Good Vibrations – A Light in the Darkness'. Arthur Magee, who had been a true and valued friend of mine ever since we had first met, set the whole thing up and it was held at Belfast's Mandela Hall on 25 April 2008. We had the recently reformed Undertones as headliners, with support from local bands Panama Kings and Shame Academy, while actor James Nesbitt agreed to compere. It was amazing!

Even more exciting was when, a matter of days before the gig, I heard that Arthur had received a letter of support and congratulations from none other than former US President Bill Clinton. It turned out that Arthur had tried to contact a number of high-profile people to let them know about the concert and Clinton had actually responded to wish us luck.

Good Vibrations
30th Anniversary

Clinton of course was no stranger to Northern Ireland. He had been here several times and had played a significant role in bringing about the Good Friday Agreement of 1998, admitting in his letter that 'Northern Ireland holds a special place in my heart.' But it was what he said about Good Vibrations that really made me proud.

In his letter he praised the fact that not only had we helped individual musicians realise their dreams but that we had given young people something positive to say 'yes' to.

I have to say that when Arthur told me he had received a letter from Clinton, my immediate fear was that my protest credentials had gone out the window! Getting letters of congratulations from American Presidents was not something I had anticipated, but in reality I was, and still am, chuffed to bits. I still tell everybody how happy I am to have received Clinton's support.

The anniversary concert held even more significance for me than just commemorating old victories though. The Undertones decided to give me the profits they made from the event, and the money they raised not only enabled me to move to much-needed new premises in Winetavern Street that July, but was also enough for me to pay six months rent up-front and replenish my stock.

It meant a huge amount to me that The Undertones did that. It had never been my intention to make money from the bands, but when the chips were down and I needed some help, The Undertones were there for me. It felt like an acknowledgement of what I had done for them all those years ago and of what we had been through together. It was a very special gesture.

I was pleased to finally be moving from the Haymarket store, and relocating to Winetavern Street was made all the more special by the fact that I already had a history with these new premises. My new store had once been the family home of the McCann brothers, Sean and Paul, whom I had known from my folk club days back in the sixties. Back then, their mother had run a second-hand clothes store from the house and I had

Waiting for customers outside the new shop

been there many times.

Over the years, the McCann brothers established a prominent law firm in Belfast, while the house on Winetavern Street lay empty, so I made contact with Sean and expressed my interest in setting up shop there. 'The shop's yours,' he said, 'we'll have it cleaned up and then it's yours.' I was thrilled. It is a great building, in a brilliant location and it was fitting to set up my new store in a place that housed some of my oldest memories. With this in mind, there was really only one name I could have given the store – Good Vibrations.

We cleaned the place up, and decided to mark the grand opening on 26 July 2008 with a huge party. I rang Billy Harrison and asked him to sing a few songs to mark the occasion, and Joby Fox, bassist for The Bankrobbers, even played a song he wrote especially for the day entitled 'The Ballad of Terri Hooley'. It was a wonderful day and we had around one hundred people come to the door for the big event, but more importantly for me, it meant that once again I was back behind the counter with a Good Vibrations sign over the door. Life really does come full circle.

If I'm honest though, I must admit that the retail business has become increasingly difficult. Vinyl may have made a bit of a comeback, but it's hard to generate enough business to justify premises in the city centre. I may have to resort to selling online, after all that's where all the serious collectors are these days, and I think 'Good Vibes online' could have a future. We'll just have to wait and see if 'Good Vibes on the street' has the same.

All of a sudden there seemed to be an interest in Belfast's musical heritage – not just in punk but also in the work of people like Van Morrison, and I wasn't the only person who noticed this. It was about a month or so after Good Vibes opened, and I was having a pint in The John

All dressed up for my debut as tour guide, September 2008

Hewitt pub with a friend of mine, Sean Kelly. Sean runs the fantastic Cathedral Quarter Arts Festival, which is centred in one of the oldest parts of Belfast and which is now a thriving entertainment area with bars and restaurants. He too wanted to acknowledge Belfast's rich musical history, and he suggested I put together a tour of the city's musical hotspots.

I thought it was a fantastic idea and straight away I agreed to do it. In September 2008, an incredible seventy people gathered to take part in my first walking tour. Looking back I think I may have been carried away by my enthusiasm for the subject and overdid it – I took those people halfway around the city! From the site of the first shop, to the site of the old Maritime Hotel, down into Cathedral Quarter and back to The John Hewitt for a well-deserved pint. The whole thing lasted for three hours, and by the time we had finished only twelve people had gone the distance! I still do the odd tour every so often, though I've had to refine – and shorten! – the route of course.

But people are still so interested in the history of Good Vibes, and all the bands we helped. The tours made me realise that we have been such an important part of this city that I thought I would put together a sort of museum, pulling together whatever memorabilia I could. I have dedicated the upstairs floor of the store to this task, but it's slow going. So much of my own material was lost in the fire that I'm reliant on others coming forward with whatever they have. It's going to be a long-term project, but I think it will be important to have a reminder of what Good Vibes achieved and to preserve it for the future.

Kevin Carson (L) and Michael Rafferty (R) from The Minnows join me to toast the success of their new album

The Good Vibrations store and name were not the only things to make a comeback in 2008, I am also happy to say that September of that year also marked a re-launch of the Good Vibrations label when The Minnows – formerly tiBeriuS' minnoWs – came to me to ask if they could launch their comeback album, *Leonard Cohen's Happy Compared to Me,* with us. They had been working on the album since August 2000, but it had been a slow process. The band, more mature now with full-time jobs and families to consider, had had to grab rehearsal time and studio time when they could. But they knew they wanted to release the album on the Good Vibrations label.

While we had released some singles over the previous two decades, this was to be the first album in seventeen years released on our label, and it felt good. The band agreed to pay for everything themselves, so it wasn't quite the set-up it had been in the seventies, but they were breathing life into the label again and for that I was grateful.

In the end, the album wasn't released until April 2010, but it was well worth the wait – the first time they played it for me, I loved it. It is, without doubt, the band's best work to date. It received great critical acclaim and, now that the label is properly up and running, I'm looking forward to them releasing the follow-up with us – I'm really very fond of those boys.

Onstage with The Moondogs, 17 April 2010

Having the label up and running again gave me a new impetus and I felt that the label was ready once more to fund the recording and the release of local artists. So I was over the moon when, in early 2010, over thirty years after they had released their single, 'She's 19', with us, The Moondogs signed up to release their new album with Good Vibrations. They have a load of new material, and we plan to throw some new versions of the original singles into the mix, for the sake of nostalgia.

I have always liked The Moondogs – they reformed back in 2000 and have been writing fantastic songs ever since. They still record under their original line up, but more importantly, they still sound amazing live! On 17 April 2010, they headlined the Good Vibes 'Burnt Out, Still Rocking' party which we held in the Oh Yeah! Centre to mark the sixth anniversary of the fire in North Street Arcade. Introducing them on-stage made me feel like we were rolling back the decades, which was just about the most exciting thing I could imagine. There's life in the old Moondogs yet!

I want to see some new bands record on Good Vibes too, to give our local talent the head start it deserves. And knowing that The Moondogs support a reunion with the label gives me hope that maybe one day The Undertones will once again record for Good Vibes – and why not? The ethos behind the label remains the same, I'm still as passionate about local bands as I was in 1978 and, more than thirty years after we kicked it all off, it would be wonderful to have the Derry boys back under my wing. At least this time they should be old enough to wipe their own arses!

And the 'old music', as I call it, has undergone a bit of a revival of late. I was delighted to see the release of *The Good Vibrations Story*, an anthology album with a selection of Good Vibes' artist and songs. It had a limited release on Dojo Records, but every copy flew out of the shop in no time at all!

Of course, I still get a huge buzz from playing live. I gig around the town and I still pull in a crowd – I always try to send everybody home happy. This year I plan to play in Belgium, France and Germany– I'll need Jimmy on guitar of course! – but details have yet to be confirmed so perhaps by the time you read this I'll be on my comeback European tour! I just find it incredible that there are people on the continent who are still interested in listening to my tuneless meanderings.

On patrol with Gary Lightbody.
He's the one on the right!

I still do a monthly DJ set too, and the highlight of that side of my career came in June 2010, in the days that followed Snow Patrol's massive gig in Bangor, County Down. The lads had put on the largest gig ever staged in Northern Ireland, with more than forty thousand fans packed into the town's Ward Park for the band's triumphant homecoming. Bangor has always been seen as the band's spiritual home, despite Nathan Connolly being from Belfast, and Tom Simpson and Paul Wilson coming from Scotland. They had showcased a host of local bands, before taking the stage for one of the best live shows I've ever seen. Being an old man, I watched from the VIP tent – I don't think I could have stood up to being shoved and pushed around by all those enthusiastic fans!

Anyway, the following night I was doing my monthly DJ set at The John

Hewitt pub, and some of the band and their entourage came down for a few pints. When the bar closed, the party moved on to the band's hotel, and it was there that Jonny Quinn – who has been a great friend to me for many years and, despite his enormous success, has never forgotten his roots – asked if I would come along to Glasgow the following weekend where the band were playing a big open-air gig at Bellahouston Park. It turned out that this was to be the last date of their tour and it also happened to coincide with Gary Lightbody's birthday weekend, and Jonny wanted me to DJ at the afterparty to celebrate.

My immediate reaction was, 'I can't,' as I was booked to play Greg Cowan's fiftieth birthday party. But the more I thought about it, the more I knew Greg wouldn't mind and so I told Jonny I would do it. The next thing I knew, I woke up in Jonny's hotel room with a bottle of twenty-five-year-old malt whiskey in my hand – I couldn't have been happier!

The following weekend I went to Glasgow, where the band played to twenty-seven thousand fans in another fantastic gig – those boys are really very special. Inevitably we partied long into the night, with yours truly spinning the discs at Gary's birthday/afterparty. I felt invigorated and full of energy, and I really appreciated what Jonny, Gary and the boys had done for me. They made an old man very happy. Gigging with one of the biggest bands in the world when you are over sixty years of age is the stuff of dreams. I felt as though they had given me yet another chance to do what I love best.

Through Jonny too I was finally able to see the Sex Pistols perform live in November 2007 – it was one of the greatest nights of my life. They were, after all, the band that started it all.

Like them or loathe them, the Sex Pistols re-wrote the history of music. They took ownership of youth culture and turned it on its head. Of course, living and preaching that level of anarchy would take its toll, and a combination of big business and bad management meant that while they made a huge dent in the system they couldn't beat it, and they split up in 1978.

I had always regretted not seeing them play. I was called 'The Godfather of Belfast Punk', and yet I'd never seen the band that started the revolution! They had never played in Northern Ireland, which I think was a great pity – Belfast, more than any other city, had epitomised the punk spirit – but in 2007 they announced a reunion tour, which was to feature five nights at the Brixton Academy.

Jonny was living in Crouch End in north London at the time, and was down at his local boozer one night, when he was approached by this bloke who asked, 'You from Belfast?' When Jonny confirmed his background, the man introduced himself as Jimmy Lydon, brother of John Lydon (aka Johnny Rotten).

'Do you know a man called Terri Hooley?' he asked. 'Know him?' said Jonny, 'I used to be his drummer!' It turned out that Jimmy had been over to Belfast a few times during the late seventies and early eighties, and had known a few of the bands.

Jimmy said it would be a great idea to bring me over to see the band play in Brixton and within minutes Jonny was on the phone telling me the story and offering to fly me over. I was thrilled! I managed to blag a ticket for Jimmy Symington too, and before we knew it we were on our way to Brixton to see the Pistols.

Time may have passed and the lads were certainly a lot slower than they had been in the seventies, but their passion was still there, Rotten's eyes blazed with defiance and, despite their image as a thrash/punk band, they were actually a very tight unit. 'Anarchy in the UK' is a classic, in the same way that 'Teenage Kicks' is a classic. Both are totally timeless.

Me and Glenn Patterson

Jimmy and I were treated like kings that night. It's a gig I'll never forget. In many ways it was the missing piece in the punk jigsaw for me. I'm not going soft, but I reckon there is a place for nostalgia and that was a night packed with fond memories. The Brixton Academy is a great venue, and there were more than a few forty-somethings who dug out the old studded dog collars for that one night, before slipping them back into their pockets and going home to the kids, job and mortgage – ever wonder what punk was all about?

It certainly wasn't about running for political office, that's for sure! But in May 2010 that was exactly the position I inadvertently found myself in when I discovered, to my amazement, a Facebook campaign to have me installed as Lord Mayor of Belfast! Now, before you accuse me of being the ultimate sell-out, I should say that my sole election pledge would have been to put on a huge open-air gig on the lawn of Belfast City Hall, to legalise cannabis for a day and to put on a free bar! Strangely enough, however, that didn't guarantee my place in the big seat, but I was touched by the love that the people of Belfast had shown me by starting the campaign anyway.

I feel as though my life has started all over again. In the past few years I have met a whole new generation of people who have just discovered Good Vibrations and what we are all about. In 2009, Glenn Patterson came to me with a movie script that he had written along with *Hot Press* journalist Colin Carberry, a script that told the story of my life.

The idea of a Terri Hooley movie was not a new one, it had been kicking about for around a decade actually, but it was one I thought would never get off the ground. One night in 2000 I had been in The Crown Bar, having a drink when I ran into Glenn. He introduced me to a group of people from RTÉ and we all got to talking. The more I told them about my life, the more interested they seemed to become in me. Glenn tells me that it was at this point that he realised the potential in my life story and so he immediately started work on a script.

I was sceptical. Would anyone really be interested in watching a movie about me? As it turned out, there was interest from a couple of film companies in Dublin, but I insisted that the film be the work of Belfast writers and directors – I've always felt it was really important to support Northern Irish industry – and so it died a death. I was disappointed of course, but I managed to put all thoughts of it out of my head, and thought no more about it. At least, that was until Glenn produced a complete film script and told me that plans were in motion to make the movie a reality. It turned out that he and David Holmes – the Belfast-born DJ who has gone on to compose film scores for Hollywood blockbusters such as *Ocean's Eleven* – had been working together and had managed to secure funding proposals and enough capital to film a pilot. I began to think that this could actually work. We struck a deal on the movie during a night of heavy drinking in the Errigle Inn – there's no better way to do business than sealing a deal over a table of tequila slammers!

They've already finished filming the pilot, which was directed by Lisa Barros D'Sa and Glenn Leyburn – the directorial team behind *Cherrybomb* – and I've even met the man who is playing me! Richard Dormer is a very fine actor, who won critical acclaim for his one-man show *Hurricane*, which told the story of the late snooker legend, Alex Higgins.

It's odd to think about my life being made public in this way, and indeed through this book. When I look back on all those wild times I had, I can see the good I did, but I can also see all the bad. My personal relationships often suffered as a result of all the partying, and my relationship with my daughter was a definite casualty of it all.

When Ruth and I broke up it was very difficult, though we did our best to remain positive. I remember writing a letter to Ruth just saying how important it was for us to stay friends, for Anna's sake. I know that I made mistakes and I am so grateful to Ruth that she remained a friend. But there is always a consequence for a child when parents part ways, and Anna and I just drifted apart. It has taken a lot of bridge-building and a lot of work on both sides, but thankfully Anna and I have managed to get back on track

Me, Michael and Anna,
Bangor, 2009

and establish a close relationship. I think the turning point was when she and I went to see Oasis at the Limelight in Belfast in 1994. They were brilliant that night and Anna and I bounced out of that gig laughing and chatting like the best of friends. I was flabbergasted to realise that we were on the same wavelength. My dad had never taken me anywhere and it was at that moment that I realised how important a father's relationship is with his children – we have been close ever since.

I remember taking her over to Scotland, where she was going to university, and telling her that the first thing she had to do was join the Young Conservatives! 'There'll be so few of them in Scotland,' I said, 'and they'll all be loaded. Don't listen to your mum – get married, take their money and get divorced, and then you can get married to someone you actually love!' Of course she didn't listen to me, but then, I didn't really expect her to.

I have made sure not to make the same mistakes with my son Michael and he too is a great friend, even calling me Terri rather than Daddy. I'll always remember his first day at nursery school being particularly difficult – for me, not for him! I cried at the gate as he wandered in without so much as a backward glance. The tears were just rolling down my face.

He lives with his mum but I make sure to spend time with him every week and every so often we will take some odds and ends to 'The Black Market' which is held at The Black Box – a great music venue in Belfast's city centre – set up a stall and do our best to sell them on. Michael is a great haggler too – on a good weekend he'll make around £60, which is more than I take in the shop most days! I see so many of my own personality traits in him, and I'm happy to see that he has inherited my interest in music. I'm so very proud of him, and I love him beyond words.

Of course, my family life has never run particularly smoothly. If the relationship with my dad was awkward, then my relationship with my brother was fairly destructive. I don't really talk about him often; he died over ten years ago at his home in England following years of drug and alcohol abuse. I don't remember feeling particularly sad, but I did regret the fact we had not had a better relationship. I do remember trying to be there for my mother when she got the news. She had known before his death that John had become involved in drugs and, while that may have been a disappointment, he was still her son and his death hit her very hard. My dad however was so distraught at how his favourite son's life had turned out that he couldn't even bring himself to go to the funeral.

I think that's why I tend to count all the friends I have made as my real family, a 'family' that numbers in the thousands. Friendship is very important to me and I feel blessed to have known so many wonderful people throughout my life. But it also means that when I lose someone I feel it acutely. I have lost so many dear friends over the years. In 2006, I lost thirty-seven friends and in 2009 I lost both my parents.

So I consider myself lucky that I have been able to count some of my own personal heroes as friends. People like the incomparable John Peel – who will always be top of my hero list – along with the legendary Phil Lynott and Bob Marley. I have been privileged to have not only worked with some of my heroes, but I've gotten drunk with them, done drugs with them, and fallen out with them.

But the real heroes of this story have to be the many people who have looked after me throughout my life and, in the case of Good Vibes, the bands and the thousands of kids who swarmed to the shop, and who packed The Harp and The Pound every week – most of whom ended up sleeping on my living room floor!

Over the years bands like The Beastie Boys, Mötley Crüe and many others have become huge fans of the music we put out on the label. When REM visited Belfast in

February 2005, Michael Stipe and guitarist Peter Buck came back onto the stage and, before a frenzied audience, struck the opening chords of 'Teenage Kicks'. Stipe sang the opening lines but, within seconds, he had given up as eight thousand fans, accompanied by Buck, sang the song for him. He just stood back and listened – it was electrifying. That night really drove it home to me that this was our song, Belfast's signature tune, and it was down to our work at Good Vibrations.

We had done something that broke every rule in the book and the fact that we are still going strong is a minor miracle. I look back and wonder how we all managed it, because I never had a plan when Good Vibes started, but the whole point of setting up the label was to leave a legacy – which is something I think we achieved. As my ex-wife Ruth always used to say, 'Do not do for money that which you cannot do for love.'

What a load of bollocks!

The 'Hooleygang' outside the Oh Yeah! centre after the press launch for the Good Vibrations concert, 2008. From L-R: Niall Kennedy, Greg Cowan, Stuart Bailie, John O'Neill, Stuart Bell, Gary Lightbody, Terri Hooley, Billy Doherty, Claire Archibald, Michael Bradley, John T. Davis, Arthur Magee, Bryan Collis and Glenn Patterson

WHY HOOLEY IS SO HARD TO BEAT
STUART BAILIE

It's the morning after the night before, the body feels fragile, and Terri Hooley has lost his glass eye. And so we have to pick over the debris of the party, lifting up cans and stepping over ashtrays, hoping to find the missing body part. We search through the stack of reggae records and check under the fridge.

Finally, Terri pulls his arm out from the back of the sofa, clutching the lost prosthetic. He gives it a quick wipe on the sleeve of his jumper and jams it back in the socket. Belfast's greatest double act is reunited.

Through much of the bad times, Terri and his eye provided the blackest entertainment. When the murder gangs ran amok in Belfast, Terri would stand on-stage at The Pound Club and The Harp Bar, barking out the lyrics of the Sonny Bono tune 'Laugh at Me'.

Outside the violence was random, but in the relative safety of those venues, Hooley would pluck out his false eye and clutch it in his hand like a voodoo spell, staring into the hearts of the punk kids, demanding that they all see the light.

Sometimes he might even sing the old Tim Rose song, the one made famous by Jimi Hendrix. By the time he'd got to the end of 'Hey Joe' he would be foaming and furious, chanting his own coda to the murder ballad: 'UVF, IRA, how many men did you kill today?' And in truth, we could not answer.

He's a part-time poet, meshing together American beat literature and Belfast blarney. At a party in London, he once invited an acquaintance into the bathroom. The guy thought he was going to be offered drugs, but instead, Hooley recited a lyric called 'Be My Friend'. This became another of his party pieces, an act of compassion from a city of conflict.

If a stranger wanted to know the Terri essentials, you'd probably answer that he was the guy who set up a record shop called Good Vibrations in Belfast. His rickety room on Great Victoria Street became a meeting place for the lost tribes of Ulster, the people who valued music and culture more than the dead hand of sectarianism.

And when punk rock arrived, it gladdened his old hippy heart and his keen sense of anarchy. In 1978, he released 'Big Time', 'Teenage Kicks' and a stack of lesser classics. He made us famous for something outside the usual agenda. And because he was such a rubbish businessman, he was bankrupt by 1982.

But that was temporary. Terri has returned many times, surviving bomb blasts, heart attacks and beatings by racketeers. He had to quit his shop on Howard Street when the peace dividend gave him soaring rates.

He was burnt out of North Street Arcade by arsonists, another repellent act in a city that deserves better. Now Terri runs Good Vibrations in Winetavern Street, the last of the independents.

Many of his stories have been so embroidered over time that the facts are hard to recognise. But we can probably agree that he had angry words with Bob Dylan and John Lennon, that there was a discourse with Bob Marley and a messy night or two with Phil Lynott. But rather than sweat over accuracy, we should celebrate the spirit of Hooley. To bring 'Teenage Kicks' into the world was a good idea, but his decision to press up a bunch of records was only part of a bigger idea.

Good Vibrations came about at a time when we had no confidence about ourselves and our art. He showed the value of self-expression, how to be fearless. And that's the real legacy.

We're not going to petition for his sainthood just yet. Terri is lovely when he's sober but when the brandies take effect he can be tiresome. It's all part of the roaring boy persona, the gusto and the grandstanding and the stories that you've heard scores of times before.

Some of it hides insecurity. Other parts of the character are driven by his anti-Midas tendencies, the urge to sabotage a good thing and to avoid complacency. Hooley will never be a rich man, and he's too volatile to be embraced by the Ulster establishment, but sometimes youth culture, guitars and insolent voices define a city more than any other form, and you can make that case for Terri and Belfast. His style will outlast the guys in the suits and their shabby deals. His logic will survive them all. He has made an actual, positive difference. In the kingdom of the blind, Terri Hooley is king.

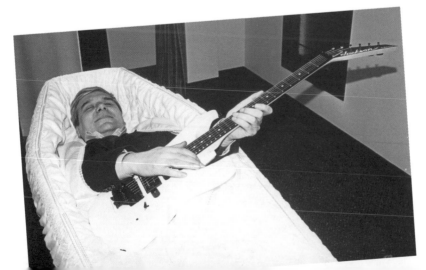

ACKNOWLEDGEMENTS

A FEW WORDS OF THANKS FROM TERRI ...

As a young boy with very strict parents, I was never really that outgoing – I hated school and instead preferred to spend my days sitting in my room listening to music. As such, I was never really part of any gang but, when I grew older, I met many women who, not only led me astray, but took me to art galleries, exhibitions, concerts and, quite simply, changed my life.

So I would like to say thanks to three very wonderful women in particular – Ruth, Eithne, and Claire. Thank you for putting up with my partying and my antics, and for trying (unsuccessfully) to keep me away from all the madness. Opposites do attract.

I would also like to thank my two children, Anna and Michael – this book is dedicated to you. I hope I was a lot more caring and loving than my father ever was to me.

In particular I would like to thank Richard Sullivan whose idea it was to do this book in the first place. I questioned his wisdom in starting such a project and worried that he might wind up in a mental institution by the end of it, but thankfully his sanity is still in tact. Which is even more surprising considering he had to deal with so many of my lunatic friends.

And to those friends, past and present, sorry there were some stories that we had to leave out.

Thanks to Gary, Jonny, Jimmy, Glenn, Stuart, Greg, Brian, John, Chris, David, and John T. for their contributions to the book and my apologies to Harry Orr, Biggy Bigmore, Darren Chittick and anyone else who contributed stories but, due to lack of space, were left out.

Thanks to John Carson, Frankie Quinn, Peter Johnson and everyone else who allowed us to use their photographs and artwork. My biggest regret is that we no longer have the fantastic sixties memorabilia that I had once collected to use in the book. Blame that on the arsonists who burnt down North Street Arcade and, along with it, my own personal history and the history of Good Vibrations. See you in hell.

Thanks to Alex Harper, Bryan Collis and Roy Wallace (the other hooleygans and my backup team) for all their love, help and support. And to Rosie McMichael and Naomi Wilson for doing their best to keep me on the rails and always having a room ready for me when I need one.

Thanks to David, Glenn, Lisa, and Chris for the movie, *Good Vibrations*. I hope I am still around to see the finished product. The pilot was spot on, and you made an old man very happy.

Thanks to the staff of The John Hewitt (my second home and office), to all at the Oh Yeah! centre and to every musician, artist and poet who has ever made me feel alive.

Finally, a big thank you to everyone who ever bought a record in Good Vibrations – please support your local independent bookshop and record shop while you still have one. We are a dying breed.

Hope you enjoy the book.
One Love

... AND FROM RICHARD

For my part I want to dedicate my work on this book to Val, Niamh, Jacob and Roly. Without your love, support, humour and interest this would never have happened – thank you.

Thank you Terri for entrusting me with your life, it has been an incredible pleasure.

I want to acknowledge the help of Brian Young – Brian your encyclopaedic knowledge and readiness to help were invaluable. Thanks to Michael Rafferty for filling in a lot of gaps, to Jimmy Symington for being Terri's friend, to Bryan Collis for keeping order in Terri's shop and to Alex Harper for the cups of tea and unswerving loyalty to the Godfather of Punk.

Special mention to Patsy Horton, Julie Steenson, Lisa Dynan and especially Michelle Griffin at Blackstaff Press – thanks for taking us on, we hope you enjoyed it as much as us.

And to all the people I have met in the writing of this book, I thank you.

PICTURE ACKNOWLEDGEMENTS

Every effort has been made to trace copyright holders of images before publication. If notified, the publishers will rectify any errors or omissions at the earliest opportunity. Where there is no information listed for an image, it is because the publishers have been unable to trace the copyright holder. The publishers and authors would especially like to thank Brian Young for all his help in sourcing images.

Preliminary material

2-3 Photograph by Alwyn Greer
8 © Lisa Dynan
10 © Michael Donald

One in the Eye

12-21 All images reproduced by kind permission of Terri Hooley
24 © Belfast Telegraph

Parties and Politics

28 Reproduced by kind permission of Michael Callaghan
32 Reproduced by kind permission of the Communist Party of Ireland
35 Reproduced by kind permission of Terri Hooley

Bombs, Bullets and Ex-Beatles

38 © Norman Craig
44 Reproduced by kind permission of Terri Hooley
45 Reproduced by kind permission of Terri Hooley
46 Reproduced by kind permission of Terri Hooley
47 Reproduced by kind permission of Terri Hooley

Good Vibrations

48-9 © Lisa Dynan
51 © Belfast Telegraph
52 © Lisa Dynan
55 Reproduced by kind permission of John Carson

Big Time Punks

58 Photograph by Alwyn Greer
60 © UrbanImage.tv/Adrian Boot
61 © Norman Craig
62 (top) © Barry Young
(bottom) Provided courtesy of Brian Young
64 Picture by Conor McCaughley
66 Reproduced by kind permission of Good Vibrations
67 © Alastair Graham
68 Provided courtesy of Brian Young
72 Provided courtesy of Brian Young
73 Provided courtesy of Brian Young
75 (top) © Liz Young
(bottom) Reproduced by kind permission of Brian Young

Working with Outcasts

78 (bottom) Reproduced by kind permission of Good Vibrations
79 © Alastair Graham
80 Reproduced by kind permission of Good Vibrations
81 Reproduced by kind permission of Good Vibrations
82 (top) Reproduced by kind permission of Good Vibrations
(bottom) Reproduced by kind permission of John Carson
84 Provided courtesy of Brian Young
86 Reproduced by kind permission of Good Vibrations

Teenage Kicks

88-9 © Lisa Dynan
91 © Fin Costello/Redferns/Getty
92 Reproduced by kind permission of Good Vibrations
94 Reproduced by kind permission of Good Vibrations
100 Reproduced by kind permission of Good Vibrations
103 Reproduced by kind permission of Good Vibrations
105 © Sean Hennessy, www.hennessyphotography.co.uk
106 Provided courtesy of Brian Young

Hitting the Road

108-9 © Lisa Dynan
110 Reproduced by kind permission of Good Vibrations
111 (top) Reproduced by kind permission of Good Vibrations
112 (top) Reproduced by kind permission of Good Vibrations
113 © Alastair Graham
114 Reproduced by kind permission of Good Vibrations
115 (top) © Sean Hennessy, www.hennessyphotography.co.uk
(bottom) Reproduced by kind permission of Good Vibrations
116 Reproduced by kind permission of Good Vibrations
118 Reproduced by kind permission of Good Vibrations
120-1 Reproduced by kind permission of Good Vibrations
123 Reproduced by kind permission of Good Vibrations

INDEX
Of people, bands and venues

Italicised page reference
indicates an image

Appreciating an exhibit at the 2009
Trans Festival, Waterfront Hall, Belfast